The European Digital Economy

The "digital economy" is a conceptual umbrella referring to markets, organizations and their networks that are based on digital technologies, communication, data processing and e-commerce. It is multidimensional and its dynamic structure must be analysed from various dimensions, such as economic – changes in the nature of resources, production factors and economic processes; technological – technological progress viewed from a macroeconomic perspective vs. technological innovation viewed from a microeconomic perspective; regulatory – challenges facing regulators, new risks affecting the institutional order; and sociological – changes in society's functioning principles, attitudes towards work and human relations.

The purpose of this book is to analyse the effectiveness of digital technologies as well as the fundamental factors that contribute to technological progress in the long run. It also examines structural and qualitative shifts in economies and societies. It investigates many research questions, such as the gap between the level of digital economic development in European Union countries; digital transformation and its impact on workplace skills development patterns; and also the legal framework for data as resource. The book approaches these issues from a multidisciplinary perspective, from law to economics and sociology. It focuses on definitional discussions, the measurement challenges, drivers for digital transition, the impact on labour relations, digital skills and education, data reuse and data extractivism.

This is a comprehensive introduction to the different contexts from which the digital economy can be addressed, offering an innovative method for studying this complex phenomenon, and as such, it will be a valuable resource for students, scholars and researchers across a range of disciplines.

Judyta Lubacha is an Assistant Professor in the Department of Economics and Innovation of the Jagiellonian University, Krakow, Poland.

Beata Mäihäniemi is a University Researcher, Faculty of Law, University of Lapland, Finland.

Rafał Wisła is a Professor of Economics in the Department of Economics and Innovation of the Jagiellonian University, Krakow, Poland.

Routledge Open Business and Economics

Routledge Open Business and Economics provides a platform for the open access publication of monographs and edited collections across the full breadth of these disciplines including accounting, finance, management, marketing and political economy. Reflecting our commitment to supporting open access publishing, this series provides a key repository for academic research in business and economics.

Books in the series are published via the Gold Open Access model and are therefore available for free download and re-use according to the terms of Creative Commons licence. They can be accessed via the Routledge and Taylor & Francis website, as well as third party discovery sites such as the Directory of OAPEN Library, Open Access Books, PMC Bookshelf, and Google Books.

Note that the other Business and Economics series at Routledge also all accept open access books for publication.

Managing Generation Z
Motivation, Engagement and Loyalty
Edited by Joanna Nieżurawska-Zając, Radosław Antoni Kycia and Agnieszka Niemczynowicz

Higher Education Institutions and Digital Transformation
Building University-Enterprise Collaborative Relationships
Marcin Lis

Organizing Sustainable Development
Edited by Aneta Kuźniarska, Karolina Mania and Monika Jedynak

The European Digital Economy
Drivers of Digital Transition and Economic Recovery
Edited by Judyta Lubacha, Beata Mäihäniemi and Rafał Wisła

For more information about this series, please visit: Routledge Open Business and Economics – Book Series – Routledge & CRC Press

The European Digital Economy

Drivers of Digital Transition and Economic Recovery

Edited by
Judyta Lubacha, Beata Mäihäniemi and
Rafał Wisła

Routledge
Taylor & Francis Group
LONDON AND NEW YORK

First published 2024
by Routledge
4 Park Square, Milton Park, Abingdon, Oxon OX14 4RN

and by Routledge
605 Third Avenue, New York, NY 10158

Routledge is an imprint of the Taylor & Francis Group, an informa business

The open access license of the publication was funded by the Priority Research Area Society of the Future under the programme "Excellence Initiative – Research University" at the Jagiellonian University in Krakow.

British Library Cataloguing-in-Publication Data
A catalogue record for this book is available from the British Library

ISBN: 978-1-032-58459-1 (hbk)
ISBN: 978-1-032-58458-4 (pbk)
ISBN: 978-1-003-45016-0 (ebk)

DOI: 10.4324/9781003450160

Typeset in Sabon
by codeMantra

Contents

Figures

Tables

Contributors

Urszula Ala-Karvia is a Doctoral Researcher of Social Sciences at the Ruralia Institute, Faculty of Agriculture and Forestry, University of Helsinki. She has been interested in sustainability of public services, multi-actor engagement and international cooperation. Her ongoing PhD focuses on demographic changes of Finnish society through urban-rural perspectives.

Helena Anacka is a PhD candidate in Economics, since 2015 related to the Faculty of Management and Economics, Gdańsk University of Technology (Poland). She is a co-author of several academic publications and conference proceedings, e.g., "Digitalization Process and Its Impact on Economic Growth: A Panel Data Study for Developing Countries" (Routledge, 2022); "Greencoin: A Proenvironmental Action-Reward System" (AMCIS, 2021); "Greencoin: Prototype of a Mobile Application Facilitating and Evidencing Pro-Environmental Behavior of Citizens" (Elsevier, 2021). Helena has an international academic experience: she made a traineeship in the Directorate General for Budget at the European Commission, studied at Universidade Técnica de Lisboa, Jagiellonian University and Universität Vechta summer school. Her research interests concentrate on the ICT, economic development, AI, digitalization and digital skills. Helena works as a researcher in a Polish-Norwegian research grant concentrated on a green currency pilot project in Poland (the National Centre for Research and Development).

Mateusz Biernacki is a PhD candidate in Economics and Finance at the Doctoral School in the Social Sciences, Jagiellonian University in Krakow (Poland). He is author and co-author of academic publications in the field of market labour and productivity such as Determinants of Spatial Differentiation of Labor Productivity in Poland (2022) and Determinants of Unemployment in Peripheral Regions (2023). His research interests concentrate on the digital economy and labour productivity.

Christopher W. Chagnon is a Doctoral Researcher of Global Development Studies at the University of Helsinki Faculty of Social Sciences. He is a board member of the Finnish Society for Development Research, a member of the Global Extractivisms and Alternatives (EXALT) Initiative and co-hosts the EXALT Podcast. He has previously co-authored the article "From Extractivism to Global Extractivism: The Evolution of an Organizing Concept" (*Journal of Peasant Studies*, 2022) and the chapter "Extractivism at Your Fingertips" (Routledge, 2021) in *Our Extractive Age: Expressions of Violence and Resistance*. He has a background in Chinese politics and Africa-China relations. His current research is on personal data extractivism in the global south, focusing on the case of Zambia. Prior to starting his doctoral research, he had over ten years of work experience in international development, market research and education spanning four continents.

Manuel Rivera Fernández is a Professor of Civil Law at the University of Seville. He has researched on the central matters of Private Law, being the author of numerous monographs and scientific articles. To highlight his work in the field of Patrimonial Law, Personal Law, Family Law and Inheritance Law, he has directed numerous doctoral theses and is part of various research groups, the last multidisciplinary one financed by the European Union on The Impact of Digitization of the economy on the skills and professional qualifications and labour relations. He has been substitute Magistrate of the Provincial Court of Cádiz, participating as a speaker in more than 300 sentences. He is also an arbitrator of the Real Estate Arbitration Court of Seville and of the Cadiz Chamber of Commerce (Real Estate Arbitration Section), having been appointed arbitrator by the Superior Court of Justice of Andalusia in various cases. He has been an evaluator for the National Agency for Evaluation and Prospective of Projects and Research Groups since 2004 and also carries out advisory and reporting activities for legal professionals and public and private entities.

Silvia Gaiani is a Senior Researcher (Sustainable Food Systems) at Ruralia Institute, Faculty of Agriculture and Forestry, University of Helsinki. She holds two PhD degrees, one in International Cooperation and Policies for Sustainable Development and the other in Food Politics and Economics, both from the University of Bologna, Italy. Her current research focuses on innovation and entrepreneurship in the transition towards sustainable food systems.

Sophia E. Hagolani-Albov is a Doctoral Researcher in the Faculty of Agriculture and Forestry at the University of Helsinki. She also works closely with the University of Helsinki Global Development Studies and the EXALT Initiative in the Faculty of Social Sciences. To date she has co-authored 16 academic articles and book chapters, including "From Extractivism to Global Extractivism: The Evolution of an Organizing Concept" (*Journal of Peasant Studies*, 2022), "Rethinking the (Wool) Economy Local" (Palgrave McMillan 2022) in *Local, Slow and Sustainable Fashion Fibres: Wool as a Fabric for Change* and "Extractivism at Your Fingertips" (Routledge, 2021) in Our

Extractive Age: Expressions of Violence and Resistance. Sophia's academic work explores different facets of extractivism, the socio-cultural aspects of transformative alternatives and food system redesign. She is the co-host of the EXALT Podcast, launched in 2019, which is a monthly conversation with scholars, activists and artists about extractivisms and alternatives.

Ewa Lechman is a Professor of Economics, since 2002 working at Faculty of Management and Economics Gdańsk University of Technology. Since 2017, she is the Vice-Dean for Development, Director of the University Scientific Council for Social Sciences and PhD Programme Director. Her extensive research interests concentrate on economic development, ICT and technological progress, and its role in reshaping social and economic systems and various aspects of poverty and economics in developing countries. She coordinates and participates in international research and educational projects and also works as an independent expert assisting with innovation assignments, including the evaluation of small and medium enterprise proposals, EU-financed programmes and policy design regarding innovativeness, digitalization, education and social exclusion. She was the 2013 winner of an Emerald Literati Network Award for Excellence and is a member of the editorial boards of international journals on technology diffusion, the digital economy and economic development. She serves as a permanent referee in *Policy&Internet* (Oxford University Press), *Technological Forecasting and Social Change* (Elsevier), *World Development* (Elsevier), *Technology in Society* (Elsevier), *Journal of Applied Research and Technology* (Elsevier), *Social Indicators Research* (SpringerNature), *Journal of Business Cycle Research* (SpringerNature), *Journal of Development Studies* (Taylor&Francis), *NETNOMICS* (SpringerNature), *Neural Computing and Applications* (SpringerNature), and *Eurasian Economic Review* (SpringerNature). In 2017 2019, she was nominated by Elsevier as outstanding reviewer. She currently coordinates and/or is the main investigator in three research grants on ICT diffusion trajectories and technological take-off (National Science Centre), exchange-traded funds development (National Science Centre) and technological development for financial markets (CERGE-GDN).

Myriam González Limón is an Associate Professor in the Department of Economic Analysis and Political Economy at the University of Seville and earned her PhD in Economics (University of Seville). She holds a degree in Economics (UNED) and a degree in Law (University of Seville). She is a member of the SEJ548 Research Group, Big Data and Business Intelligence in Social Media. Her main lines of research are the Labour Market, the Economics of Culture, economic-labour analysis with a gender perspective, Big Data in Social Media, tourism destination image and teaching innovation in university economics subjects. She is a member of the Advisory Board of journals indexed in Journal Citation Report, member of the Advisory Board of journals indexed in Journal Citation Report and reviewer of papers for international conferences and scientific journals. She is a member of the Asociación Libre de Economía (AldE) and of the Asociación de Mujeres Investigadoras y Tecnólogas (AMIT).

Mª del Milagro Martín López is a Professor at the University of Seville, PhD of Business Administration and Management, Vice Dean of Teaching Innovation at the Faculty of Labour Sciences, University of Seville (2004–2008), Dean of the Faculty of Labour Sciences from 2009 to 2017, expert of the Economic and Social City Council of Seville from 2015 to date, President of the Economic and Social Council of the City Council of Seville from 2016 to date, main coordinator of Project No. VP / 2012/001/0068. Department: DS EMPL.B.1. European Commission and entitled "Les Relations professionnelles dans le contexte du développement de la Sous-Tritance" and national coordinator of the project VP/2018/004/0006 (Call for proposals "Improving expertise in the field of industrial relations". European Commission). "The impact of the digitalisation of the economy on professional competences and qualifications, and its impact on working and working conditions" with financial support from the European Union. She is Master Program Coordinator in Management and Development of Human Resources.

Judyta Lubacha is a researcher and works as an Assistant Professor in the Department of Economics and Innovation of the Jagiellonian University in Krakow (Poland). Her research is focused on innovative activities and regional development. She received many national and international scholarships and research grants: PRELUDIUM grant financed by the National Science Center; DAAD Research Grant for PhD students and young scientists; Polish National Bank Research scholarship for PhD students; and Special Award of the Minister of Regional Development in the competition of master's theses "Now Poland Promotion". Currently, she works in the field of sustainable development and circular economy. In 2023, she received three-year grant for the project: Economic and institutional factors influencing the implementation of the circular economy model in enterprises of the manufacturing sector.

Agata Luśtyk is a PhD candidate in Economics and Finance at the Doctoral School in the Social Sciences, Jagiellonian University in Krakow (Poland). She is author and co-author of academic publications in the field of innovative potential and labour productivity, such as Assessment of the innovative potential of Polish voivodeships and the probability of its change (2022) and Determinants of spatial differentiation of labor productivity in Poland (2022).

Beata Mäihäniemi is a University Researcher, Faculty of Law, University of Lapland and is also the author of the book *Competition Law and Big Data.*

Imposing Access to Information in Digital Markets published in 2020. She is an international expert in competition law and has authored over 20 publications in this area. She has been teaching competition law, European law and Internet Regulation for over ten years. She has been involved in two national projects on AI that involve elements of competition law. She has authored few national reports on the recent developments, and she actively participates as an expert in competition law and data governance in national workshops and conferences.

Alejandro Díaz Moreno is a Professor of the Department of Civil and Private International Law at the University of Seville. He is the author of more than 50 scientific articles and more than 150 case law reviews. He earned his PhD in Private Law from the University of Seville. He is the Dean of the Faculty of Labor Sciences. He is the President of the Association of Centers and Faculties of Labor Relations and Human Resources (ARELCIT). The issues that he deals with are in the field of credit protection and the satisfaction of the creditor's interest, jurisdictional competence as well as problems arising in practice like the delay in commercial operations and its impact on the guarantees and traditional mechanisms of commercial credit and the treatment of some of the multiple problems raised by the recent insolvency reforms. He is a permanent collaborator of the *Journal of Patrimonial Civil Law*. He is a coordinator and Lead Researcher of the EC project, The impact of digitization of the economy on the skills and professional qualifications and labor relations, Call for proposals: Improving expertise in the field of industrial relations (GRANT_NUMBER: VP/2018/004/0006).

Johanna Niemi (Niemi-Kiesiläinen) is a Professor and the Dean, Faculty of Law, University of Helsinki. Niemi has worked as a professor at the Universities of Turku and Umeå and as a visiting professor at Lund University, Sweden. She is a Doctor Honoris Causa at Uppsala University and has been Fulbright Scholar at the University of Wisconsin, Madison Law School. She was the member of the Scientific Committee of the EU Fundamental Rights Agency 2013–2018 and Academy of Finland Research Council for Culture and Society 2016–2018. Her research interests include criminal procedure, consumer insolvency, human rights and the construction of gender in legal discourses.

Małgorzata Niklewicz-Pijaczyńska is a researcher and works as an Assistant Professor in the Department of General Theory of Economics, Faculty of Law, Administration and Economics, University of Wrocław. She is the author of numerous publications in the field of economic and legal problems of industrial and intellectual property, the functioning of patent systems, inventiveness and innovation in economic development and the tasks of the knowledge-based economy. In 2020, she received the Award of the Polish Minister of Education and Science. The award was granted within the competition held by the Polish Patent Office for the monograph Patent system in knowledge management: economics of codified technical knowledge.

Yevheniia Polishchuk is a Professor in the Corporate Finance and Controlling Department of Kyiv National Economic University named after Vadym Hetman (Ukraine) and is the author and co-author of over 100 academic publications including Government early policy responses on COVID-19 challenges in central and eastern Europe: SME support (2022), SMEs debt financing in the EU: On the eve of the coronacrisis (2020), Smart-contracts via blockchain as the innovation tool for SMEs development (2019), Fintech platforms in SME's financing: EU experience and ways of their application in Ukraine (2018) and Barriers and opportunities for hi-tech innovative small and medium enterprises development in the 4th industrial revolution era (2017). Her research interests are FinTech development, economic shocks and crisis, regional development and smart specialization. In 2015, she was rewarded with President Prize for Young Scholars in Ukraine. She is the Bachelor Program Coordinator in Investment Management (2019–2022) and United Nation Development Program expert in SMEs development and COVID-19 impact.

Amalia Verdu Sanmartin is a Postdoctoral Researcher at the Turku Institution for Advance Studies (TIAS). She does interdisciplinary research with a focus on discrimination, teaching methods, legal knowledge and legal subjects. She is currently working in a project called *The Person on the Edge: Disrupting Normative Legal Knowledge in the Digital Age* with a focus in the intra-actions between the digital and physical space through blended education.

Rafał Wisła is a Professor of Economics in the Department of Economics and Innovation of the Jagiellonian University in Krakow (Poland) and is also the author and co-author of over 80 academic publications such as *Innovation in the Pharmaceutical and Medical Technology Industries of Poland* (2018), *Developmental Diversification of Contemporary Europe* (2016) and *Regional Patterns of Technology Accumulation in Central and Eastern Europe Countries* (2014). Recently, he has co-edited and contributed to *Economic Transformation in Poland and Ukraine* (Routledge, 2020), *The Socioeconomic Impact of COVID-19 on Eastern European Countries* (Routledge, 2022) and *The Solow Model of Economic Growth* (2023). He is the Head of the Department of Economics and Innovation at the Institute of Economics, Finance and Management, Jagiellonian University in Krakow and also Doctoral Program Coordinator in Economics and Finance at Jagiellonian University (2019–2023). The issues that he deals with are the differentiation of spatial economic development in Europe and innovation activity from a regional perspective.

Michał Włodarczyk is a doctoral student at the Faculty of Management and Social Communication, Jagiellonian University (Krakow, Poland). He is the author and co-author of academic publications in the field of financial innovations, new technologies and the fintech sector, such as *Between Social Responsibility and Potential Profit. The Technological Giants' Dilemma* (2018) and *Financial Clusters and Fintech Agglomerations – Location Factors* (2020). He is also a co-founder of *StaćMnie*, a scientific YouTube channel focused on financial education and popularizing economics among young people.

Anna Zachorowska-Mazurkiewicz is an Associate Professor at the Institute of Economics, Finance and Management and a Director of the Doctoral School of Social Sciences at Jagiellonian University in Krakow, Poland. She holds a PhD in Economics. Her research interests focus on heterodox economics. She is the author and co-author of more than 80 academic publications, including the most recent Women's work and its conceptualization in Post-Keyensian Institutionalism, [in:] Ch. J. Whalen (ed.) (2022) *A Modern Guide to Post-Keynesian Institutional Economics*, London: Edward Elgar, pp. 339–358. In years 2013–2016, she was a leading researcher in the project *Innogend – Innovative Gender as a New Source of Progress*.

Aleksander Żołnierski is an Assistant Professor in the Department of Microeconomics, Institute of Economics of the Polish Academy of Sciences. He is the author and co-author of over 50 publications on innovation, information management, organizational culture and SMEs sector. Next to academic and research activity, he is involved in advisory projects, using in practice the knowledge from research on innovation, communication and social capital. He is also engaged in business-related organizations and successfully applied academic and R&D knowledge in economic practice.

Introduction

Judyta Lubacha, Beata Mäihäniemi and Rafał Wisła

Societies and economies are not digitally neutral. Technological progress is a disruptive process that stimulates the emergence of a new status quo. Technology and technological change enrich and reshape socio-economic systems, raising their responsiveness and adaptability to further technological development.

The "digital economy" is a multidisciplinary conceptual "umbrella" referring to markets, organizations and their networks that are based on digital technologies, communication, data processing and e-commerce. The digital economy is multidimensional, and its dynamic structure must be analysed considering its various aspects: economic (changes in the nature of resources, production factors and economic processes), technological (technological progress viewed from a macroeconomic perspective vs. technological innovation viewed from a microeconomic perspective), regulatory (challenges facing regulators and new risks affecting the institutional order) and sociological (changes in society functioning principles, attitudes towards work and human relations).

The purpose of this book is to analyse the effectiveness of the implemented digital technologies as well as fundamental factors that contribute to technological progress in the long run. It also analyses structural and qualitative shifts in economies and societies. The following research topics are investigated and discussed: the gap between the level of digital economic development in the EU countries, digital transformation and its impact on the development patterns of labour skills and the legal framework for using data as a resource.

The book is the result of interdisciplinary workshops, namely, (1) "Digital Economy", organized at the Jagiellonian University in Kraków, 23 June 2022, and (2) The Interdisciplinary Insights into Digital Economy, organized at the University of Helsinki on 1 December 2022. During the workshops, we had the chance to present our research to scholars representing other disciplines in a way understandable to specialists from outside our own research orbit. This approach is also visible in the result, that is, the monograph itself: the editors, who conduct research in two different disciplines, prepared the volume in the spirit of interdisciplinarity. Selected chapters are peer-reviewed

DOI: 10.4324/9781003450160-1

by scholars from other disciplines. This interdisciplinary cooperation has been one of the most rewarding endeavours we have recently undertaken.

The book aims at approaching the topics discussed from a multidisciplinary perspective, ranging from law to economy and sociology. The monograph confirms that, on the one hand, digitalization is a complex phenomenon which alters the economy and society while law does not always keep up with these changes. On the other hand, changes in legislation shape the environment in which companies operate, and new or amended laws may either stimulate or inhibit the development of an economic sector.

In our monograph, we focus on definitional discussions, the problems of measurement, drivers of digital transition, changing labour relations, digital skills and education, data reuse and data extractivism. We closely consider selected aspects of the digital economy, many of which are hot topics. The strength of the monograph also lies in the rich background of the team of authors that consists of researchers from eight European academic centres.

The book is divided into three parts: Measuring the Digital Economy, Sources for Developing the Digital Economy and Nature of Resources.

In Chapter 1 "The dimensions of the digital economy and society", Judyta Lubacha, Rafał Wisła, Michał Włodarczyk and Anna Zachorowska-Mazurkiewicz present and discuss different dimensions and the extent of the impact of digital transformation on the economy. The authors also look into opportunities and risks arising from the digitalization of economic and social processes.

Chapter 2 "Measuring the digital economy with 'digital economy' tools" by Aleksander Żołnierski presents emerging methods of monitoring the use of digital economy that include not only artificial intelligence or big data analysis but also a wide range of technologies of the digital economy itself. The described methodology is increasingly employed in a number of research projects but has not been used on a large scale to date. It can eliminate many imperfections of commonly used quantitative methods. The chapter analyses the potential offered by three of them: (1) big data analysis of unstructured data, (2) analysis based on Google Trends used in many scientific studies and (3) beacon technology which has new applications, e.g., in monitoring the work environment in Industry 4.0.

The main objective of Chapter 3 "Differentiation of the digital economic development in Europe" (Mateusz Biernacki, Agata Luśtyk and Rafał Wisła) is to examine the variation in the digital economic development in Europe. The first section of this chapter contains a review of proposals aimed to measure the digital economy, considering various approaches to its definition. The second section discusses two methods designed to identify changes in the digital economy from a macro perspective and gives the characteristics of data used in the following sections. The third section presents research results with a discussion of their limitations and downsides.

In Chapter 4 "Digital innovation hubs as drivers for digital transition and economic recovery: the case of the Arctic Development Environments

Cluster in Lapland ", Silvia Gaiani and Urszula Ala-Karvia describe the increasingly important role that Digital Innovation Hubs (DIHs) play in the European digital economy where supply chains are systematically digitalized, traditional business models are transforming, companies work in an integrated way and smart distributed production has become a new standard. This chapter first adds to the general discussion on DIHs as supportive ecosystems and underlines their role as drivers of regional competitiveness, innovation capacity and digital transition. Second, it focuses on Finland, the country with the highest IT skills in the world, and specifically on the Arctic Development Environments Cluster which has recently been approved by the European Commission as the first official DIH in Lapland.

The analysis conducted in Chapter 5 by Alejandro Díaz Moreno, Mª del Milagro Martín López, Myriam González Limón and Manuel Rivera Fernández concerns digital transformation and its impact on labour relations. Digital transformation is of such magnitude and is happening so fast in recent years that it is having a major effect on the competitiveness and growth of companies. Digital transformation is changing the nature of work and the structure of the labour market. Digital technologies, on the one hand, minimize production costs by replacing workers with computers and robots and, on the other hand, are related to the balance in the labour market. Digitalization of the economy is a social process that is still under construction and has accelerated in recent years as a result of the pandemic. It involves a new way of understanding the forms of working and the organization of work itself, and therefore has an impact on the complex world of labour relations.

The study contained in Chapter 6 by Helena Anacka and Ewa Lechman concerns the digitalization and digital skills development patterns. It aims to shed light on digitalization and digital skills dynamics in Europe between 1980 and 2022. The authors have identified three research goals: (1) to identify digitalization trajectories in European countries, (2) to identify digital skills development patterns in European countries and (3) to examine digitalization and digital skills inequalities across countries in Europe. Their empirical sample comprises 27 European economies, and the time span of the analysis is set for the period between 1980 and 2022. Statistical data on digitalization and digital skills are extracted from the ITU and Eurostat databases.

In Chapter 7 "Virtual reality in legal education. Challenges and possibilities to transform normative knowledge", Amalia Verdu Sanmartin and Johanna Niemi explore the intersection between digital education and law, explaining how they challenge each other while coming together in a continuous becoming process affecting the substance of the law, the legal profession and education. The chapter is organized so that Part 2 introduces virtual reality, and Part 3 discusses how VR is transforming the classroom into a smart learning environment. Part 4 explores the possibilities of using virtual reality in legal education.

The aim of Chapter 8 "The patent system and the problem of innovation diffusion in the digital economy" (Małgorzata Niklewicz-Pijaczyńska) is to indicate the most problematic, from the perspective of digital management, areas that determine the functioning of patent systems. It also analyses a new function which, once implemented, will make patent regulations an important player in the global process of innovation diffusion. The chapter is based on a critical analysis of the source literature in the field of economics and law. The main conclusions of the chapter state that with the information function implemented, patent systems show a significant potential for a wide spectrum of applications in the process of innovation diffusion. However, in order for this role to be performed in an optimal way, it is necessary to urgently verify the applicable patent rules and thoroughly improve the IT infrastructure so that they respond to the challenges of the digital economy to a greater extent than before.

In Chapter 9 "Behind the transparency of 'data reuse'", Beata Mäihäniemi assesses the framework for the reuse of personal data by gatekeepers, currently being shaped in the EU. The starting point is provided by the question whether data should be seen as property or commons. Current EU-wide regulations such as the General Data Protection Regulation do not create a property right as regards data, although some, such as competition law, are based on the idea that data is an economic good that can be re-materialized and commodified. Moreover, how does the abundance of data affect possible data sharing? It seems that information on the origin of datasets must only be provided when sharing sensitive data. However, the recently introduced EU-wide proposals of the Data Act and the Digital Markets Act are rooted in the idea of "data altruism". The Data Act also aims at empowering users, while the Digital Markets Act imposes several obligations on gatekeepers. The chapter analyses in-force and upcoming regulations in the light of the data as property, commodity/commons divide. What is the legal framework for facilitating the reuse of personal data by gatekeepers? Which pieces of the puzzle are missing?

Chapter 10 "Data extractivism: social pollution and real-world costs" (Christopher W. Chagnon and Sophia E. Hagolani-Albov) utilizes the concept of extractivism to highlight the socio-cultural damage done by data extractive systems in Europe and around the world. Just as previous industrial revolutions relied on resources like coal and oil, the digital revolution has sparked an insatiable demand for its own resource—personal data. Rather than using open-pit mines, data extraction depends on proliferating devices that do their digging by embedding themselves ever deeper into our lives and societies. This desire for data has led to modes of extraction that cause environmental pollution and what could be termed "social pollution", which causes damage to societies and individual lives.

In Chapter 11 "FinTech future trends: secondary data review", Yevheniia Polishchuk analyses how the phenomenon of digitalization has also affected the financial sector, how the emergence of such an industry as FinTech has forced financial intermediaries to adopt the changes we are witnessing now. Currently, investments in FinTech are an integral part of the development strategy of banking institutions and large companies operating outside the market of financial services. Despite the rapid development of the FinTech industry, it faces challenges such as the COVID-19 shock, innovations in FinTech regulation, competition from banks, as well as a lack of specialists with the skills that are required in the FinTech industry. In addition, the image of consumers of financial services is changing, and the role of socially significant projects is growing. The need to identify signals that indicate future developments arises on the part of businesses from the FinTech industry when formulating their strategies. The secondary data review method is used to summarize the reports from various reliable organizations, the main trends in future development of the FinTech industry, providing useful evidence for the decision-making process. The DEEP software has become the main methodological tool for identifying and studying various sectors related to the FinTech industry, factors determining forecast development trends that bring both opportunities and risks.

Acknowledgements

The publication has been supported by a grant from the Faculty of Management and Social Communication under the Strategic Programme Excellence Initiative at Jagiellonian University.

We would like to thank the Jagiellonian University for funding open access and proofreading to the monograph. We also appreciate UNA Europa Network for facilitating the exchange of researchers among universities in network. We would like to express our thanks to Mr. Alexander Mörelius-Wulff from the Legal Tech Lab, University of Helsinki, for his assistance in editing the book and to Mr. Wojciech Rynduch-Walecki for copy editing. Our warm thanks go to Ms. Kristina Abbotts from Routledge for ensuring smooth cooperation on the publisher's part, to the Jagiellonian University for sponsoring our workshop in Kraków and partly that in Helsinki and to the University of Helsinki Legal Tech Lab for funding the Helsinki workshop.

Part I

Measuring the digital economy

1 The dimensions of the digital economy and society

Judyta Lubacha, Rafał Wisła, Michał Włodarczyk and Anna Zachorowska-Mazurkiewicz

1.1 Introduction

The Organisation for Economic Co-operation and Development (OECD, 2020) defines the digital economy as an economic structure wherein data is a factor of production. Enterprises in this type of economy rely on digital data and its processing and use in creating value-added services. The development of the digital economy is driven by the transformation of traditional economy and the rise of the information society. Thus, the changes observed at present give reasons to propose a hypothesis about a change to the structure of mature economies where traditional resources and factors of production are being replaced by their digital equivalents (see: Nazarov et al., 2019). The increase in computer usage and the third industrial revolution initiated the production of digital data. Its exponential growth entails the need to have it systematized, stored and processed. It provides a basis for developing digital technologies (such as the Internet of Things), resulting in changes to data archiving models, data protection or broadly to the functioning of various types of organizations.

This chapter is aimed to formulate a conceptual framework for the present book. The framework consists of four aspects of the digital economy, namely, the economic dimension (a change in the nature of resources, factors of production and economic management), the technological dimension (technical progress from a macroeconomic perspective vs. technology innovation from a microeconomic perspective), the regulatory dimension (challenges to regulators) and the social dimension (a change in the functioning of society, in the approach to labour and interpersonal relationships). This chapter presents successively: a brief historical outline of the history of the digital economy with various approaches to its definition (considering its various dimensions), the sphere of influence of digital transformation on the economy and the threats and opportunities created by the digitalization of economic and social processes.

1.2 The emergence of the digital economy

The digital revolution began in the mid-1980s with the emerging mass market for personal computers. The 1990s saw a rapid development of digital

DOI: 10.4324/9781003450160-3

design tools and robotic manufacturing equipment. As of the turn of the 20th and 21st centuries, digitalization processes are driven by massive growth in outsourcing and offshoring. International coordination and corporate interoperability are being rapidly improved at present. An increasing number of diverse computing devices and computer programs are used in business processes, including services, transportation or precision agriculture (UNCTAD, 2017).

The current state of economic relationships, termed the digital economy, is still considered to be in its emerging phase (Chen & Wang, 2019). The emergence process of the digital economy is described by Katz (2017) by distinguishing its three waves. The first wave is associated with the use and management of information systems aimed at automating data processing. They are applied to monitoring and reporting of business performance. A significant aspect of this wave is the popularization of telecommunication technologies, such as broadband (fixed and mobile) access to the Internet. The second wave entails the diffusion of the Internet and the development of digital platforms (new markets and search engines). The third wave is the key phase for shaping the digital economy. The third wave consists in automating routine tasks and processes at various levels: individual organizations, their networks and public policies.

The Federation of German Industries in its 2015 report identifies four major factors of digital transformation of Europe's economies: (1) digital data, (2) automation, (3) connectivity and (4) the digital customer interface (Table 1.1).

Analysing the contents of Table 1.1, a hypothesis may be proposed about a change to the paradigm of production factors. Digital data in the age of digital economy is equivalent to raw materials for manufacture.

Table 1.1 Levers of digital transformation

	Levers	*Enabling technologies*	*Applications*
Digital transformation	Digital data	• Big data • Wearables • Internet of Things	• Demand forecasts • Data-based routing • Predictive maintenance
	Automation	• Robotics • Additive manufacturing	• Drones • Autonomous vehicles
	Connectivity	• Cloud computing • Broadband Internet	• Smart factory • Pure digital products • Remote maintenance
	Digital customer access	• Social networks • Mobile Internet/ apps	• E-commerce • Infotainment • Fourth-party logistics

Source: Roland Berger, The digital transformation of industry (2015). https://www.rolandberger.com/publications/publication_pdf/roland_berger_digital_transformation_of_industry_20150315.pdf (30.08.2022).

Automated, robotic production lines and digital organizations form a new labour market, and scalable communication networks represent relational, social and structural capital. The increase in computer usage and the third industrial revolution initiated the production of digital data. Exponential growth in data production entails the need to have it systematized and stored. The inventions that initiated the fourth revolution (e.g., the Internet of Things) entail inevitable changes in personal data archiving and protection. Opinions are voiced that personal data protection should be considered a human right. Digital technologies may be perceived as a disruptive innovation that changes the status quo (Kerber, 2016).

1.3 The digital economy as a research subject

The term "digital economy" was first used by Tapscott in 1996. He used it with reference to the age of networked intelligence characterized by a rapid development of the sector of information and communication technology (ICT). Tapscott (1996) argued that the digital economy combines intelligence, knowledge and creativity, thus being capable of creating "the wealth of nations" and supporting their development.

The first publications on the digital economy appeared in the WOS database in 1993 (Figure 1.1). The number of such publications did not exceed 100 papers annually until 2015. As of 2016, the number of publications on

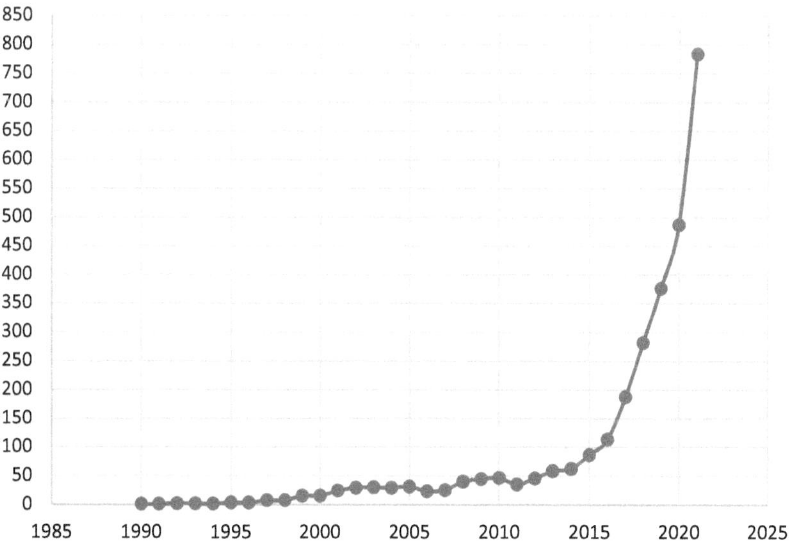

Figure 1.1 Number of publications for "digital economy" query from 1990.

Source: Own calculations based on Web of Science (2022).

this topic has increased by 30%–60% year by year. In 2022, until September of that year, as many as 674 papers on the digital economy were published.

From 1990 to September 2022, the Web of Science database collected 3,950 papers with "digital economy" as their keyword. The largest set includes papers dedicated to the areas of Business and Economics (27%) and Communication (12%). Such research fields are found within the range between 2% and 4% as Government and Law, Environmental Science and Ecology and Sociology and Education. This indicates the interdisciplinary nature of the subject discussed (Figure 1.2).

In the first two decades of research on the digital economy (Figures 1.3 and 1.4), the studies focused mainly on technology topics and the use of the Internet and ICT. Such concepts as e-commerce, e-government or information society were introduced in 2000–2009.

An analysis of keywords occurring jointly in 2010–2019 (Figure 1.5) compared to prior years shows a significant increase in associating the concept of digital economy with other areas of the social system, not limited to its economic aspects. Several fields of research developed in 2010–2019: (1) the digital economy combined with collaborative economy and sharing economy; (2) information society, the use of digital tools in teaching and digital skills; (3) property rights, intellectual property and piracy; (4) social media

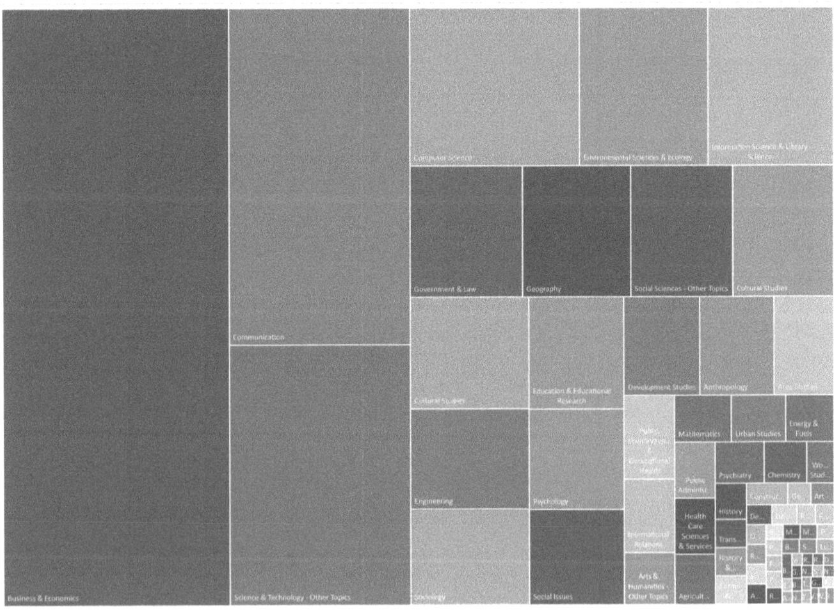

Figure 1.2 Share of research areas represented in the articles for "digital economy" query.

Source: Own calculations based on Web of Science (2022).

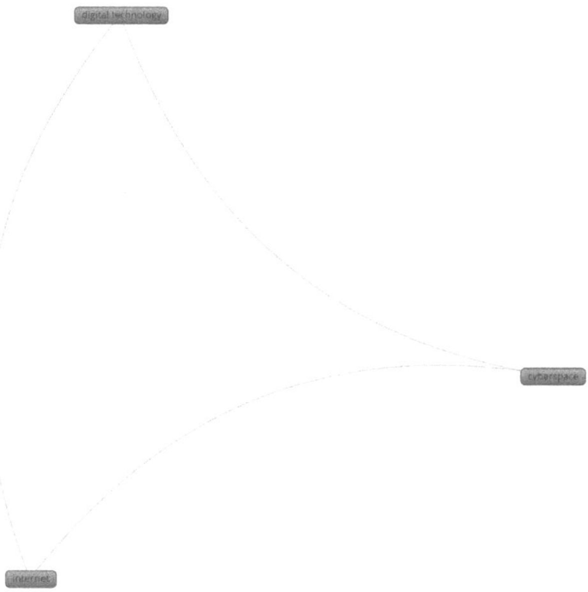

Figure 1.3 Map of the keywords occurrence for "digital economy" query in 1990–1999.

Source: Own elaboration based on Web of Science (2022), prepared in VOSviewer.

Figure 1.4 Map of the keywords occurrence for "digital economy" query in 2000–2009.

Source: Own elaboration based on Web of Science (2022), prepared in VOSviewer.

and their use in advertising, and the question of personal data protection; and (5) big data and digital tools used in regulation.

The years after 2020 were affected by the COVID-19 pandemic as the virus characteristics limited society's activity in the real world and caused a transfer of numerous tasks into the virtual world. Therefore, many studies on the digital economy also discussed the COVID-19 pandemic

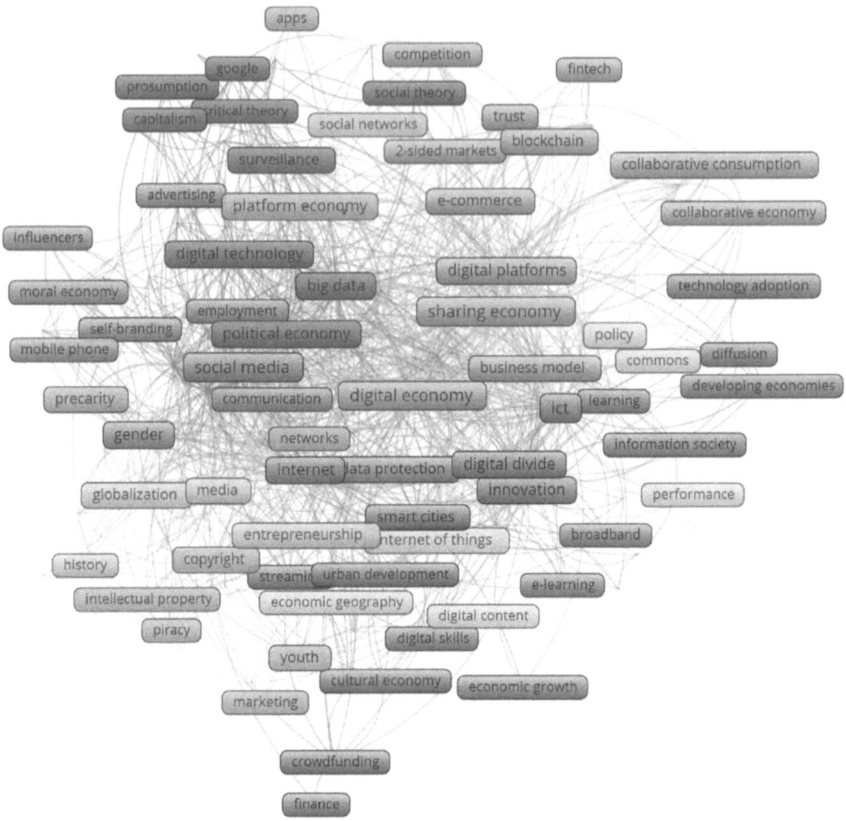

Figure 1.5 Map of the keywords occurrence for "digital economy" query in 2010–2019.

Source: Own elaboration based on Web of Science (2022), prepared in VOSviewer.

(Figure 1.6). The COVID-19 pandemic caused accelerated implementation of numerous digital solutions in the economy, management, finance and education. Other important fields of research appeared in 2020–2022: (1) changes to the labour market – platform economy, gig economy, crowdsourcing and precarity; (2) changes in digital products and services – digital trade, fintech, mobile money, e-government and associated emotions; (3) necessary amendments to legislation on personal data and privacy protection, on algorithm use and on improving security in using Internet applications; (4) the rise of cryptocurrencies; and (5) the development of Economy 4.0 combined with the topics of a circular economy and a sustainable business model.

Figure 1.6 Map of the keywords occurrence for "digital economy" query in 2020–2022.

Source: Own elaboration based on Web of Science (2022), prepared in VOSviewer.

1.4 A comparison of approaches to defining the digital economy

The conducted review of the main research topics in the area of digital economy gives its picture as a multi-dimensional and dynamic structure that should be analysed considering its economic, technological, regulatory and social aspects. All those aspects are discussed in the further chapters of the book.

From an economic perspective, the digital economy is founded on a digital form of trade (Teo, 2001). Digital information transfers have dramatically changed the nature of management processes in enterprises (D'Ippolito et al., 2019). Given this observation, Cheon and Kim (2003) define the sphere of digital economy as an economy in which the production, sales, and consumption of goods and services depend on the network of electronic means based on an intermediary information flow. Thus, digital technologies and broadband network access can be identified as the core of the digital economy (Banning, 2016). In this approach, the digital economy is an economic form of production in the digital technology sector. It is driven by the development of the information and communication industry, which directly translates into growth in electronic commerce (Lane, 1999).

The digital economy can be understood as a kind of umbrella concept describing digital markets, technologies and communication, data processing and e-commerce (Nathan et al., 2013). The growing number of interrelations between the traditional (offline) and the digital economy makes the boundary between them increasingly difficult to define. The difficulty becomes greater as the influence of the digital economy grows beyond business, to include the area of lifestyles in society (e.g., the sharing economy, algorithms and big data) (Capobianco & Nyeso, 2018). The digital economy with its multiple dimensions and internal dynamics requires a flexible approach to its definition (Barefoot et al., 2018). However, an excessively general and easy-to-modify description of the digital economy can present problems in analysis and observation due to the boundaries of the research subject being blurred and changing in time.

The material basis for the digital economy is provided by the processes and products offered by the ICT sector that pervade all areas of the economy and society in a majority of developed countries (Lazanyuk & Revinova, 2019): the banking system – mobile and online banking and electronic payment; trade – auction and sales platforms; energy – coordinating fuel supplies, energy purchase and remote reading of consumption meters; transport – advanced logistics, real-time vehicle tracking and autonomous vehicles; education – remote teaching/learning; health – teleconsultation, teleoperations, surgical robots and patient records (e.g., Internet patient account in health service); offices – online access to data, documents and requests.

The structure of the digital economy can be analysed at its three levels (UNCTAD, 2017). The core refers to the ICT and IT sectors. It includes telecommunications, software development, computer hardware manufacture and offering IT services. This level is considered from the perspective focusing on specific technologies, such as 3D printing, blockchain, 5G or the Internet of Things. The narrow scope includes digital platforms, the sharing economy and digital services (e.g., Facebook and Google). This level employs specific technologies to create innovative processes, new methods of distribution or to change the approach to fundamental concepts in economics, like utility and ownership. The broad scope of the concept of digital economy extends beyond advanced technology industries (e-agriculture, e-administration, e-business and Industry 4.0). It includes the sphere of finance (fintech and open banking), e-commerce and the labour market (gig economy) (Figure 1.7).

The digital economy is distinguished from the traditional economy by Valenduc and Vendramin (2016) as the diminishing role of geographical location, no longer providing a competitive advantage; the key role played by digital platforms; the great importance of network effects; and the use of big data. Digital transformation also initiated the fourth industrial revolution, conceptualized by Klaus Schwab (2017). It is based on digital data, the combination of sensors and data warehouse analysis made by artificial

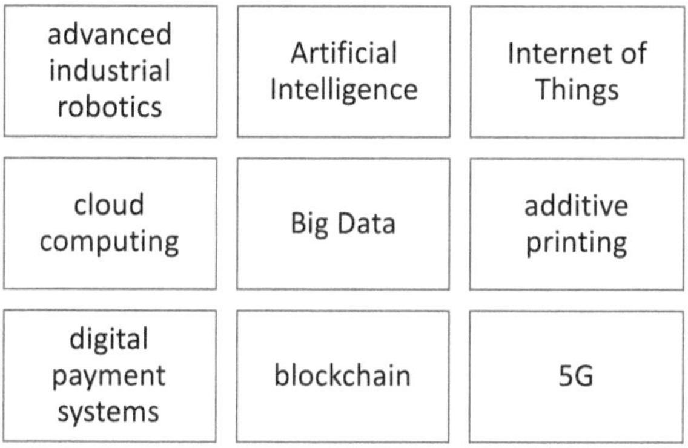

Figure 1.7 Key digital technologies.
Source: UNCTAD (2017).

intelligence (Industry 4.0). Adaptation of digital technologies in production and services causes changes in the production process. The digital economy determines the quality of economic growth and development. Digital transformation of a traditional economy is sufficient to produce desirable effects (Zhao et al., 2020). ICTs provide foundations for the digital economy. Therefore, it is important to identify various types of digital technologies (Nathan et al., 2019), namely, IT hardware (e.g., drones, industrial robots and wearables) and digital content (software, online advertising, design, online media and online business).

The digital economy is now replacing the economy based on natural resources. An enormous challenge is posed by establishing adequate formal institutions (a regulatory infrastructure) designed to lay down rules for market play, a new deal, e.g., for the digital data market. Wiebe (2017) emphasizes the need for regulating the right to trade in industrial data and its protection in the digital age. Considering that big data, which involves collecting and processing large data sets, represents an essential component of the digital economy, immediate decisive actions are indispensable. During the following years, the rise of industrial robots, autonomous vehicles the growing automation of numerous processes will cause an increase in the number of data producers.

The OECD (2020) identifies many areas where digitalization and innovation based on digital data will affect competitiveness. The digital economy was selected as a strategic theme for the OECD Competition Committee, with a focus on four sub-streams (Capobianco & Nyeso, 2018): (1) the relationship between the digital economy, law and innovation; (2) challenges posed to antitrust tools and approaches; (3) practical challenges to competition enforcement; and (4) development and evolution of specific industries.

By using ICT and virtual resources (software and algorithms), businesses can easily expand their operations (this is termed flexible scalability of activity). This capability is described as a cross-jurisdictional scale without mass. The technology companies actively participate in the economies of numerous countries, influencing social processes and decisions made by people. They ignore constraints imposed by local (national) laws (Śledziewska & Włoch, 2020). This gives reasons for introducing a digital tax payable by the "digital giants" in the member states of the EU. Not waiting for a joint initiative to introduce a "digital tax" and aiming to protect their domestic markets from being monopolized by American and Chinese corporations, Spain imposed a 3% tax on "digital revenue" generated in the Spanish market, and Great Britain imposed a similar 2% tax. Such measures are taken to achieve the community objective of creating a single digital market in the European Economic Area and thus facilitating the free movement of digital goods, increasing productivity and improving access to information.

The solutions used to regulate the digital economy include regulatory test environments known as regulatory sandboxes. Their concept consists of creating special and isolated areas for testing the potential consequences of a new technical solution to be introduced. Such sandboxes facilitate performing an "experiment" in a safe manner, rapid verification by the regulator of the consequences of an innovation, reducing the barriers to entry faced by innovators and accelerating the pace of implementation of a solution.

This is done in the spirit of mitigating risks to consumers of digital services. Currently, regulatory sandboxes are operating in more than 20 countries. A regulatory sandbox has been operated by the Financial Supervision Authority in Poland since 2018. The European leader and pioneer is the British regulatory body the Financial Conduct Authority (FCA) that has improved the regulation process, making Great Britain an inspiring example of fintech development. On average, one-third of the applications for participating in the FCA sandbox are approved and admitted to testing (Marchewka-Bartkowiak, 2019).

The development of the digital economy is also characterized by significant changes in work organization. A new global division of labour across value chains, the new business model of online platforms, reflecting the increasing capacity to extract value from big data, and the digital renewal of the informal economy are fostering new forms of work and employment (Valenduc, 2019, p. 79). There is ICT-based nomadic work with digital nomads characterized by two specific work practices: they make extensive use of computers, smartphones, cloud services and the Internet, and their working time is not spent solely on the premises of the employer (p. 68). Another change is linked to online platforms that have enabled on-demand work. Such work relies on the continued employment relationship with an employer but without continuity of job, pre-defined working hours or level of remuneration. The employer calls on the worker only when needed (p. 70). There is crowd working that refers to work carried out through online platforms which allow organizations or individuals prepared to solve specific problems or supply specific services or products in exchange for payment (Green et al., 2013); in other words, work is "externalized to the crowd" (Valenduc, 2019, p. 71). And finally prosumers – individuals who both produce and consume digitized information – carry out work by supplying data and services without being paid for it, but for which salaried employers were previously partly responsible (p. 73).

Participation in the digital economy appears to be characterized by social stratification. According to Eichhorn et al. (2020, p. 396), digital inequality research has shown that individuals cannot simply be categorized as users and non-users of online services – or haves and have-nots. Rather, individuals can be distinguished along various dimensions of access. The "digital divide" describes not only the difference between those who are connected to the digital world and those who are not, or those with "digital readiness skills" and those without them, but also widening inequality within groups and places that are connected (Sturgeon, 2021, p. 50). Notwithstanding the elimination of the classic elements of the digital divide, such as barriers to ICT adaptation, use of social media or the uptake of current e-government services, new chasms have appeared, e.g., regarding privacy, cybersecurity or the major challenge of how to deal with fake news and other forms of cyber manipulation (Bánhidi et al., 2020, p. 43).

The idea that the digital economy will advance with great rapidity creates worry about dislocations, especially from rapid reductions in demand for labour-intensive and routine jobs from automation, autonomy and artificial intelligence (Sturgeon, 2021, p. 35). According to Heikki Hiilamo (2022, p. 2), with economic globalization, technological change will have an impact across the globe with potential political repercussions. An increase in precariousness, unemployment and inequality may lead to widespread discontent which is a breeding ground for xenophobia, populism and political violence (Hiilamo, 2022). Thus, the role of policy is crucial. Policy makers have an obligation to shape digital technologies in ways to protect citizens and key institutions from abuse or damage and mitigate market concentration (Sturgeon, 2021, p. 50).

Knowledge, skills and competencies desired in the labour market change over time. Today, the following competencies are indicated as particularly important: collaboration, communication, digital literacy, citizenship, openness, capability of problem solving and critical thinking (Voogt & Roblin, 2012). The development of knowledge society has led to an accelerated growth in the importance of soft skills. However, ITC literacy has become equally essential (Lewin & McNicol, 2015). The ability to effectively function in a technology-rich society has become crucial (Eshet-Alkalai, 2004). Aiming to classify the desired 21st-century skills, Claro et al. (2012) indicate (1) the mastery of ICT applications to solve cognitive tasks at work, (2) skills supporting higher order thinking processes and (3) skills related to cognitive processes favouring continuous learning.

1.5 The sphere of influence of an economy's digital transformation

The fourth industrial revolution was triggered mainly by the development of the Internet. It enabled global and instant communication between people, and between people and machines, using cyber-physical systems. The transformation process of the industry is triggered by social, economic and political changes (Lasi et al., 2014), in particular, by pressure on shortening consecutive phases of the innovation development process. High innovation capability is becoming an essential success factor for many enterprises, enabling them to shorten "time to market". Individualization on demand and a change from a seller's into a buyer's market have been observed for decades, due to market saturation. Buyers wish to define the conditions of transactions, and this requires that individualized products be offered. Flexibility means growing flexibility in product development and manufacturing processes. Decentralization means that organizational structures are reduced to introduce faster decision-making procedures in response to sharp market fluctuations. Resource efficiency (increase in prices for resources) is caused by their shortage. Ecological aspects grow in importance, entailing a transition of manufacturing processes towards a sustainable industrial model.

Digital transformation is based on the development of the Internet and ICT. They enable developing new products in a digital form, their virtual distribution, and the emergence of new enterprise models and industries. ICT, generation by generation, offers an increasing range of functionalities, also reducing the cost of their purchase which leads to their growing accessibility.

The development of the Internet has made it possible to provide services through digital channels (Table 1.2). Automated services can be provided remotely and with a minimum participation of humans. The time of day and geographical location are irrelevant. The Internet, mobile devices (smartphones and tablets) or satellite television are used for the purposes of entertainment (music, films and games), education (remote teaching, websites, magazines and ebooks), communication (video conferencing, chats, forums and social media), physical exercise (online training sessions with a coach) and even telework (call centres and hotlines, consultancy, freelancing and financial services). Investment in advanced distribution networks of digital services became crucial, especially in the times of the COVID-19 pandemic and lockdowns.

The development of ICT in agriculture has led to an improvement in the standard of living in rural areas, more efficient plant growing and animal breeding methods. Due to technological progress, farmers are provided with precise and current information or dedicated services opening opportunities for more profitable digital agriculture (e-agriculture). The term e-agriculture refers to the conceptualization, design, development, evaluation and application of innovative ways to use ICT in rural areas (Mahant et al., 2012). As a result, digital technologies make it possible to conduct precision and

Table 1.2 The most important areas of digital services

Service	*Directions of further development*
E-health	The possibility of remote medical consultation, arranging online a visit to a health centre or receiving an e-prescription
E-work	Using the Internet to conduct remote recruitment of workers, to cooperate, complete projects and access corporate data resources
E-learning	Language courses, professional training, tertiary education, remote classes at schools, private tutoring and electronic textbooks
E-logistics	Services that support the supply chain, coordination of drivers and business partners and real-time tracking on a map of current locations of specific shipments and parcels
E-finance	The possibility of completing all tasks in the areas of finance, banking, investment and insurance with the use of dedicated software and Internet access
E-commerce	Buying and selling products over the Internet, discussed in more detail in a dedicated section below
E-administration	The provision of public services using ICT. This includes the possibility of filing applications with authorities and submitting requests by email, and even of taking popular vote over the Internet
E-culture	Access to scanned paintings and to other works of art in a digital format (also using augmented and virtual reality). This gives people with disabilities or those living in the provinces the opportunity to experience culture

Source: Flis et al. (2009).

computer-aided farming. The data collected (from agricultural machinery, e.g., on machine locations indicated by the Global Positioning System, analysis of weather and soil conditions) facilitate precise planning of soil fertilization and plant protection from pests, storms or droughts. This finally results in getting larger volumes of quality crops while managing the costs of agricultural produce (Gozdowski et al., 2007).

Another industry that has undergone a revolution due to technological progress is finance. Through the digital transformation of financial services, a new sector emerged, known as fintech (a portmanteau of "financial technology"). The term fintech, as regards market players, refers to the entities coming from the technology industry. They possess necessary know-how and technical resources useful in offering innovative financial products. In this narrow definition, the fintech industry includes only new technology companies characterized by a considerable degree of flexibility, innovation and their focus on a competitive advantage over traditional banks, gained from technology. In a broader definition, fintech may also include the digital giants that offer financial services and even the traditional banks that invest in digital solutions (Harasim & Mitręga-Niestrój, 2018).

1.6 Opportunities and threats presented by digitalization

Digital transformation of economies in numerous countries entails heightened expectations for economic growth and an improved standard of living. Simultaneously, fears are voiced of a reduction in the number of jobs, increasing inequalities and threats to information security. However, the digitalization of economies has become a major social objective (Lazanyuk & Revinova, 2019). This process was accelerated by the coronavirus pandemic in 2020–2022. The digital economy offers the following advantages according to the World Bank (2016): a reduction in the cost of information, and thus in transaction costs; promoting innovation; increasing efficiency achieved by faster and more convenient operations and services; a better integration, as the services previously unavailable are now within reach to a greater number of consumers; and job opportunities.

Vatamanescu et al. (2017) argue that the digital economy raises questions regarding the consumer protection mechanisms, the protection of privacy, the intellectual rights and the competition policies. In this respect, the EU authorities express concern about the inconveniences caused by digital transformation and its effect on the consumers and the business environment. Simultaneously, despite a rapid increase in business spending on ICT, the digital economy (understood as mobile technology, the Internet and cloud computing) has not yet generated any visible improvement in productivity (Van Ark, 2016). However, it must be reminded that the digital economy is still in its initial phase. Its effect on productivity may only be assessed from a wider historical perspective.

Technological progress may take place on condition that the development level in the preceding phase is sufficiently high. The convergence effect is observed in the industrial age and in industrial technologies. The digital revolution is the motor of divergence (growing revenues relative to scale), which is not directly observable in national accounts. For example, gross domestic product does not include a fragment of quantitative changes taking place in the age of emerging digital economy. Such spheres as online entertainment, open-source software or freeware are ignored. The digital age cannot be perceived as a simple continuation of the industrial age. The changes are observable, but the challenge lies in their measurement.

1.7 Conclusion

This chapter was aimed at providing a general conceptual framework for the present book. The proposed historical outline of the digital economy with various approaches to its definition, the discussed sphere of influence of digital transformation on the economy, leads to the following conclusions.

First, as of the turn of the 20th and 21st centuries, digitalization processes are driven by massive growth in outsourcing and offshoring. International coordination and corporate interoperability are being rapidly improved at present. Economic processes are determined by the growing diversity of digital devices and computer programs. However, it must be remembered that the current development phase of the digital economy is still to be regarded as its beginnings (with a relative shortage in software, a huge potential of artificial intelligence for influencing transformation and frequently immature automation of production processes). Second, the digital economy is driven by the development of ICT. Digital technologies and broadband access to the Web form the core of the emerging digital economy. "Digital economy" can be understood as a kind of umbrella concept describing digital markets, technologies and communication, data processing and e-commerce. Third, the characteristics distinguishing the digital economy from the traditional economy include the diminishing role of geographical location, the key role of digital platforms and network effects and the use of big data. The key factor determining future developments is AI. Fourth, the most important challenges for the development of the digital economy in the short run are posed by enforcing the competition law, taxation, data ownership, intellectual property, privacy, profiling and statistical/algorithmic discrimination.

References

Bánhidi, Z., Dobos, I. & Nemeslaki, A. (2020). What the overall Digital Economy and Society Index reveals: A statistical analysis of the DESI EU28 dimensions. *Regional Statistics, 10*(2), 42–62. doi:10.15196/RS100209.

Banning, M.E. (2016). Shared entanglements – Web 2.0, info-liberalism & digital sharing. *Information, Communication and Society, 19*(4), 489–503. doi:10.1080/1369118X.2015.1061573.

Barefoot, K., Curtis, D. & Jolliff, W. (2018). *Defining and Measuring the Digital Economy* (Bureau of Economic Analysis, U.S. Department of Commerce, Working Paper 3/15/2018). Retrieved June 29, 2022, from: https://www.bea.gov/sites/default/files/papers/defining-and-measuring-the-digital-economy.pdf.

Capobianco, A. & Nyeso, A. (2018). Challenges for competition law enforcement and policy in the digital economy. *Journal of European Competition Law & Practice, 9*(1), 19–27. doi:10.1093/jeclap/lpx082.

Chen, Y. & Wang, L. (2019). Commentary: Marketing and the sharing economy: Digital economy and emerging market challenges. *Journal of Marketing, 83*(5), 28–31. doi:10.1177/0022242919868470.

Cheon, B.Y. & Kim, H.W. (2003). *Digital Economy and Job Creation*. Korea Labor Institute.

Claro, M., Preiss, D.D., San Martín, E., Jara, I., Hinostroza, J.E., Valenzuela, S., Cortes, F. & Nussbaum, M. (2012). Assessment of 21st century ICT skills in Chile: Test design and results from high school level students. *Computers & Education, 59*(3), 1042–1053. doi:10.1016/j.compedu.2012.04.004.

D'Ippolito, B., Messeni Petruzzelli, A. & Panniello, U. (2019). Archetypes of incumbents' strategic responses to digital innovation. *Journal of Intellectual Capital, 20*(11), 662–679. doi:10.1108/JIC-04-2019-0065.

Eichhorn, T., Jürss, S. & Hoffmann, C.P. (2020). Dimensions of digital inequality in the sharing economy. *Information, Communication and Society, 25*(3), 395–412. doi:10.1080/1369118X.2020.1791218.

Eshet-Alkalai, Y. (2004). Digital literacy: A conceptual framework for survival skills in the digital era. *Journal of Educational Multimedia & Hypermedia, 13*(1), 93–107. Retrieved June 29, 2022, from: https://www.learntechlib.org/primary/p/4793/.

Gozdowski, D., Samborski, S. & Sioma, S. (2007). *Rolnictwo precyzyjne*. SGGW. ISBN: 978-83-7244-858-3.

Green, A., de Hoyos, M., Barnes, S.-A., Baldauf, B. & Behle, H. (2013). *CrowdEmploy: Crowdsourcing Case Studies. An Empirical Investigation into the Impact of Crowdsourcing on Employability*. European Commission Joint Research Centre, Institute for Prospective Technological Studies, JRC Technical Reports EUR 26351, Publication Office of the European Union. Available at: https://publications.jrc.ec.europa.eu/repository/handle/JRC85751.

Harasim, J. & Mitręga-NIestrój, K. (2018). Fintech – dylematy definicyjne i determinanty rozwoju. *Prace Naukowe Uniwersytetu Ekonomicznego we Wrocławiu, 531*, 169–179. doi:10.15611/pn.2018.531.15.

Hiilamo, H. (2022). *Participation Income. An Alternative to Basic Income for Poverty Reduction in the Digital Age*. Edward Elgar. doi:10.4337/9781800880801.

Katz, R. (2017). *Social and Economic Impact of Digital Transformation on the Economy* (ITU, GSR-17, Discussion Paper). Retrieved September 10, 2022, from: https://www.itu.int/en/ITU-D/Conferences/GSR/Documents/GSR2017/Soc_Eco_impact_Digital_tra nsformation_finalGSR.pdf.

Kerber, W. (2016). Digital markets, data, and privacy: Competition law, consumer law and data protection. *Journal of Intellectual Property Law & Practice, 11*(11), 856–866. doi:10.1093/jiplp/jpw150.

Lane, N. (1999). Advancing the digital economy into the 21st century. *Information Systems Frontiers, 1*(3), 317–320. doi:10.1023/A:1010010630396.

Lasi, H., Fettke, P., Kemper, H., Feld, T. & Hoffmann, M. (2014). Industry 4.0. Business & information. *Systems Engineering, 6*, 239–242. doi:10.1007/s12599-014-0334-4.

Lazanyuk, I. & Revinova, S. (2019). Digital economy in the BRICS countries: Myth or reality? [conference paper]. *Proceedings of the International Scientific and Practical Conference on Digital Economy (ISCDE 2019)*. doi:10.2991/iscde-19.2019.97.

Lewin, C. & McNicol, S. (2015). Supporting the development of 21st century skills through ICT [conference paper]. In T. Brinda, N. Reynolds, R. Romeike & A. Schwill (Eds.), *KEYCIT 2014: Key Competencies in Informatics and ICT* (pp. 181–98). University of Potsdam. Retrieved September 10, 2022, from: https://publishup.uni-potsdam.de/opus4-ubp/frontdoor/deliver/index/docId/7032/file/cid07.pdf.

Mahant, M., Shukla, A., Dixit, S. & Patel, D. (2012). Uses of ICT in agriculture. *International Journal of Advanced Computer Research, 2*(1), 46–49.

Marchewka-Bartkowiak, K. (2019). Regulacyjne środowisko testowe (regulatory sandbox) – doświadczenia i perspektywy. *Studia BAS, 1*(57), 61–75. Retrieved June 15, 2022, from: http://orka.sejm.gov.pl/WydBAS.nsf/0/23F5FA0EA2F618E8C12583E1003527F1/$file/Studia_BAS_57.pdf.

Nathan, M., Rosso, A., Gatten, T., Majmudar, P. & Mitchell, A. (2013). *Measuring the UK's Digital Economy with Big Data*. National Institute of Economic and Social Research. Retrieved June 15, 2022, from: https://www.niesr.ac.uk/wp-content/uploads/2021/10/SI024_GI_NIESR_Google_Report12.pdf.

Nathan, M., Vandore, E. & Voss, G. (2019). Spatial imaginaries and tech cities: Place-branding east London's digital economy. *Journal of Economic Geography, 19*(2), 409–432. doi:10.1093/jeg/lby018.

Nazarov, D.M., Fitina, E.K. & Juraeva, A.O. (2019). Digital economy as a result of the genesis of the information revolution of society [conference paper]. *Proceedings of the 1st International Scientific Conference "Modern Management Trends and the Digital Economy: from Regional Development to Global Economic Growth" (MTDE 2019)*. doi:10.2991/mtde-19.2019.67.

OECD (2020). *A Roadmap toward a Common Framework for Measuring the Digital Economy*. OECD Publishing. Retrieved June 15, 2022, from: https://www.oecd.org/sti/roadmap-toward-a-common-framework-for-measuring-the-digital-economy.pdf.

Schwab, K. (2017). *The Fourth Industrial Revolution*. Crown Business. ISBN: 9781524758868.

Sturgeon, T.J. (2021). Upgrading strategies for the digital economy. *Global Strategy Journal, 11*(1), 34–57. doi:10.1002/gsj.1364.

Śledziewska, K. & Włoch, R. (2020). *Gospodarka cyfrowa. Jak nowe technologie zmieniają świat*. Wydawnictwo Uniwersytetu Warszawskiego. Retrieved June 15, 2022, from: https://delab.uw.edu.pl/wp-content/uploads/2020/04/Katarzyna-%C5%9Aledziewska-Renata-W%C5%82och-Gospodarka-cyfrowa.pdf.

Tapscott, D. (1996). The digital economy: Promise and peril in the age of networked intelligence. *Academy of Management Perspectives, 10*(2), 156–168. doi:10.5465/ame.1996.19198671.

Teo, T.S.H. (2001). Understanding the digital economy: Data, tools, and research. *Asia Pacific Journal of Management, 18*(1), 553–555. doi:10.1023/ A:1012879426983.

UNCTAD (2017). *Information Economy Report 2017: Digitalization, Trade and Development*. United Nations. ISSN 2075-4396. Retrieved June 15, 2022, from: https://unctad.org/system/files/official-document/ier2017_en.pdf.

Valenduc, G. (2019). New forms of work and employment in the digital economy. In A. Serrano-Pascual & M. Jepsent (Eds.), *The Deconstruction of Employment as a Political Question* (pp. 63–80). Palgrave, Macmillam. doi:10.1007/978-3-319-93617-8.

Valenduc, G. & Vendramin, P. (2016). *Work in the Digital Economy: Sorting the Old from the New* (ETUI Research Paper – Working Paper 2016.03). doi:10.2139/ssrn.2770405.

Van Ark, B. (2016). The productivity paradox of the new digital economy. *International Productivity Monitor, 31*(3). http://www.csls.ca/ipm/31/vanark.pdf.

Vatamanescu, E.M., Nistoreanu, B. & Mitan, A. (2017). Competition and consumer behavior in the context of the digital economy. *Amfiteatru Economic, 19*(45), 354–366. Retrieved June 15, 2022, from: https://www.econstor.eu/bitstream/10419/169076/1/aej-v19-i45-p354.pdf.

Voogt, J. & Roblin, N.P. (2012). A comparative analysis of international frameworks for 21st century competences: Implications for national curriculum policies. *Journal of Curriculum Studies, 44*(3), 299–321. doi:10.1080/00220272.2012.668938.

Wiebe, A. (2017). Protection of industrial data – A new property right for the digital economy? *Journal of Intellectual Property Law & Practice, 12*(1), 62–71. doi:10.1093/jiplp/jpw175.
Web of Science (2022). *Social Science Citation Index.* Retrieved May 20, 2022, from https://www.webofscience.com/wos/woscc/basic-search
World Bank (WB) (2016). *Digital Dividends Report.* Retrieved June 29, 2022, from: http://www-wds.worldbank.org/external/default/WDSContentServer/WDSP/IB/2016/01/13/090224b08405ea05/2_0/Rendered/PDF/World0developm0000digital0dividends.pdf.
Zhao, T., Zhang, Z. & Liang, S.K. (2022). Digital economy, entrepreneurship, and high quality economic development: Empirical evidence from urban China. *Frontiers of Economics in China*, 2022, *17*(3), 393–426, doi:10.3868/s060-015-022-0015-6

2 Measuring the digital economy with "digital economy" tools

Aleksander Żołnierski

2.1 Introduction

Measuring the digital economy is mostly based on quantitative methods (see G20 DETF, 2018; IMF, 2018; ITU, 2020; OECD, 2020). They are used to create various rankings, and so popular in both economic journalism and scientific publications (see Chakravorti & Chaturvedi, 2019; European Commission, 2022; Fraunhofer Institute FOKUS, 2021; UNCTAD, 2021). Indeed, international comparisons and statistics identifying local leaders in digitalization and at the same time showing the distance between economies with the highest degree of use of digital technologies, and those where more traditional solutions dominate, provide a useful tool, supporting not only policymakers. For instance, the DESI (Digital Economy and Society Index) methodology used by the Directorate-General for Communication Networks, Content and Technology measures the actual implementation of the Digital Single Market (DSM) strategy, a set of policies aimed to make Europe fit for the digital age (European Commission, 2015). Measurements of DESI (European Commission, 2022) are based on integrated indicators and represent the main method of both measuring the scale of digitalization in the European Union countries and examining the scope and degree of implemented strategies related to the digitalization of the economies of these countries. Such tools make it possible to evaluate the digitalization level of economies and the development of the digital economy not only by considering individual countries, groups of countries and regions but also at the meso-economic level – within industries. Integrated indicators focus on the digitalization process in the economy, measurement of the ICT sector, the use of broadband internet, security and e-commerce, the use of ICT by citizens and their security and competencies in this area, as well as online public services. However, the question is whether the tool (be it DESI or another, based on currently used methods) describes the dynamically changing landscape and not only technological issues relating to the digital economy; whether it can be used to identify the most important areas of change.

The problem is that the measurements used are not based on a clear definition of the digital economy, and the methodology employed is founded on an

DOI: 10.4324/9781003450160-4

ostensive definition. In a word, it examines those areas of the socio-economic spectrum where the expected impact of digitalization is discernible. Presumably, these issues stem from the lack of a rigorous definition of the field of research and the vague description of the digital economy itself.

The digital economy is not a new concept. Some years ago we observed the phenomena related to economic applications of digital technologies, termed a "new economy". Technology-based economies emerged, wherein new digital technologies facilitating more extensive and efficient business were referred to as the digital economy, the knowledge economy or the data economy. The term itself, as used in the book "The Digital Economy: Promise and Peril in the Age of Networked Intelligence" and popularized by Tapscott in 1995, was still far from being unambiguous (Tapscott, 2015). Tapscott wrote about it in the context of the new information medium:

> A new medium of human communications is emerging, one that may prove to surpass all previous revolutions [...] in its impact on our economic and social life. The computer is expanding from a tool for information management to a tool for communications. The internet and World Wide Web are enabling a new economy based on the networking of human intelligence. In this digital economy, individuals and enterprises create wealth by applying knowledge, networked human intelligence, and effort to manufacturing, agriculture, and services. In the digital frontier of this economy, the players, dynamics, rules and requirements for survival and success are all changing.
>
> (Tapscott, 2015, XXIII)

Tapscott argues that the spread of new practices used by industries to ensure economic growth is becoming noticeable (Tapscott, 2015, 362). However, all these concepts refer to the knowledge-based economy or, for short, the knowledge economy, where information becomes the basic factor in creating a modern and competitive product.

Initially, the conceptualization of characteristics describing the digital economy principally focused on its social and economic aspects (knowledge management, ICT applications in enterprises, education of workers in the economy or the degree of internationalization), to evolve in time, with the widespread use of the Internet of Things (IoT) technology and analysis of big data sets, with the development of data processing technologies, into an approach based rather on technical sciences, computer science and mathematics. Despite the increasing use of the term "digital economy", a precise definition of this phenomenon still leaves room for discussion among scientists and theorists, as well as business practitioners. Thus, with the development of technology, including data collection techniques and big data analysis, the approach to conceptualizing the digital economy has changed – beginning with knowledge management, to structures and networks, ending with security issues and all types of crypto and tokenization applications.

Three primary components of the concept of the digital economy were distinguished by Mesenbourg (2001, 2), namely, the supporting infrastructure, electronic business processes (how business is conducted) and electronic commerce transactions (selling of goods and services online). Contemporary concepts describe the digital economy as a type of economy focused on the flow of intangible goods with zero marginal cost (Rifkin, 2014). The digital economy is also closely related to the applications of digital technologies, known for nearly a decade as Industry 4.0. Bukht and Heeks (2017) emphasize, that "definitions are always a reflection of the times and trends from which they emerge", and define the digital economy as an economy of digital services and platforms, with its core formed by the digital (IT/ICT) sector (that consists of four components: hardware manufacturing, software and IT consulting, information services and telecommunications). Bukht and Heeks (2017) also distinguish a broad scope (digitalized economy) as a sum of the above-mentioned items and e-business, e-commerce, Industry 4.0, precision agriculture and algorithmic economy, with the presence of sharing economy and gig economy. The broad scope is related to the development of the Industry 4.0 concept. It seems that the concept of the digital economy also evolved from the earlier concepts of the knowledge economy and the knowledge-based economy, following the development of digital technologies, especially the applications of artificial intelligence (AI) in economic practice. Industry 4.0 is a concept describing value creation with the use of digital technologies (Schwab, 2018). Industry 4.0 is based on cyber-physical systems enabling real-time connection of the physical and the virtual world, supported by intelligent data analysis systems. Cyber-physical production systems enable such functions as condition monitoring, preventive diagnostics and maintenance and autonomous machine control. On the one hand, Industry 4.0 is used for management in dynamically changing environmental conditions; on the other hand, it is based on technological changes, such as automation, digitization and networking within machine and human and product environments along the entire value chain. The main trends of development are big data and analytics, AI, augmented reality, digitalization of supply chains, cybersecurity and the IoT (Sweeney, 2018).

As mentioned above, the research and analysis of the digital economy is mostly based on quantitative studies covering the scope of dissemination of ICT in economic entities, households and among individual users. This approach is "boosted" by social research methods (e.g., surveys) to analyse the effects of ICT applications. It covers the whole spectrum, from social and economic issues to social psychology, education and employment. Measurement tools are used both to create an aid policy and to monitor the condition of the economy, including the potential demand for high-skilled workforce (jobs) from the high-tech and IT industries in the near and somewhat more distant future.

The described tools are reliable measuring instruments and show a clear, although not multidimensional reality. However, in view of the dynamically changing socio-technological aspects of the digital economy, they leave much to be desired. First of all, as tools that rely on a specific method of collecting data, on the one hand, they generate problems resulting from time delay; therefore, they are not ideal for assessing the current situation of the digital economy. On the other hand, the data used for statistics is collected as part of social research (i.e., surveys) and thus may be distorted by the interviewer error. The most serious issue, however, is that in each case, they reflect the mindset concerning the digital economy of planners and politicians, and even if researchers and practitioners are involved in the tool design process – measurement tools are not appropriate for an accurate identification of new phenomena related to the digital economy. In this respect, information about both new, fast-growing technologies and competencies being developed is lost.

The tools commonly used measure what in the digital economy was already visible a year or several years ago and are unfit for the identification and measurement of new phenomena and contemporary changes within the economy. An example is provided by many high-end technology issues related to Industry 4.0. Despite the fact that the existing tools allow to identify the scope of use of technologies based on AI, blockchain, or robotics and automation, and on implementing cyber-physical systems, they do not support reliable measurement of phenomena caused by the use of specific types of these technologies (e.g., the scope of application of tools related to access protection, monitoring or even ecotechnology).

Not only do surveys or statistical research provide a measurement tool but the data used for analysis also comes from the internet or sensors and devices of the IoT. An example is provided by lighting systems that use various sensors to optimize power consumption by office and manufacturing floor lighting.[1]

An important point is that the dynamic digitalization processes taking place today make it difficult to research and analyse the subject of digital economy using the existing and most common research methods. It seems that the applied measurement tools and concepts ignore the wide spectrum of possibilities offered by digital technologies themselves and by the methods using behavioural analysis that are increasingly popular in the field of commercial research.

The emerging new methods for monitoring the technological and socio-economic environment of digital economies, in particular the methods using AI, business intelligence systems, big data and information refining, are increasingly being used in many research projects, but their widespread use will take time. On the one hand, official statistics grapple with a number of problems which make the task of monitoring a dynamically changing environment particularly difficult; the complexity of economic processes increases the wealth of data to be analysed, and the analysis process itself becomes more and more complicated. On the other hand, at each stage of operation, organizations generate information whose bulk is placed in various forms in the virtual space. Identifying this information, refining and analysing it appears to be the key to effective monitoring of changes in the economy.

Internet data resources provide material for qualitative research. The use of big data tools, in which information from several or over a dozen million sources is analysed, allows to combine the advantages of quantitative and qualitative methods. So far, in research focusing on economic topics, in particular on the subjects of innovation, economy and ecology, or in the analysis of stock exchange trends where the collected information is qualitative, extensive social research was used: surveys, interviews etc. This also applies to issues (not only of a qualitative nature) relating to the digital economy. The method based on the "digital economy" approach, including the tools for refining information and big data, eliminates any imperfections of the above-mentioned representative methods – in practice, analysing a million or 10 million records does not affect the cost of the study. It turns out that systematic scanning of available unstructured data in the environment may become a strategically important activity of economic process researchers. This is especially so due to the growing complexity of available information and business data, primarily related to new technologies.

The process underlying the analyses with the use of big data refining and analysis tools is a multi-stage process. The first step is to identify offline and online digital resources, including internet sources, object databases and streaming media. The next stage is collecting the identified resources by an online bot, which is a specialized ICT system for targeted monitoring and data collection from indicated websites or other data sources. Identified and collected resources are subject to a query in search of selected keywords – cores and sentiments that define a given keyword. The next step is to transform cores or words into matrices (to transform them as elements of an "algebraic structure"). Matrices are used to compute statistics. The frequency of occurrence of individual cores and sentiments (or words) in the analysed corpus is calculated. The columns constitute a statistically verified reference point for the selection of sentiments (words and phrases) of an evaluative nature that accompany the topics under study.

The new approach is useful in analysing multiple characteristics of the digital economy. It includes the analysis of keywords referring to new and emerging technologies, the analysis of the content (discussions) on social networks related to the economic and social aspect of digitalization, of discussion among both specialists and scientists, and managers and users – information technology experts etc. It is important that big data analytical tools are already used by many institutions (e.g., in the United States) to predict, inter alia, the financial condition of stock market companies or even the likelihood of crimes.[2] What can be achieved by implementing "digital economy" tools to measure digital economy issues is getting easy access to current data on research and development and innovation activity within digital economy areas (in a geographic, regional, technological and industrial sense).

Further possibilities include monitoring the situation in terms of human resources involved in digital economy processes and the situation in terms of the competitiveness of the digital economy entities and industries.

2.2 Big data analysis and the data refining method

As regards unstructured data sets analysis, a number of useful methods already exist, like rough set theory, theory of approximation and fuzzy rough sets theory (Tran & Huh, 2022). In many cases, the information analysing system allows to integrate unstructured data with structured one (Balabin et al., 2022). To monitor and analyse the digital economy environment of high complexity, a knowledge management system must be built. Such systems are increasingly based on AI, big data analysis and information refining as well as business intelligence technologies (Cetera et al., 2022).

Unstructured data analysis requires effective data management methods also in the case of databases derived from IoT sources (Azad et al., 2020). The challenge is to "create, transfer, pool, integrate and exploit knowledge resources" (Frishammar & Richtnér, 2008). Methods based on digital economy tools principally employ the data acquisition technology. The examples of methods of refined data and unstructured data analysis found in the literature are focused on unsupervised text processing (Jain et al., 2021). The text mining technology is widely used, from management and social sciences to medicine and biomedical data analysis.

The first attempts to explore the online data and big data acquired from structured scientific data repositories resulted from the need to shorten the time of big data processing. The information collected from the online "behavioural" sources is characterized by independence from the observer and its growing volume. One of the first steps in exploring the online sources is to distinguish valuable sources of information for identifying the issues to be analysed. A data processing system is needed to facilitate automatic collection of source data as well as statistical processing. Collected and analysed data is used for quantitative analysis and visualized to obtain a better description of results. A modular design of the data processing system is created to meet the requirements of scalability. Scalability applies to both the infrastructure of the system itself and the use of distributed task processing. The application of a specific tool results from the needs of the research area and the range of tests – each particular search is heuristic in its nature and is practically a separate, unique study.

Identifying valuable information sources relies on using methods fitting the analysed theory and is always dictated by the research problem. The key issues are related to both the research area and the types of data sources. Finally, a practical method must be worked out for collecting and exploring data and selecting tools used for information refining (see Figure 2.1).

The use of big data analysis begins with encoding plain text in the UTF-8 standard. Data converted to this form and input information provided in the

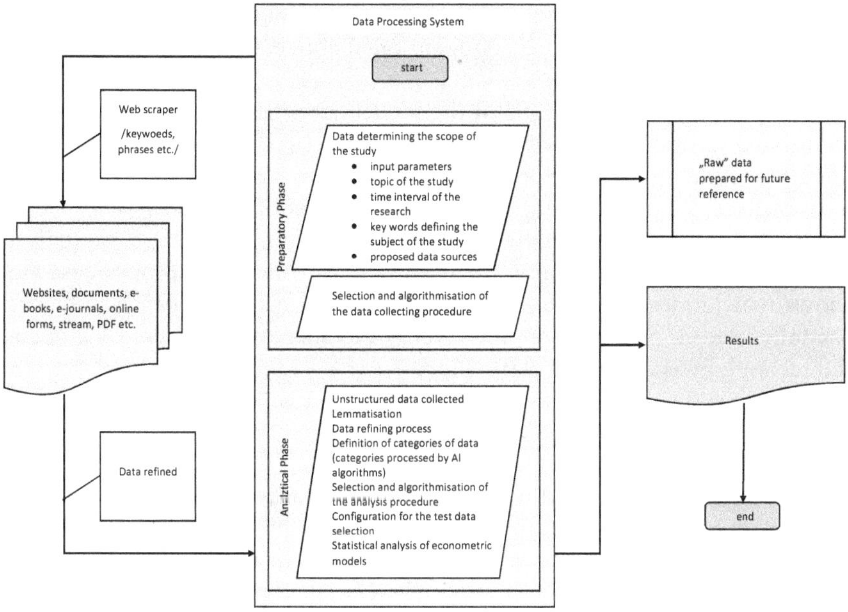

Figure 2.1 Data processing procedure: refining unstructured data online.

Source: Own research.

form of URL links directing to internet sites with data needed are collected by automated online tools. The data processing system contains an analytical warehouse accepting data sources as RSS feeds. The utility program performs data extraction and converts the non-text file to a text file (in a UTF-8 format). A research project generates a database of sources both from many different services and in different formats. This creates a need to check the sources for completeness before starting computations. The most common method is based on comparing individual items from the list of data sources intended for analysis to the sources appearing in the database (see Cetera et al., 2022).

The next step is to launch analysis, and this is usually associated with using the R scripting language (R Core Team, 2021). It is important to create an automatic data classifier, enabling the necessary use of supervised learning and natural language processing algorithms as part of the analysis being carried out. To guarantee the high quality of analysis results, the script is strengthened by integrating measures of its effectiveness. Finally, a confusion matrix is created to evaluate the results of the model. The trained machine learning model accuracy is about 0.84. Structured data is subject to a statistical analysis. This includes the following sequence of operations: tokenization, quantitative analysis, TF-IDF statistics, bigram analysis, correlation analysis and cluster analysis. The required high confidence level is determined not only by choosing adequate statistical tools but also indirectly by the machine learning model. As mentioned above, the accuracy of the data processing system is 0.84.

A good application example of the model described above is a system for identifying technology trends (Cetera et al., 2022). The system is designed to identify technological development within specific areas and to evaluate the level of technological development. The tools identifying technology trends represent one of the first applications of data refining and big data analysis in a country that is not among the world's most innovative economies. This shows that modern analytical tools of the digital economy can also be successfully used in places where the level of advancement and use of Industry 4.0 technology is not particularly high.

2.3 Google Trends as a trend prediction tool

The use of predictive capabilities provided by data from the internet is growing in popularity. Some studies indicate that Google Trends can be used as an effective source of data indicating the interest of stock investors (Huang et al., 2020). Google Trends is a service by Google that allows users to obtain information on the number of all queries in the Google search engine for a specific term or phrase in a selected period and for a selected geographic area. The selected period can be freely defined and thus the data obtained in time series (since 2004). Google Trends in a specific, selected period of time returns information about the relative number of queries.

For example, researchers analysing data from Google Trends use the Kaplan-Meier estimate to gauge trends in S&P 500 in a term's Granger causality. A correlation is observed between S&P 500 trends and dynamics of queries (indicated in Google Trends). This depends on the specific term searched and, above all, the sentiment related to the term being searched. Google Trends itself is an indicator of investor interest, but the dynamics of changes in queries about individual values depends on the evaluative sentiment appearing around the term or phrase searched (specific securities, shares of stock, bonds or other financial instruments; e.g., Bayer, SAP, Apple and Microsoft Corporation).

Google Trends can also be used to analyse the response to environmental crises. Researches in this area reflect the ever wider and more complex possibilities of analysing the communication ecosystem. The analysis of Google Trends in this context indicates the consequences of interactions that occur between social media, "traditional" mass media and queries in the Google search engine (Matei et al., 2021). The analysis of queries in the Google search engine, as "powered" in a kind of secondary way by media users' responses to press and TV news and activity on Twitter, indicates that Google Trends may also be a valuable source of data for predicting trends in the natural environment. Internet users, both individual and collective, increasingly create data within new information channels outside of mainstream media.

This is especially true in crisis situations, when social media becomes one of the main information channels (due to the up-to-date information published there by users). For example, by analysing the time series, the correlation between each pair of the following variables was investigated – soil moisture, Twitter activity, search engine trends and media reports on drought. Based on, inter alia, Autoregressive Moving Average models, a statistically significant correlation was established between geological conditions and activity in the Google search engine, media coverage and the number of tweets.

Researchers also use Google Trends to predict price trends in grain futures (Gómez Martínez et al., 2021). Gómez Martínez et al. (2021) used data from soybean and corn futures contracts (at the Chicago Mercantile Exchange) to evaluate the potential of a tool based on data from a search engine. The researchers proved that there was a potential in terms of price forecasting and proposed that the analysed possibilities be used by individual traders as well as investors and trading companies. Over the years, multiple investment strategies have been developed for the analysis of raw materials prices in the agricultural sector, mainly based on the methods of fundamental analysis and on selected indicators of technical analysis. Gómez Martínez et al. (2021) propose methods based on behavioural finance, primarily analysing investor sentiment and indicators based on big data and social media. Behavioural finance focuses on the analysis of individual investor behaviour and on the psychological aspects of behaviour that influence investment decisions in capital markets. Accurate predictions of the price level of soybeans and corn based on online data – primarily Google Trends – have become possible. Gómez Martínez et al. (2021) demonstrate how individual investors and traders can predict market price fluctuations by using the available data of Google Trends as a tool to work out their own strategy.

The use of online data on investor and consumer sentiments instead of information "traditionally" obtained through surveys and personal interviews has become a common tool for marketers and market researchers. It is also useful for more sophisticated analyses of economic and social issues. As Google Trends contains data based on queries, entered practically from the beginning of this tool's existence, researchers have used it as a kind of substitute tool for opinion polls or sentiment surveys. Google Trends has proved to have considerable potential for forecasting many economic and financial variables. Researchers have used it to explore such issues as unemployment, inflation and fluctuations in the stock market, as well as the value of cryptocurrencies, the dynamics of exchange rates or – more than a decade ago – consumer sentiment and consumption rates. Wilcoxson et al. (2020) examine the possibility of using Google Trends to analyse exchange rates and forecast rates for the US dollar and ten other currencies. The study covers the period from January 2004 to August 2018 and shows that Google Trends can also be an important prediction tool in this case.

There are studies showing that analyses based on Google Trends data can produce more accurate forecasts than traditional (and reliable) surveys (Zhu et al., 2012). But researchers indicate that the data from Google Trends has a certain limitation, namely, accessibility of the internet. Not everyone who has access to the internet and uses the global web will use the Google search engine. When using Google Trends, it should therefore be remembered that the data contained therein defines "only" the active population of internet users who use the Google search engine. Despite these limitations, data from Google Trends makes it possible to accurately predict investor behaviour and provides good material for analysing the psychological aspect of currency markets. Some researchers, including Zhu et al. (2012), find no systematic difference in the opinions expressed in standard polls between internet users and non-users. It turns out that public opinion – and therefore also investors' preferences – can be studied based on the analysis of search queries in the search engine; however, it should be remembered that the strength of the correlation between "opinion" and "query" probably depends on the analysed problem.

Another research team analysed the potential of using Google Trends for sales forecasts (Fritzsch et al., 2020). Fritzsch et al. (2020) combined standard time series models with Google Trends data. Sales forecasts, from the producer's point of view, form a basis for strategic planning. If the data used is imprecise or false, the forecasts can cause shortages of supply (the forecast demand falls below its actual volume) on the one hand; on the other hand, they can increase inventory costs (the forecast demand exceeds its actual volume). Traditional time series models aimed at predicting sales tend to rely on historical data. Fritzsch et al. (2020) prove that this problem can be solved by using (up-to-date) data from search engines. This data also describes business-related issues and is available online in real time. It should be noted that Google Trends data was first used in econometrics in 2009 (Choi & Varian, 2009; Choi & Varian, 2012). The available Google Trends data that can be used for sales forecasts (at a product level) mainly covers online products. This is because customers enter the product they are looking for in the search engine and then go to the websites of online stores or manufacturers offering this product for online sale. Fritzsch et al. (2020) focused on the data for two (Sennheiser) products that are offered for sale in a traditional market. Therefore, the researchers had to demonstrate a link between sales data and Google Trends data. The results indicate that the data from Google Trends may be helpful in obtaining a more precise sales forecast.

The development of internet technologies contributes to the rapid increase in the availability of online data. For over a decade, researchers have had access to new and rich data sets which for some time have been supplemented by analyses of economic and social issues, made using "traditional" survey tools (Woo & Owen, 2019). Woo and Owen (2019) augmented the set of data from the Michigan Consumer Sentiment Index (MCSI) and the Conference Board Consumer Confidence Index (CCI) with data from Google Trends analyses. Their research focused on the potential of online data for economic forecasts. Unlike surveys, Google Trends data indicates economic consumer behaviour (e.g., pre-purchase activity). They studied data on consumption of both durable and fast-moving consumer goods and services. The research proved the high usefulness of the data from Google Trends and the high quality (accuracy) of the trends, exceeding the results of the MCSI and CCI research on private consumption forecasts. Moreover, the use of data from Google Trends reduces the cost of analyses – this data is available to virtually every internet user, and also has another very desirable value – it is possible to obtain data updated on a daily basis in a relatively long time series. Woo and Owen (2019) proved that surveys (of consumer sentiment) as a basis for predicting actual economic behaviour are not the best tool for consumption forecasts. Such surveys give relatively trivial results and are also criticized for their opacity in terms of cause-and-effect relationship (consumer sentiment-consumption decisions) and high correlation with other macroeconomic indicators (it turns out that macroeconomic indicators explain 70% of MCSI variation). In the case of Google Trends, a direct correlation between search engine queries and individual consumption was demonstrated.

The development of analytical methods based on big data and advanced IT tools results, on the one hand, from the increase in computing power of IT systems, and on the other hand, it is related to the generation of massive data sets by organizations and individuals in many economic sectors. Big data is generated by telecommunications, IT producers, organizations operating in the field of healthcare, pharmaceutical companies and the financial sector. In addition to these sectors, data is generated by internet users and amassed by institutions interested in (and able to use) big data related to user behaviour. In recent years, technologies have been developed that allow the analysis of big data "extracted" from streaming media. Already in 2015, it was estimated (Tsui & Zhao, 2017) that the average network user generates 2.5 trillion bytes of data per day (behavioural data, such as tweets, likes, comments, blogs and media streams, e.g., on YouTube). Behavioural big data (BBD) contains a large amount of information revealing individual behaviour, sentiment and multiple interactions. Researchers define BBD as very large and rich multidimensional data sets on human behaviour, actions and interactions that have become available to companies, governments and scientists. BBDs are generated (and often shared) in processes related to management in public health institutions, marketing and market research, business monitoring or in Recency, Frequency and Monetary Value analysis and Customer Relationship Management methods etc. In the United States, BBD is used by government agencies to improve the decision-making process. In large cities around the world, cameras and sensors are used to record traffic and human activity – the data is used not only to manage urban traffic but also to detect and prevent crime. In some countries, for example, in China, extreme monitoring measures are adopted to identify people who may pose a threat in the eyes of a totalitarian regime, mainly due to their actual or potential initiatives for democracy and human rights. For several years, this type of data has been used to identify and monitor the spread of various types of epidemics.

The analysis of large data sets requires not only adequate IT resources and systems but also an appropriate degree of expertise and competence of individuals supervising and using such system. This competence must be based on specific skills combining knowledge of computer science with expertise in other fields – such as engineering or economics and behaviourism or social psychology. In practice, it is important to combine specialist expertise in a particular field with the skills and knowledge required to exploit the potential of using BBD for analysis in that field. Knowledge of statistics and econometrics is also crucial for creating models using BBD.

It is known that the enormous complexity of human behaviour is not advantageous to either the efficiency or the accuracy of BBD-based predictions. The complexity of behaviours makes greater demands on the advancement of algorithms, IT systems and also on analysts, compared to those systems that focus on the analysis of data from production or financial systems. Such complexity affects the scope of data necessary for modelling not only the size and efficiency of IT resources needed but also the level of complication in terms of the modelling tools used – relating to correlation, causality, variability, dynamics, sentiment analysis etc.

2.4 Beacons technology

In June 2013, Apple introduced iBeacon as part of iOS 7 at its Worldwide Developer Conference. Beacons are mainly used to initiate interaction between the customer or visitor and the place of their interest (a shop, hospital, university, library, museum etc.) (Maxin, 2015). Already in 2013, this technology was well developed and had many practical applications; Titan installed 500 beacons in Manhattan phone booths for "maintenance purposes", and in December, Apple activated beacons in all 254 of its US shops to provide customers with in-store notifications about items, product reviews, and deals. Beacons can also be used for navigation in areas where the GPS signal fades. Beacon technology, designed for sending direct messages to in-store customers, from its very beginning created a wave of excitement among retailers and marketing leaders (plotprojects.com, 2022).

To effectively use the full capability of beacons, a dedicated mobile (or computer) application is needed. The signal transmitted by beacons and intercepted by a smartphone or laptop allows the customer to get a commercial or a piece of necessary information. More advanced technologies are now being developed for gathering and processing data collected by smartphones interacting with beacons. An individual moving around the place of their interest can be informed about the details of a particular object or its current status. For this purpose, the smartphone generates data collected by the system supervising the network of beacons (Softensy, 2022). Although the technology has not yet established a strong foothold in retailing, it enables collecting huge data sets that not only suit the needs of marketers but also contribute to understanding consumer behaviour (van de Sanden et al., 2019).

In 2014, over 50 of the top 100 US retailers tested beacons in their shops; in Europe, beacon technology was trialled in the UK where in-store customers had to have an app downloaded to receive information from beacons. The customers were tracked to find what time they spent looking at an item and their method of purchase. Using the data collected from retailers' beacons, a more accurate and personalized marketing strategy could be implemented. A year later, Google launched Eddystone, a competitor to Apple's iBeacon. Google Beacon – compatible across platforms – was designed to provide location-based content to mobile devices. Google improved beacon technology by making it possible for people to use the feature without downloading any applications (Wordstream, 2021).

The global smart beacon market generated more than $3 billion in 2020 and is expected to reach a whopping value of $103.94 billion by 2030, growing at a CAGR of 37.70% from 2021 to 2030 (plotprojects.com, 2022). The technology provides marketers with a more precise apparatus intended to both encourage engagement and validate the purchase mindset of in-store consumers (PR Newswire US, 2015). More advanced beacon technologies focus on user experience design, digital product design, digital/online marketing, marketing analytics and brand marketing (PR Newswire US, 2019).

Proximity marketing is a way of communication between business and customer. Development trends of the proximity market are based on building trust among customers with the use of the approved, accustomed technology which readily available to customers (in portable devices). These portable devices (mainly smartphones, but also laptops, smartwatches and other personal IT devices) have determined the methods used to influence the consumer's behaviour. Proximity targeting shapes the marketing strategies adopted by companies (Giurea, 2015). The evolution of proximity marketing is enhanced by the implementations of the Bluetooth beacon technology (BBT). Some researchers noticed growing concern about privacy among customers, although BBT fosters customers' reception of relationship marketing programmes. The "technological" approach makes difficult an understanding of consumer behaviour in some areas; it is all about consumer cognition, evaluation and receptiveness behaviours (Lin et al., 2022). Expectations about the development of proximity marketing are growing high. In 2016, it was expected to be worth USD 52.46 billion by 2022 (PR Newswire US, 2016).

Beacons as devices are characterized by low energy consumption (nowadays they can be reinforced by energy harvesting), can be installed almost anywhere and transmit signals using Bluetooth technology. When a smartphone with a dedicated application is located in the area of operation of a beacon, it can take a programmed action. Beacons are primarily intended for marketing purposes but also allow to collect large data sets used by marketers, traders and market analysts. Beacon technology allows object tracking in real time and helps to organize production and distribution channels with the aim of implementing Industry 4.0 solutions. It can be used both to better locate employees or customers and to integrate logistics processes. Beacon supports solutions for informing the traffic network users about the environment. This technology aims to provide the user with precise and real-time information and to raise the level of safety in traffic (Periša et al., 2019).

The technology has also a wide range of applications in medical research. A Bluetooth low energy beacon-based algorithm helps to remotely measure the social behaviour of individuals with Autism Spectrum Disorder (ASD). A study was conducted on the social behaviour of people with ASD, based on an algorithm that estimated signal strength from implemented beacons, and was used to assess the development of objective sociability features and eventually support decisions regarding drug efficacy in ASD (Kriara et al., 2021). The beacons technology can efficiently be applied not only to monitor the location of medical equipment or even the patients themselves but also, e.g., to track the position of tools in production processes in a smart factory. School and university teachers can automatically check attendance in their classes and send students warnings and additional information on lectures. During a pandemic or other security threats, a net of beacons helps to avoid queues and dangerous situations during public gatherings. The technical potential of the beacon helps to monitor the distance and to navigate the customer within the sales area and to keep statistics on the occupancy of selected rooms. As a technology that has grown to become the foundation of the IoT, beacons unlock the potential of Industry 4.0 and bring it closer to the user.

2.5 Conclusion

The process of changes towards a wider use of big data methods, including BBD, is evolutionary rather than revolutionary. The beginnings of big data analytics can be traced back to the 1970s (Big Data Framework, 2021; Dataversity, 2021). In the 1970s, machine learning methods and computer-based methods began to play an important role in economics and statistics. In the 1980s, the amount of analysed data grew rapidly, mainly due to improvements in computer performance. The concept of "very large databases" emerged, distinguishing separate large data sets from conventional ones. Scientists also used the term "massive data". The 1990s saw further rapid development of big data analytical methods, defined as the first wave of big data analysis. These methods began to be used in various scientific disciplines; from data mining through statistical learning to discovering statistical correlations in large data sets known as knowledge discovery in database. Still, in the 1990s, big data analytics was used primarily by the academic world. The effectiveness of big data methods and the success of methodologies using big data analytics contributed to the dissemination of these methods in areas beyond strictly scientific applications, including primarily industry.

In the new millennium, big data methods have successfully developed across a range of disciplines and applications: from business analytics and disciplines related to computer science to engineering (including bioinformatics and health informatics). Big data applications are increasingly used in academia, education and industry. Nowadays, there are many methods of monitoring the digital economy that use digital technologies, but their spread is not as wide as that of "traditional" methodologies based on statistical data and surveys. Three selected new methods are described in this chapter.

By using analyses of non-structured data collected from online sources, it is possible to obtain information on the advancement and proliferation of digital technologies in economies. Thanks to this methodology, it is possible to analyse data at the level of industries as well as that of entire economies. The data analysis techniques that employ big data tools allow to assess the state of new technologies and technological challenges and the use of existing digital solutions.

Data analysis with Google Trends extends the knowledge of socio-economic phenomena, technology and public health, based on behavioural statistics. Google Trends data analysis is a cheap and fairly common method of determining trends and turning points in the analysed areas of human activity related to digital economy. The method used by the scientific community has been extensively tested and is continually improved in the field of applied statistical and econometric research, and combined with other methods, techniques and data sources.

Beacon technology has many new applications today. Although it is no longer widely used in its original form as a retail support tool, new applications pave the way for a reversal of the downtrend. The COVID-19 pandemic has shown that beacon technology is perfectly useful not only for indoor navigation but also in places where the GPS signal is weak or unavailable. The technology facilitates access control, identification and location of resources and – in combination with other IoT sensors – controlling the health of employees. Thanks to the beacon technology, it is also possible to study and analyse the degree of diffusion of applications used in mobile devices and to indicate the advancement of communication technologies.

New methodologies for collecting and analysing digital economy data are constantly evolving and modifying, and their use is changing just like the technologies themselves.

Notes

1 Depending on the sensor used, it is possible to monitor selected parameters of the environment with control, tracking and analysis of portable devices used by employees. During the COVID-19 pandemic, IoT sensors used for remote control of light intensity in fluorescent lamps could also be used for health monitoring of employees.

2 It is not science fiction, it is a fact! Such a programme is implemented by the police in Modesto, California.

References

Azad, P., Navimipour, N.J., Rahmani, A.M. & Sharifi, A. (2020). The role of structured and unstructured data managing mechanisms in the Internet of Things. *Cluster Computing 23*, 1185–1198. https://doi.org/10.1007/s10586-019-02986-2.

Balabin, H., Hoyt, C.T., Birkenbihl, C., Gyori, B.M., Bachman, J., Kodamullil, A.T., Plöger, P.G., Hofmann-Apitius, M. & Domingo-Fernández, D. (2022). STonKGs: A sophisticated transformer trained on biomedical text and knowledge graphs. *Bioinformatics 38*(6), 1648–1656. https://doi.org/10.1093/bioinformatics/btac001.

Bukht, R. & Heeks, R. (2017). *Defining, Conceptualising and Measuring the Digital Economy* (Manchester Centre for Development Informatics Working Paper 68). http://doi.org/10.2139/ssrn.3431732.

Cetera, W., Gogołek, W., Żołnierski, A. & Jaruga, D. (2022). Potential for the use of large unstructured data resources by public innovation support institutions. *Journal of Big Data 9*(46). https://doi.org/10.1186/s40537-022-00610-6.

Choi, H. & Varian, H. (2009). *Predicting the Present with Google Trends*. Google Technical Report. Available from: http://google.com/googleblogs/ pdfs/google_predicting_the_present.pdf.

Choi, H. & Varian, H. (2012). Predicting the present with Google Trends. *Economic Record 88*, 2–9. https://doi.org/10.1111/j.1475-4932.2012.00809.x.

European Commission. (2015). *A Digital Single Market Strategy for Europe* (Commission Staff Working Document). https://eur-lex.europa.eu/legal-content/EN/TXT/?uri=CELEX%3A52015SC0100.

European Commission. (2022). *Digital Economy and Society Index*. https://digital-strategy.ec.europa.eu/en/library/digital-economy-and-society-index-desi-2022

Frishammar, J. & Richtnér, A. (2008). Editorial. *International Journal of Technology Intelligence and Planning 4*(3), 229–233.

Fritzsch, B., Wenger, K., Sibbertsen, P. & Ullmann, G. (2020). Can google trends improve sales forecasts on a product level? *Applied Economics Letters 27*(17), 1409–1414. https://doi.org/10.1080/13504851.2019.1686110.

G20 DETF. (2018). *Toolkit for Measuring the Digital Economy*. G20 Digital Economy Task Force. Available at: https://www.oecd.org/g20/summits/buenos-aires/G20-Toolkit-for-measuring-digital-economy.pdf.

Giurea, A.M. (2015). Proximity Market, the New Trend Approved by the Consumer's Behavior. *International Journal of Economic Practices & Theories 5*(5), 462–469. https://doi.org/10.1007/s10551-019-04278-6.

Gómez Martínez, R., Orden-Cruz, C. & Prado Román, C. (2021). Google Trends as predictor of grain prices. *Economics of Agriculture / Ekonomika Poljoprivrede 68*(1), 203–211. https://doi.org/10.5937/ekoPolj2101203G.

Huang, M.Y., Rojas, R.R. & Convery, P.D. (2020). Forecasting stock market movements using Google Trend searches. *Empirical Economics 59*(6), 2821–2839. https://doi.org/10.1007/s00181-019-01725-1.

IMF. (2018). *Measuring the Digital Economy*. IMF Policy Paper. Available at: https://www.imf.org/en/Publications/Policy-Papers/Issues/2018/04/03/022818-measuring-the-digital-economy.

ITU. (2020). *Manual for Measuring ICT Access and Use by Households and Individuals*. Available at: https://www.itu.int/en/ITU-D/Statistics/Pages/publications/manual.aspx.

Jain, S., de Buitléir, A. & Fallon, E. (2021). *An Extensible Parsing Pipeline for Unstructured Data Processing* [Conference Paper]. 2021 23rd International Conference on Advanced Communication Technology (ICACT). https://doi.org/10.23919/ICACT51234.2021.9370654.

Kriara, L., Hipp, J., Chatham, C., Nobbs, D., Slater, D., Lipsmeier, F. & Lindemann, M. (2021). Beacon-based remote measurement of social behavior in ASD clinical trials: A technical feasibility assessment. *Sensors 21*(14). https://doi.org/10.3390/s21144664.

Lin, M.Y.C., Nguyen, T.T., Cheng, E.Y.L., Le, A.N.H. & Cheng, J.M.S. (2022). Proximity marketing and bluetooth beacon technology: A dynamic mechanism leading to relationship program receptiveness. *Journal of Business Research 141*, 151–162. https://doi.org/10.1016/j.jbusres.2021.12.030.

Matei, S.A., Kulzick, R., Sinclair-Chapman, V. & Potts, L. (2021). Setting the agenda in environmental crisis: Relationships between tweets, Google search trends, and newspaper coverage during the California drought. *PLOS ONE 16*(12), 1–19. https://doi.org/10.1371/journal.pone.0259494.

Mesenbourg, T.L. (2001). *Measuring the Digital Economy*. Bureau of the Census. Available at: https://www.census.gov/content/dam/Census/library/working-papers/2001/econ/umdigital.pdf.

OECD. (2020). *A Roadmap toward a Common Framework for Measuring the Digital Economy, Report for the G20 Digital Economy Task Force*. OECD Publishing. Available at: https://www.oecd.org/sti/roadmap-toward-a-common-framework-for-measuring-the-digital-economy.pdf.

Periša, M., *Cvitić, I.*, Peraković, D. & *Husnjak, S.* (2019). Beacon technology for real-time informing the traffic network users about the environment. *Transport 34*(3), 373–382. https://doi.org/10.3846/transport.2019.10402.

PR Newswire. (2015, 9 June). Verve mobile acquires beacon technology platform fosbury to further link mobile marketing to offline retail performance. *PR Newswire US*. https://www.prnewswire.com/news-releases/verve-mobile-acquires-beacon-technology-platform-fosbury-to-further-link-mobile-marketing-to-offline-retail-performance-300096144.html.

PR Newswire. (2016, 27 September). Market for proximity marketing by location, technology, hardware, software, service, application - Global forecast to 2022. *PR Newswire US*. https://www.prnewswire.com/news-releases/market-for-proximity-marketing-by-location-technology-hardware-software-service-application---global-forecast-to-2022-300335258.html.

PR Newswire. (2019, 22 August). Beacon hill technologies launches new practice area – Digital & creative. *PR Newswire US*. https://www.prnewswire.com/news-releases/beacon-hill-technologies-launches-new-practice-area—digital—creative-300906024.html.

Rifkin, J. (2014). *The Zero Marginal Cost Society: The Internet of Things, the Collaborative Commons, and the Eclipse of Capitalism*. Palgrave Macmillan. ISBN: 9781137280114.

Schwab, K. (2018). *Shaping the Fourth Industrial Revolution*. World Economic Forum.

Sweeney, S. (2018). The next step to Industry 4.0 adoption. *Manufacturers' Monthly*.

Tapscott, D. (2015). *The Digital Economy: Rethinking Promise and Peril in the Age of Networked Intelligence*. McGraw-Hill Education. ISBN: 0070622000.

Tran, D.T. & Huh, J.H. (2022). Building a model to exploit association rules and analyze purchasing behavior based on rough set theory. *The Journal of Supercomputing 78*. https://doi.org/10.1007/s11227-021-04275-5.

Tsui, K.L. & Zhao, Y. (2017). Discussion of 'analyzing behavioral big data: Methodological, practical, ethical, and moral issues'. *Quality Engineering 29*(1), 79–83. https://doi.org/10.1080/08982112.2016.1210981.

UNCTAD. (2021). *Digital Economy Report 2021.* United Nations Publications. https://doi.org/10.18356/9789210058254.

van de Sanden, S., Willems, K. & Brengman, M. (2019). In-store location-based marketing with beacons: From inflated expectations to smart use in retailing. *Journal of Marketing Management 35*(15/16), 1514–1541. https://doi.org/10.1080/0267257X.2019.1689154.

Wilcoxson, J., Follett, L. & Severe, S. (2020). Forecasting foreign exchange markets using Google Trends: Prediction performance of competing models. *Journal of Behavioral Finance 21*(4), 412–422. https://doi.org/10.1080/15427560.2020.1716233.

Woo, J. & Owen, A.L. (2019). Forecasting private consumption with Google Trends data. *Journal of Forecasting 38*(2), 81–91. https://doi.org/10.1002/for.2559.

Zhu, J.J.H., Wang, X., Qin, J. & Wu, L. (2012). *Assessing Public Opinion Trends Based on User Search Queries: Validity, Reliability, and Practicality* [Conference Paper]. 65th Annual Conference of the World Association for Public Opinion Research, China. https://scholars.cityu.edu.hk/en/publications/publication(54cc3372-239d-40cd-8e3f-1a6e875ecfd7).html.

Electronic sources

Big Data Framework (2021, 18 March). A Short History of Big Data. https://www.bigdataframework.org/knowledge/a-short-history-of-big-data/.

Chakravorti, B. & Chaturvedi, R.S. (2019, 5 September). Ranking 42 Countries by Ease of Doing Digital Business. *Harvard Business Review*. https://hbr.org/2019/09/ranking-42-countries-by-ease-of-doing-digital-business.

Dataversity (2021, 20 September). A Brief History of Analytics. https://www.dataversity.net/brief-history-analytics/.

Fraunhofer Institute (2021, 6 May). German Index of Digitization 2021. https://www.fokus.fraunhofer.de/en/news/fokus/dps/D-Index_2021_05.

Maxin, J. (2015, 30 November). 12 Crucial Questions Answered on Beacons' Growing Influence on the Retail Industry. OpenXcell. https://www.openxcell.com/blog/12-crucial-questions-answered-on-beacons-growing-influence-on-the-retail-industry/.

Plot Project (2022, 20 June). Beacon Technology: What Is Beacon Technology | Best Solutions in 2022. https://www.plotprojects.com/blog/beacon-technology-why-the-market-is-booming/.

R Core Team (2021). R: A Language and Environment for Statistical Computing. R Foundation for Statistical Computing [Electronic Source]. https://www.R-project.org/. Access 8.10.2021.

Softensy (2022). What Is Beacon Technology and How to Use It in Your App. https://softensy.com/what-is-beacon-technology-and-how-to-use-it-in-your-app/.

Wordstream (2021, 25 November). 5 Things You Need to Know about Beacon Technology. https://www.wordstream.com/blog/ws/2018/10/04/beacon-technology.

3 Differentiation of the digital economic development in Europe

Mateusz Biernacki, Agata Luśtyk and Rafał Wisła

3.1 Introduction

The digital economy is a conceptual "umbrella" referring to markets, organizations and their networks that are based on digital technologies, communication, data processing and e-commerce (see Nathan et al., 2013). The term denotes a multidimensional, dynamic structure that must be analysed considering its various dimensions, such as economic aspects (changes in the nature of resources, production factors and economic processes), the area of technology (technological progress viewed from a macroeconomic perspective vs. technological innovation viewed from a microeconomic perspective), regulatory measures (challenges facing regulators, new risks affecting the institutional order) and sociological phenomena (changes in society functioning principles, attitudes towards work and human relations).

The Organisation for Economic Co-operation and Development (OECD, 2020) defines the digital economy as an economic system wherein data is used as a factor of production. Businesses operating in this type of economy use or process digital information aiming to increase its value (create value added). The enterprises adopt new business models enabled by new market conditions (digital services, digital distribution channels and digital networks) (OECD, 2020).

The digital components (digital resources and IT infrastructure) drive the digital economy value chain; new industry sectors and new business models emerge. The new value chain opens new spaces and promotes the consolidation of growth areas and job creation (Zhenlong, 2021). Digitalization dramatically modifies the very nature of products, the value creation process and the competitive environment in business. Based on the network-centric view, the firms may achieve a competitive advantage by actively shaping the digital environment and by interconnecting in the digital environment (Koch & Windsperger, 2017).

Carlsson (2004) emphasizes that the digital economy is more about new activities and products than about higher productivity. Its key resources include information and a series of economic and social activities that people carry out using the Internet and related technologies (Turcan et al., 2014). Continual

DOI: 10.4324/9781003450160-5

technological progress and growing data repositories and flows can be indicated as the key trends shaping digital transformation on a global scale.

The terminological context outlined above and in Chapter 1 gives rise to a fundamental question about a method suitable for quantifying the dynamics of these changes at various levels of economic analysis. The International Monetary Fund (IMF, 2018, pp. 2–6) indicates the lack of generally agreed understanding and definition of the digital economy as a major hurdle to reliable measurements of changes associated with that economy. The IMF (2018) distinguishes the concept of the digital sector and that of the digital economy. The concept of the digital sector is limited to the core activities of digitalization, such as ICT goods and services, online platforms and platform-enabled digital services, including the sharing economy. Considering enormous difficulties in quantifying the dynamics of changes in the digital economy environment, interdependencies observed in that economy and their characteristics, the IMF (2018) proposes to focus measurement efforts on a concrete range of economic activities at the core of digitalization.

In this chapter, we will not follow this recommendation. Instead, we propose an original method for a quantitative description of changes in the digital economy from a macroeconomic perspective. For this purpose, the taxonomic analysis will be used. The first section of this chapter contains a review of proposals aimed to measure the digital economy, considering various approaches to its definitions. The second section discusses two methods designed to identify changes in the digital economy from a macro perspective and gives the characteristics of data used in the following sections. The third section presents research results with a discussion of their limitations and downsides. The last section contains a summary.

3.2 A review of proposed methods for measuring the digital economy

The current approach to measuring the digital economy, adopted by international organizations (G20, 2018; IMF, 2018; OECD, 2020), is broad and addresses its various aspects: infrastructure, employment, applications, social change and innovation.

The infrastructural context consists of physical, service and security infrastructure. The measurement methods use such indicators as access to mobile and landline telephone networks, the development of next-generation access, the number of broadband service subscribers and the number of active mobile Internet subscribers. But in addition to accessibility and affordability, such factors as the connection quality and Internet transmission speed (both in mobile and DSL technologies) play an important role in measuring the individuals' and enterprises' capability of participating in the development of the digital economy. The OECD (2020) also discusses the concept of Internet of Things (IoT), i.e., an ecosystem of applications and devices that connect and exchange data with their environment and with each other without human intervention. The OECD (2020, p. 21) expects that the IoT will become a central element of the digital economy in G-20 countries.

The aspect of employment, digital competencies and labour market is operationalized using the following indicators (OECD, 2020, pp. 72–73):

- the number of jobs in the ICT sector,
- the proportion of enterprises that employ ICT specialists,
- the number of individuals teleworking from home,
- Eurostat Digital Skills Indicator,
- ICT usage in schools,
- the number of tertiary graduates in natural sciences and engineering,
- value added by information industries,
- information industry-related domestic value added,
- labour productivity in information industries,
- ICT contribution to labour productivity growth,
- ICT goods exports and imports,
- ICT services exports and imports.

The category of emerging applications, i.e., technological innovation, is quantified in terms of e-commerce or robotization in manufacturing (robot intensity) (OECD, 2020, pp. 28–34).

The social dimension of the digital economy is understood as using digital technologies to improve general well-being and the quality of life and to enhance communication capabilities. The principal quantifiers of changes include here the percentage of Internet users and the percentage of individuals using the Internet to interact with public authorities. The digitalization and automation of procedures are aimed to simplify those interactions and provide easy access to various official forms and means of efficient completion of government procedures (OECD, 2020, pp. 23–26).

The International Telecommunication Union (ITU, 2020, p. 4) describes access by individuals and households to ICT infrastructure as a factor accelerating social development and stimulating economic changes. The concept of the digital economy is understood as available digital infrastructure, digital products, their accessibility and society's digital skills. The ITU (2020, pp. 47–49) proposes a list of ICT household equipment indicators. These indicators include, e.g., the proportion of households with multichannel television, the proportion of households with Internet, household expenditure on ICT, the proportion of individuals using the Internet, the proportion of individuals who purchased goods or services online, the number of individuals with ICT skills and total household expenditure on ICT. The ITU adopts the following principal indicators of ICT infrastructure development and access to that infrastructure (2020, p. 235)

- fixed-telephone subscriptions per 100 inhabitants,
- mobile cellular telephone subscriptions per 100 inhabitants,

- fixed broadband Internet subscriptions per 100 inhabitants (broken down by speed),
- active broadband Internet subscriptions per 100 inhabitants,
- Internet throughput per inhabitant (bits/second/inhabitant),
- fixed broadband Internet prices per month,
- mobile cellular telephone prices and TV broadcasting subscriptions per 100 inhabitants.

Bukht and Heeks (2017) indicate temporal changes in conceptualizing the digital economy. They result from the development of infrastructure and its use (the Internet as a leading technology, mobile networks and cloud computing). Kling and Lamb (2000, pp. 295–324) identify four areas of the digital economy: highly digital goods and services (e.g., online education), mixed digital goods and services (e.g., books), IT-intensive services or goods production (e.g., accounting) and the segments of the IT industry that support these three segments of the digital economy (e.g., the computer networking industry). Bukht and Heeks (2017) also emphasize the importance of measuring the digital economy. They propose such measures as value added by the ICT sector, employment in the IT/ICT sector and comparing labour productivity in highly digital sectors with that in the traditional economy. Similarly, ITU (2020, pp. 236–237) uses a macro perspective to propose the proportion of ICT specialists in total employment, ICT sector share of gross value added, ICT goods imports as a percentage of total imports and ICT goods exports as a percentage of total exports.

The G20 DETF (2018) indicates that sound measurement is crucial for policymaking, as it helps to produce precise diagnostics, assess the potential impact, monitor progress and evaluate the efficiency and efficacy of implemented actions. The digital economy is believed to have a great potential for transforming jobs, hence the rapidly growing demand for measurement tools and indicators. The G-20 member states are encouraged to disclose measurements characterizing the digital economy in their national statistics, using various methods for monitoring the digitalization level. 30 key indicators are recommended, divided into four main thematic areas: (1) infrastructure, (2) empowering society, (3) innovation and technology adoption and (4) jobs and growth. In addition to these four areas, the report authors emphasize the importance of measuring such indicators as expenditure on research and development (R&D), machine learning, AI-related technologies and cloud computing services used by enterprises (G20 DETF, 2018, pp. 37–41, 48).

Currently (G20 DETF, 2018, pp. 4–8), multiple hurdles are identified for the systematic collection of comparable statistical data in the discussed area. Main obstacles include differences in data collection methodologies and approaches and a limited range of surveys. The methodological differences are evident in the currently used indicators aimed to measure the digital economy. It is not enough to improve the existing indicators; new measures and data collection methods must be identified. There are areas with internationally recognized standards for statistical data collection, but states have insufficient capabilities and resources to systematically implement those standards and then distribute the figures obtained.

The recommendations proposed by the authors of the G20 DETF report (2018) include:

- experimenting with concepts and data gathering within existing measurement frameworks,
- exploiting the potential of existing survey and administrative data,
- adding questions to existing surveys,
- augmenting existing surveys with topic-specific modules,
- developing short turnaround surveys to meet specific needs,
- defining policy needs and, in cooperation with other stakeholders, setting priorities for internationally comparable measurement,
- using the potential of big data for developing indicators to measure the digital economy.

The authors of the above recommendations (G20 DETF, 2018, p. 10) indicate a series of crucial actions aimed to improve the quality of presented measurements.

The International Standard Industrial Classification, like the Central Product Classification, adopts a definition of the digital economy understood as the ICT, media and entertainment sectors. In general, typically for an initial phase in defining new categories, numerous approaches are observed to the conceptualization of the digital economy. However, even the impressive number of proposed definitions and their variations are insufficient to embrace the dynamic growth in digital products and services. Those definitions frequently fail to include new categories, leading to an underestimated value of economic activities based on digital products. The variation and elasticity of definitions pose an obstacle in research, which requires accurate measurements or temporal and spatial comparisons. The challenges include (1) capturing the fast-changing quality of digital services, (2) distinguishing between revolutionary and evolutionary developed digital products, (3) measuring e-commerce and (4) measuring the sharing economy (IMF, 2018, pp. 7, 17).

3.3 Data

Most of the cited authors agree that in measuring the global economy, the most useful information is provided by ICT[1] and IC[2] sector data, being both globally applicable and comparable. Consequently, seven variables are proposed to construct a taxonomic indicator of the development of states' digital economy. These include:

X_1 – percentage of the ICT personnel on total employment in the country
X_2 – percentage of value added (at factor cost) in the ICT sector on GDP,
X_3 – the value of the import stream of IC sector products,
X_4 – the value of the export stream of IC sector products,
X_5 – percentage of enterprises that employ ICT specialists,
X_6 – business expenditure on R&D (BERD) in ICT sector as percentage of total R&D expenditure,
X_7 – percentage of enterprises' total turnover from e-commerce sales; without financial sector.

The ICT and IC sectors are distinguished in line with the currently applicable *Statistical classification of economic activities in the European Community* (Eurostat, 2008, pp. 164–170, 224, 252–255, 308). Imports and exports of IC products are calculated as the value of foreign trade in products manufactured by the information and communication sector (IC: 58–63). The figures are collected from the databases published by the European Statistical Office (Eurostat) and cover the years 2012–2019. This is the largest time interval for which figures are available in all of the selected categories. The following method was employed in imputing missing data for individual years:

- if the value is unavailable at a period endpoint, i.e., for the year 2012 or 2019, it is replaced with the value for the nearest year,
- if the value is unavailable in between the endpoints, it is replaced with the mean from adjacent years,
- if more than one value are missing in a sequence, all subsequent replacement values are equal and imputed as above.

Separate taxonomic indicators are constructed in four selected groups of states. These include:

- EU15+1 – member states of the European Union prior to its enlargement in 2004 plus Norway,
- EU15 – member states of the European Union prior to its enlargement in 2004,
- EU13 – the states that joined the European Union after 2003,
- EU28 – all member states of the European Union in 2019.

Certain states are excluded from the EU15+1 and EU15 groups, due to the absence of figures, namely, Ireland, Luxembourg, Portugal and Sweden (hence, the same omissions in the EU28 group). Cyprus was excluded from the EU13 index for the same reason. The EU28 index covering the entire European Union does not include the five indicated states but includes the United Kingdom (that did not withdraw from the European Union until 2020).

3.4 Presentation of analysis results

3.4.1 Descriptive statistics

The first proposed variable describes the proportion of employment in the ICT sector in the total state's employment level. The economies that are characterized by a high indicator of technological and digital development should report a high percentage of employment in that sector. In all countries covered by the study, the proportion ranged on average[3] from 1.4% in Greece to 4.4% in Malta. Almost all countries disclosed in the analysed period an increase in the indicator, ranging from about 0–0.1 percentage points (hereinafter: pp) (the Netherlands, Finland and Hungary) to 1.3–1.6pp (Estonia and Latvia). The only exception is provided by Denmark, with a drop in ICT personnel ratio by 0.5pp. A substantial majority of the EU states were characterized by a moderate but stable increase in ICT personnel, reaching an annual average of 0.06pp and 0.5pp over the analysed period of eight years. No correlation was observed between the rate of increase in employment ratio and its value for the first year analysed, i.e., a high or low base level had no effect on future rises in employment.

The second discussed variable describes the proportion of ICT value added in the state's GDP. Variation in this variable is considerably greater than that in ICT personnel percentage and ranges on average from 2.1% in Greece to 7.4% in Malta. The remaining countries mostly fall within the interval 3%–5%, disclosing average annual growth of about 0.1pp. Falls in that proportion were observed in five countries over the period of eight years: Spain, Italy, Denmark, Slovakia and Malta (from −0.1pp to −0.8pp). The remaining states achieved a growth reaching on average 0.5pp, with its largest value observed in Bulgaria and Latvia (2pp). The percentage of ICT sector employment and ICT value added on GDP are correlated. A substantial majority of countries characterized by top ICT personnel proportions also belong to the group of leaders in creating ICT value added on GDP, and the countries characterized by the lowest ICT personnel indicators disclose a small ICT value added on GDP. However, exceptions are identified, such as Bulgaria. At an impressively high ICT value added on GDP, reaching 5.4% on average (the fourth highest result), the country is characterized by one of the lowest percentages of ICT personnel (2.5%, the eighth worst result). This may indicate an enormous difference between productivity in the ICT sector and in other industries.

Table 3.1 contains mean values of ICT value added on GDP, mean values of the percentage of ICT sector employment on total employment and the quotients of those indicators. The third column is described as productivity of the ICT sector in an economy. If that indicator is greater than 1, productivity in the sector is higher than in other economy sectors. Values less than 1 would indicate lower productivity in the ICT sector than in the remaining economy. Over the analysed years, the ICT productivity indicator in all countries surveyed was greater than the average in their economies, exceeding 2 in Bulgaria where only 2.5% of employees generated more than 5% of GDP.

Table 3.1 Values of variables $\mathbf{X}_1$ – percentages of employment in the ICT sector on total country's employment, $\mathbf{X}_2$ – percentages of value added in the ICT sector on GDP and ICT sector productivity indicators in the national economies

Country	*Percentage of value added in the ICT sector on GDP*	*Percentage of the ICT personnel on total employment*	*ICT sector productivity indicator*
Bulgaria	5.36	2.48	2.16
Croatia	4.17	2.36	1.77
United Kingdom	5.85	3.42	1.71
Malta	7.37	4.42	1.67
Hungary	5.80	3.55	1.63
Netherlands	4.90	3.06	1.60
Romania	3.45	2.17	1.59
Germany	4.19	2.74	1.53
Greece	2.14	1.42	1.50
Czechia	4.39	2.95	1.49
Poland	3.27	2.24	1.46
Belgium	3.94	2.72	1.45
Slovakia	4.30	3.03	1.42
Spain	3.27	2.33	1.41
Slovenia	3.61	2.61	1.38
Italy	3.30	2.40	1.38
France	4.09	2.99	1.37
Austria	3.41	2.53	1.35
Estonia	5.04	3.86	1.30
Latvia	4.33	3.39	1.28
Finland	4.63	3.75	1.24
Denmark	4.57	3.80	1.20
Lithuania	2.87	2.39	1.20
Norway	3.39	3.00	1.13

Source: Eurostat and own calculations.

A study into the percentage of imports and exports of IC products on the total country's imports and exports leads to similar conclusions regarding the dynamics and direction of changes over time. In imports, the proportion of IC products equalled on average 1.17% of the total imports value. The highest average proportions were observed in the Netherlands and the United Kingdom (3% and 2.5%, respectively), and the lowest – in Malta and Czechia (0.43% each). An increase in the discussed proportion was observed only in eight states, the remaining economies disclosed falls. In exports, the proportion of IC products equalled on average 0.4% of the total export value. The countries characterized by top average proportions included the United Kingdom and Netherlands (1.32% and 0.98%, respectively) while Malta and Italy disclosed the lowest proportions (0.06% and 0.14%, respectively). Like in nominal values, more countries disclosed an increase in the proportion of IC product exports in total exports; IC imports compared to total imports increased in 12 states, representing one-half of the analysed group. The largest increase between 2012 and 2019 was observed in Slovenia: by 0.69pp.

The fifth proposed variable is the percentage of enterprises that employ ICT specialists. The value of this indicator is comparable in most states and equals about 20% on average. The countries characterized by top values are Belgium and Finland (27% each), and the lowest values are observed in Romania and Poland (10% and 13%, respectively). Importantly, this proportion has dropped in almost all analysed countries for years. The mean indicator value in all those countries equalled 23.2% in 2012 and 20.6% in 2019, showing an average annual drop by -0.4pp. An increase was observed over the analysed period only in seven countries (Romania, Poland, Italy, France, Bulgaria, Malta and Denmark) – between 1pp and 9pp. Considering the discussed increase in the percentage of ICT personnel on total employment, a hypothesis can be proposed: the reduction was not caused by dismissing ICT specialists, but rather by a large number of newly established businesses that could not afford hiring this type of personnel in their initial phase of operation. However, this cannot be confirmed due to the absence of data.

Another variable is the BERD in ICT sector as a percentage of total R&D expenditure. This indicator dramatically varied not only from one country to another but also in individual countries over the analysed eight years. The lowest average proportions were characteristic of Slovenia and the Netherlands (10% each), and the highest – of Malta and Estonia (50% and 44%, respectively). The mean value for all countries equalled 18% in the first and 21% in the last analysed year, showing an average annual increase by 0.5pp. A drop in the proportion of expenditure was observed in eight countries and ranged from -1.5pp to -6.5pp. The increase rates were higher, reaching even 18pp in Estonia and 33pp in Bulgaria.

The last proposed variable is the percentage of enterprises' turnover from e-commerce sales on their total turnover, without the financial sector. This indicator reflects, in addition to the development level of the digital economy, such aspects as Internet access or computer use in society. The mean indicator value ranges from a modest 3% to an impressive 29%. The lowest values were observed in Greece (3.3%), Bulgaria (4%) and Romania (6.9%), the highest – in Czechia (29%), Belgium (24.7%) and Norway (21.5%). An increase in this indicator was observed in all states, except Germany, over the analysed years – the greatest in Belgium (an increase from 14% in 2012 to 33% in 2019). The indicator rose annually in all discussed states by 0.6pp on average (a total increase in the mean value from 13% to 17.4%).

3.4.2 Taxonomic analysis results

The first method used to assess the development of the digital economy in the European countries consists of the determination of a taxonomic indicator. All variables proposed above are understood as measures (but also stimulants) of the digital economic development. Following their normalization, the taxonomic approach was adopted, based on the maximum value of the total of Pearson correlation coefficients between the taxonomic indicator Sk_t^i and standardized variables $X_{i,j}$.

$M = [m_{ij}]$ represents a matrix of values of selected variables, where m_{ij} is the value of jth variable in the kth country, where $k \equiv i(\text{mod}23)$ for the countries of UE28; $k \equiv i(\text{modl}\,1)$ for the countries of UE15; $k \equiv i(\text{modl}\,2)$. This matrix consists of 184 rows and 8 columns (EU28), 88 rows and 8 columns (EU15) and 98 rows and 8 columns (EU15+1 and EU13). Given the properties of linear congruence, we obtain the equality $k = i + 23p$, further accordingly $k = i + 11p$ and $k = i + 12p$. Let X be the matrix after standardization, done using the following formula

$$X_{i,j} = \frac{M_{i,j}}{\max(M_{i,j})},$$

where the jth column of matrix M is the stimulant. In turn, in the case of dis-stimulants $X_{i,j} = 1 - \frac{M_{i,j}}{\max(M_{i,j})}$. The taxonomic indicator Sk_t^i is given by a linear combination of standardized variables and a certain vector of weights $\omega = (\omega_1, \ldots, \omega_7)$

$$Sk_t^i = \omega_1 X_{i,1} + \omega_2 X_{i,2} + \cdots + \omega_7 X_{i,7}.$$

The vector of weights $\omega = (\omega_1, \ldots, \omega_7)$ represents the argument of a function given by the formula

$$F(\omega) = \sum_{j=1}^{7} \text{cor}(X_{i,j}, X \cdot \omega),$$

where $X \cdot \omega$ is the simple multiplication of matrix X by the vector of weights ω. As a result of the above transitions and calculations, the expected taxonomic indicator is obtained. It has to be emphasized here that the determination of the vector of weights ω is rather burdensome, and optimization algorithms are used in practice.

The macro characteristics of the digital economy described above were used to construct a taxonomic indicator of the digital economic development in the defined analytical groups. The coordinates of weights in the EU15+1 group were determined using the optimization algorithm known as local multivariate optimization and had the following values:

X_1 – percentage of the ICT personnel on total employment in the country: 0.169,
X_2 – percentage of value added in the ICT sector on GDP: 0.171,
X_3 – the value of the import stream of IC sector products: 0.111,
X_4 – the value of the export stream of IC sector products: 0.084,
X_5 – percentage of enterprises that employ ICT specialists: 0.193,
X_6 – BERD in ICT sector as percentage of total R&D expenditure: 0.135,
X_7 – percentage of online sales on total sales in the enterprise sector, without financial sector: 0.137.

The greatest weights are assigned to the percentage of enterprises employing ICT specialists (0.193), the percentage of value added in the ICT sector on GDP (0.171) and the percentage of ICT personnel on total employment (0.169). Similar weights are assigned to the percentage of online sales on total sales in the enterprise sector, excluding the financial sector (0.137) and BERD in ICT sector as a percentage of country's total R&D expenditure (0.135). The least significant variables include imports of IC products (0.111) and exports of ICT products (0.084).

The greatest average value of the indicator in the EU15+1 group was achieved in 2012–2019 by the United Kingdom (0.730), followed by Finland (0.652). Six countries achieved indicators within the range of 0.590–0.525. The lowest values of the indicator were calculated for Austria (0.449), Spain (0.446), Italy (0.396) and Greece (0.361). Similar rankings according to this criterion were obtained for both 2012 and 2019. The positions in the ranking are thus highly stable, due to a relatively short time span of the analysis (Table 3.2).

The coordinates of weights in the EU15 group have the following values

X_1 – percentage of the ICT personnel on total employment in the country: 0.164,
X_2 – percentage of value added in the ICT sector on GDP: 0.169,
X_3 – the value of the import stream of IC sector products: 0.109,
X_4 – the value of the export stream of IC sector products: 0.084,
X_5 – percentage of enterprises that employ ICT specialists: 0.195,
X_6 – BERD in ICT sector as percentage of total R&D expenditure: 0.140,
X_7 – percentage of online sales on total sales in the enterprise sector, without financial sector: 0.139.

Table 3.2 Values of the taxonomic indicator of digital economic development in the EU15+1 group in 2012–2019

EU15+1 group	*Taxonomic indicator*							
	2012	2013	2014	2015	2016	2017	2018	2019
Belgium	0.501	0.497	0.505	0.543	0.553	0.580	0.591	0.609
Denmark	0.583	0.575	0.575	0.557	0.564	0.544	0.570	0.595
Germany	0.540	0.531	0.548	0.570	0.556	0.565	0.597	0.582
Greece	0.405	0.363	0.345	0.365	0.399	0.324	0.347	0.341
Spain	0.437	0.440	0.455	0.449	0.467	0.446	0.438	0.431
France	0.505	0.493	0.546	0.573	0.603	0.610	0.611	0.577
Italy	0.384	0.386	0.376	0.401	0.401	0.403	0.404	0.411
Netherlands	0.587	0.588	0.607	0.597	0.566	0.584	0.606	0.586
Austria	0.463	0.444	0.432	0.450	0.459	0.448	0.441	0.453
Finland	0.647	0.645	0.645	0.647	0.644	0.668	0.655	0.666
Norway	0.548	0.523	0.497	0.507	0.527	0.518	0.530	0.555
United Kingdom	0.766	0.753	0.731	0.739	0.720	0.692	0.706	0.728

Source: Own calculations.

The greatest weights are assigned to the percentage of enterprises employing ICT specialists (0.195), the percentage of value added in the ICT sector on GDP (0.169) and the percentage of ICT personnel on total employment (0.164). Similar weights are assigned to: BERD in ICT sector as a percentage of country's total R&D expenditure (0.140) and the percentage of online sales on the total sales in the enterprise sector, excluding the financial sector (0.139). The least significant variables include imports of IC products (0.109) and exports of ICT products (0.084).

The greatest average value of the indicator in the EU15 group was achieved in 2012–2019 by the United Kingdom (0.726), followed by Finland (0.653). Five countries achieved indicators within the range of 0.590–0.540. The lowest values of the indicator were calculated for Greece (0.363), Spain (0.445), Italy (0.345) and Austria (0.449). A comparison of the years 2012 and 2019 demonstrates that (1) the United Kingdom and Finland retained their positions as group leaders, (2) stable positions were occupied by Denmark (the fourth place in the ranking), Austria (the eighth place in the ranking) and Spain (the ninth place in the ranking), (3) Belgium moved up considerably from the seventh place (2012) to the third place (2019), (4) the Netherlands moved down from the third (2012) to the fifth place (2019) and (5) Germany, Greece, France and Italy retained similar positions in the ranking at the beginning and end of the analysed period (Table 3.3).

The coordinates of weights in the EU13 group have the following values

X_1 – percentage of the ICT personnel on total employment in the country: 0.168,

X_2 – percentage of value added in the ICT sector on GDP: 0.178,

Table 3.3 Values of the taxonomic indicator of digital economic development in the EU15 group in 2012–2019

EU15 group	*Taxonomic indicator*							
	2012	*2013*	*2014*	*2015*	*2016*	*2017*	*2018*	*2019*
Belgium	0.501	0.497	0.504	0.543	0.553	0.581	0.591	0.610
Denmark	0.581	0.573	0.572	0.555	0.562	0.542	0.569	0.593
Germany	0.539	0.530	0.546	0.568	0.553	0.563	0.594	0.579
Greece	0.408	0.365	0.347	0.367	0.401	0.326	0.349	0.343
Spain	0.437	0.440	0.455	0.449	0.467	0.446	0.438	0.430
France	0.504	0.492	0.545	0.571	0.601	0.609	0.610	0.576
Italy	0.383	0.385	0.375	0.400	0.400	0.402	0.403	0.411
Netherlands	0.584	0.585	0.604	0.594	0.564	0.582	0.604	0.584
Austria	0.463	0.444	0.432	0.450	0.459	0.448	0.440	0.452
Finland	0.649	0.647	0.647	0.649	0.645	0.669	0.656	0.667
United Kingdom	0.764	0.750	0.728	0.736	0.717	0.689	0.703	0.726

Source: Own calculations.

X_3 – the value of the import stream of IC sector products: 0.141,
X_4 – the value of the export stream of IC sector products: 0.116,
X_5 – percentage of enterprises that employ ICT specialists: 0.156,
X_6 – BERD in ICT sector as percentage of total R&D expenditure: 0.114,
X_7 – percentage of online sales on total sales in the enterprise sector, without financial sector: 0.127.

The greatest weight is assigned to value added in the ICT sector on GDP (0.178), the ICT personnel on total employment (0.168) and the proportion of enterprises that employ ICT specialists (0.156). The least significant variables include BERD in ICT sector as percentage of total R&D expenditure (0.114) and exports (0.116).

The greatest average value of the indicator in the EU13 group was achieved in 2012–2019 by Malta (0.599), followed by: Hungary (0.559), Czechia (0.528) and Poland (0.508). The lowest values of the indicator were calculated for Latvia (0.391), Bulgaria (0.388), Lithuania (0.335) and Romania (0.322). A comparison of the years 2012 and 2019 demonstrates that (1) Malta and Hungary retained their positions as group leaders, (2) Poland moved up from the fifth (2012) to the third place in the group in 2019, (3) Bulgaria moved up from the 11th place in the ranking (2012) to the seventh place (2019), (4) Croatia moved down from the seventh (2012) to the tenth place (2019) and (5) Romania occupies the last place in the ranking (2012–2019) (Table 3.4).

Table 3.4 Values of the taxonomic indicator of digital economic development in the EU13 group in 2012–2019

EU13 group	*Taxonomic indicator*							
	2012	*2013*	*2014*	*2015*	*2016*	*2017*	*2018*	*2019*
Bulgaria	0.278	0.308	0.347	0.371	0.429	0.444	0.456	0.475
Czechia	0.524	0.509	0.504	0.518	0.525	0.544	0.533	0.565
Estonia	0.452	0.450	0.461	0.472	0.496	0.507	0.526	0.547
Croatia	0.384	0.394	0.400	0.426	0.393	0.411	0.436	0.429
Latvia	0.354	0.363	0.373	0.389	0.392	0.398	0.417	0.468
Lithuania	0.335	0.310	0.299	0.318	0.318	0.372	0.360	0.371
Hungary	0.575	0.555	0.559	0.535	0.529	0.577	0.561	0.579
Malta	0.593	0.573	0.569	0.586	0.599	0.622	0.616	0.631
Poland	0.475	0.503	0.483	0.518	0.525	0.489	0.501	0.569
Romania	0.265	0.275	0.306	0.338	0.357	0.335	0.352	0.347
Slovenia	0.363	0.378	0.391	0.407	0.414	0.432	0.457	0.451
Slovakia	0.487	0.480	0.475	0.526	0.495	0.508	0.494	0.498

Source: Own calculations.

The coordinates of weights in the EU28 group have the following values

- X_1 – percentage of the ICT personnel on total employment in the country: 0.169,
- X_2 – percentage of value added in the ICT sector on GDP: 0.187,
- X_3 – the value of the import stream of IC sector products: 0.125,
- X_4 – the value of the export stream of IC sector products: 0.097,
- X_5 – percentage of enterprises that employ ICT specialists: 0.165,
- X_6 – BERD in ICT sector as percentage of total R&D expenditure: 0.129,
- X_7 – percentage of online sales on total sales in the enterprise sector. without financial sector: 0.128.

The greatest weight is assigned to value added in the ICT sector on GDP (0.187), the ICT personnel on total employment (0.169) and the proportion of enterprises that employ ICT specialists (0.165). Similar weights are assigned to BERD in ICT sector as percentage of total R&D expenditure (0.129), the percentage of online sales on the total sales in the enterprise

Table 3.5 Values of the taxonomic indicator of digital economic development in the EU28 group in 2012–2019

Country	*Taxonomic indicator*							
	2012	*2013*	*2014*	*2015*	*2016*	*2017*	*2018*	*2019*
Belgium	0.427	0.425	0.434	0.471	0.479	0.503	0.511	0.525
Bulgaria	0.260	0.290	0.326	0.341	0.404	0.416	0.441	0.456
Czechia	0.468	0.454	0.453	0.449	0.461	0.477	0.470	0.495
Denmark	0.498	0.492	0.492	0.477	0.483	0.468	0.490	0.511
Germany	0.486	0.477	0.495	0.518	0.503	0.513	0.548	0.531
Estonia	0.436	0.439	0.454	0.461	0.484	0.498	0.523	0.544
Greece	0.336	0.298	0.283	0.298	0.330	0.266	0.285	0.281
Spain	0.376	0.377	0.391	0.387	0.403	0.386	0.379	0.372
France	0.446	0.432	0.491	0.518	0.550	0.549	0.548	0.508
Croatia	0.350	0.361	0.365	0.379	0.353	0.372	0.399	0.404
Italy	0.326	0.328	0.321	0.342	0.341	0.344	0.345	0.351
Latvia	0.335	0.348	0.355	0.375	0.377	0.383	0.396	0.443
Lithuania	0.313	0.292	0.282	0.297	0.294	0.348	0.334	0.341
Hungary	0.521	0.504	0.507	0.473	0.460	0.494	0.505	0.520
Malta	0.600	0.580	0.576	0.591	0.605	0.631	0.625	0.637
Netherlands	0.523	0.523	0.545	0.531	0.499	0.517	0.542	0.523
Austria	0.425	0.377	0.367	0.384	0.391	0.381	0.375	0.385
Poland	0.294	0.289	0.283	0.309	0.335	0.334	0.347	0.413
Romania	0.216	0.232	0.254	0.280	0.297	0.277	0.297	0.298
Slovenia	0.337	0.331	0.339	0.349	0.351	0.359	0.364	0.363
Slovakia	0.408	0.402	0.383	0.421	0.407	0.431	0.417	0.429
Finland	0.539	0.536	0.537	0.539	0.537	0.557	0.548	0.558
United Kingdom	0.699	0.687	0.664	0.675	0.652	0.620	0.633	0.652

Source: Own calculations.

sector (0.128) and imports (0.125). The least significant variable is ICT exports (0.097). The weight structure and values are similar to those in the UE15+1 group.

The greatest average values of the indicator in the EU28 group were achieved in 2012–2019 by the United Kingdom (0.660) and Malta (0.605). They are followed in the ranking by Finland (0.544), the Netherlands (0.525) and Germany and France (a similar level of 0.510). In the statement of mean values for the analysed period, Poland (0.326), Lithuania (0.313), Greece (0.297) and Romania (0.269) occupy the last four places in the ranking. Events between 2012 and 2019 showed (1) stable positions of the United Kingdom, Malta and Finland as ranking leaders, (2) significant progress in Poland, from the 21st (2012) to the 15th place (2019) and (3) considerable move down in the ranking of Spain from the 14th to the 18th place, Austria from the 12th to the 17th place and Greece (from the 17th to the last place in the list) (Table 3.5).

3.5 Conclusion

The analyses conducted in this chapter lead to the following conclusions. First, the current approach to measuring the digital economy, adopted by international organizations (OECD, IMF and ITU), is broad and addresses its various aspects: infrastructure, employment and digital applications. The infrastructural context includes physical, service and security infrastructure. The aspects of employment, digital skills and labour market are operationalized using, e.g., the number of jobs in the ICT sector, the number of individuals teleworking from home or the digital skill level. Technological innovation (applications) is quantified in terms of e-commerce or robotization in manufacturing.

Second, in measuring the global economy, the most useful information is provided by ICT and IC sector data, both being globally applicable and comparable. A substantial majority of the EU states were characterized by a moderate but stable increase in ICT personnel in the years 2012–2019. The percentage of ICT sector employment and ICT value added on GDP are correlated. A substantial majority of countries characterized by top ICT personnel proportions also belong to leaders in creating ICT value added on GDP, and the countries characterized by the lowest ICT personnel indicators disclose a small ICT value added on GDP.

Third, the completed taxonomic analysis demonstrates that the UE15+1 group was characterized in 2012–2019 by highly stable ranking positions of the countries (probably due to a relatively short time span of the analysis).

Notes

1 NACE Rev. 2, (2008): ICT Manufacturing (26.1 + 26.2 + 26.3 + 26.4 + 26.8) and ICT Services (46.5 + 58.2 + 61 + 62 + 63.1 + 95.1).
2 NACE Rev. 2, (2008): Section J—Information and Communication (IC): 58–63.
3 The mean for a country in 2012–2019.

References

Bukht, R. & Heeks, R. (2017). Defining, conceptualising and measuring the digital economy. *International Organisations Research Journal*, *13*(2), 143–172. https://doi.org/10.17323/1996-7845-2018-02-07.

Carlsson, B. (2004). The digital economy: What is new and what is not? *Structural Change and Economic Dynamics*, *15*(3), 245–264. https://doi.org/10.1016/j.strueco.2004.02.001.

Eurostat (2008). *NACE Rev. 2, Statistical Classification of Economic Activities in the European Community*. European Communities. ISBN: 978-92-79-04741-1. Available at: https://ec.europa.eu/eurostat/web/products-manuals-and-guidelines/-/ks-ra-07-015.

G20 Digital Economy Task Force (DETF) (2018). *Toolkit for Measuring the Digital Economy*. Available at: https://www.oecd.org/g20/summits/buenos-aires/G20-Toolkit-for-measuring-digital-economy.pdf.

IMF (2018). *Measuring the Digital Economy*. Policy Paper, Washington, DC. Available at: https://www.imf.org/en/Publications/Policy-Papers/Issues/2018/04/03/022818-measuring-the-digital-economy.

ITU (2020). *Manual for Measuring ICT Access and Use by Households and Individuals*. ISBN: 978-92-61-30861-2. Available at: https://www.itu.int/en/ITU-D/Statistics/Pages/publications/manual.aspx.

Kling, R. & Lamb, R. (2000). IT and organizational change in digital economies. In E. Brynjolfsson & B. Kahin (Eds.), *Understanding the Digital Economy* (pp. 295–324). MIT Press. https://doi.org/10.7551/mitpress/6986.001.0001.

Koch, T. & Windsperger, J. (2017). Seeing through the network: Competitive advantage in the digital economy. *Journal of Organization Design*, *6*(1), 1–30. https://doi.org/10.1186/s41469-017-0016-z.

Nathan, M., Rosso, A., Gatten, T., Majmudar, P. & Mitchell, A. (2013). *Measuring the UK's Digital Economy with Big Data*. National Institute of Economic and Social Research. Available at: https://www.niesr.ac.uk/wp-content/uploads/2021/10/SI024_GI_NIESR_Google_Report12.pdf.

OECD (2020). *A Roadmap toward a Common Framework for Measuring the Digital Economy: Report for the G20 Digital Economy Task Force*. OECD Publishing. Available at: https://www.oecd.org/sti/roadmap-toward-a-common-framework-for-measuring-the-digital-economy.pdf.

Turcan, V., Gribincea, A. & Birca, I. (2014). Digital economy – A premise for economic development in the 20th century. *Economy & Sociology: Theoretical & Scientifical Journal*, 2, 109–115. Available at: https://ince.md/uploads/files/1455540156_14.turcan109_115.pdf.

Zhenlong, M. (2021). Digital economy value chain: Concept, model structure, and mechanism. *Applied Economics*, *53*(37), 4342–4357. https://doi.org/10.1080/00036846.2021.1899121.

Part II

Sources for developing the digital economy

4 Digital innovation hubs as drivers for digital transition and economic recovery

The case of the Arctic Development Environments Cluster in Lapland

Silvia Gaiani and Urszula Ala-Karvia

4.1 Introduction

The chapter aims to detect the increasingly important role that Digital Innovation Hubs (DIHs) play in the European digital economy where supply chains are increasingly digitalised, traditional business models are transforming, companies work in an integrated way, and smart distributed production are the new norm.

It starts by depicting the current European framework where DIHs are fundamentally changing the paradigm of industrial development by blurring the boundaries among companies, sectors, and regions, by facilitating the transfer of knowledge and the development of cooperation between science and business.

It argues that DIHs can be both subjects of a single digital space and at the same time objects of the use of digital tools: their aim is to accelerate the digitalisation of small-and medium-sized enterprises (SMEs) and the public sector – mostly through training, testing and trial services, financial advice, and support for networking – and to bring about substantial economic benefits. They are pillars in the European Commission's Digitising European Industry (DEI) strategy which aims to promote the competitiveness of European industry and the continent's carbon neutrality goals.

The chapter then focuses on Finland, a long-time forerunner in the development and uptake of digitalisation and specifically on the Lapland region where in 2021 the Arctic Development Environments Cluster was approved by the European Commission as the first official DIH in Lapland. The Artic Development Environments Cluster is presented by explaining its functioning, structure, aims, and activities.

Data for the case study were collected through a systematic mapping of secondary material, primarily from the Regional Innovation Monitor, the European Innovation Scoreboard, and a wide range of policy documents, such as smart specialisation (S3) strategies, Digital Innovation Scoreboard, and Digital Economy and Societal Index.

DOI: 10.4324/9781003450160-7

Primary data were collected through cooperation with the Artic Development Environments Cluster manager, Mr. Raimo Pyyny from Lapland University of Applied Sciences. The process was semi-structured; alongside quantitative data, the aim was to collect qualitative data based on personal reflections in terms of the role of the cluster in the region.

4.2 The European dimension of the digital economy

The term 'digital economy' has been used extensively in recent years to describe the functioning of that part of the economy which is linked to information and communication technologies (ICTs). The most important aspect of the current trend is not the shift to high-tech industries, but the way that IT can improve the efficiency of all parts of the economy, especially old-economy firms.

The digital economy may be characterised by three main factors (OECD, 2020):

- etwork effects' that lead to considerable spillovers, and these contribute to higher economic growth. The more participants use a network, the greater is its value to all who use it. The power of a network increases in proportion to the square of the number of access points to the network.
- a change in the business cycle since ICT in combination with globalisation may lower the non-accelerating inflation rate of unemployment and change the short-run trade-off between inflation and unemployment. As a result, the economy can expand for a longer period of time accompanied by low inflation rates.
- more efficient business methods linked to the use of new technologies that lead to higher trend growth.

Digitalisation has become widespread in the second half of the 1990s and it has not yet realised its full impact on aggregate productivity.

The European Commission has recently published the results of the 2022 Digital Economy and Society Index (DESI) (European Commission, 2022d), which tracks the progress made in EU Member States in digitalisation. DESI measures the progress of EU Member States towards a digital economy and society, on the basis of both Eurostat data and specialised studies and collection methods. It supports EU Member States by identifying priority areas requiring targeted investment and action.

Based on DESI Index, it seems that during the COVID pandemic, Member States have been advancing in their digitalisation efforts but still struggle to close the gaps in digital skills, the digital transformation of SMEs, and the establishment of advanced 5G networks. The findings, also presented in Figure 4.1, show that most of the Member States are making progress in their digital transformation, but the adoption of key digital technologies by businesses, such as Artificial Intelligence (AI) and Big Data remains low – at 8% and 14% respectively.

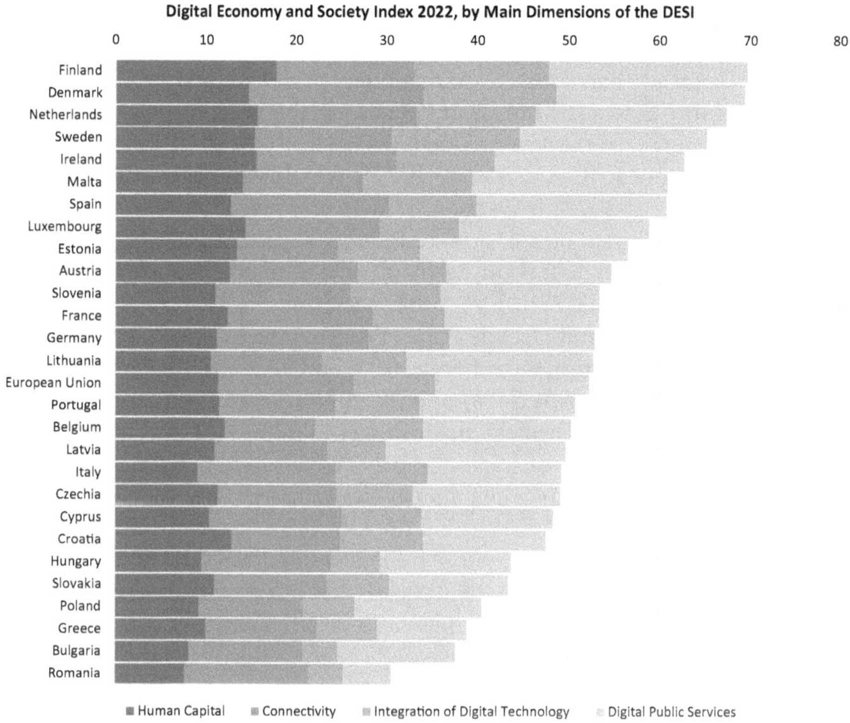

Figure 4.1 Digital Economy and Society Index 2022 by the main dimensions.

Source: European Commission (2022d).

The positive trend is that the EU continues to improve its level of digitalisation, and Member States that started from lower levels are gradually catching up, by growing at a faster rate. In particular, Italy, Poland, and Greece are substantially improving their DESI scores over the past five years, implementing sustained investments with a reinforced political focus on digitalisation. Three Scandinavian countries (Finland, Denmark, Sweden) and the Netherlands remain the EU frontrunners. However, they are faced with gaps in key areas: the uptake of advanced digital technologies such as AI and Big Data remains below 30% and there is a widespread skill shortage, which are slowing down overall progress and lead to digital exclusion.

Regarding the uptake of key technologies, during the COVID-19 pandemic, businesses have pushed the use of digital solutions, but only 55% of EU SMEs have a basic knowledge of digital tools indicating that almost half of SMEs are not availing of the opportunities created by digitalisation.

In 2021, in Europe, the gigabit connectivity grew further (European Commission, 2022b). The coverage of networks connecting buildings with glass fibre reached 50% of households, driving overall fixed very high capacity network (VHCN) coverage up to 70%. 5G coverage also went up last year to 66% of populated areas in the EU. However, an important precondition for the commercial launch of 5G is said as not complete by EC (2022a): only 56% of the total 5G harmonised spectrum has been assigned in the vast majority of Member States (Estonia and Poland are the exceptions).

In order to increase the level of digitalisation, the Digital Decade Policy Programme (European Commission, 2021), which will enter into force in Europe by the end of 2022, will set out targets organised under four cardinal points: a digitally skilled population and highly skilled digital professionals, secure and sustainable digital infrastructures, the digital transformation of businesses, and the digitalisation of public services.

According to the Digital Decade Policy Programme, by 2030, at least 80% of the European population aged between 16 and 74 should have basic digital skills (currently we are at 54%) and 20 million of ICT specialists should enter the labour market. The current shortages in filling ICT specialist vacancies represent a significant obstacle for the recovery and competitiveness of EU enterprises.

To fill in the gaps, the EU has put on the table significant resources to support the digital transformation. €127 billion are dedicated to digital related reforms and investments in the 25 national Recovery and Resilience Plans (RRPs) (European Union, 2022) that have so far been approved by the Council. Member States dedicate on average 26% of their Recovery and Resilience Facility (RRF) allocation to the digital transformation, above the compulsory 20% threshold. Member States that chose to invest more than 30% of their RRF allocation to digital are Austria, Germany, Luxembourg, Ireland, and Lithuania.

4.3 The role of digital innovation hubs in the European digital economy

Currently the main EU programme on digitalisation is the Digital Single Market package (https://eufordigital.eu/discover-eu/eu-digital-single-market/), launched on 19 April 2016. Building on and complementing the various national initiatives for digitizing industry, the Commission aims through it to create better framework conditions for the digital industrial revolution. One of the most important pillars of the Digital Single Market package is the activity to develop a network of DIHs.

DIHs are said to be 'one-stop-shops' that support companies to become more competitive with regard to their business, processes, products, or services using digital technologies (European Commission, 2022a). DIHs are based upon technology infrastructure (Competence Centre – CC) and provide access to the latest knowledge, expertise, and technology to support customers with numerous processes including piloting, testing, and experimenting with digital innovations. DIHs may also provide business and financing support to implement innovations and IT solutions, if needed across the value chain. Their aim is to facilitate the experimentation and uptake of technologies coming from six main areas: Big Data and AI, Internet of Things, Manufacturing/Industry 4.0, Robotics, HPC, and Photonics.

As proximity is considered crucial, it acts as a doorway and strengthens the innovation ecosystem. A DIH is a regional multi-partner cooperation (including organisations like universities, industry associations, chambers of commerce, incubators/accelerators, regional development agencies and even governments) and the organisational form is usually adapted to regional conditions and contexts.

A DIH can be formed from existing organisations taking on the title and/or rebranding themselves, from existing projects under Horizon 2020 programme, by bringing together several existing actors in a (new) virtual organisation or by creating an entirely new organisation from scratch. It should have or develop a dedicated expertise, based on the available local strengths and the current and emerging needs of the local industry or public sector.

The geographical scale of a DIH's focus is also a varying factor. Most DIHs are clearly regional in their original scope but recognise the need to attract expertise and experience from outside the region. A successful implementation of the DIH concept could lead in some cases to the DIH playing a prominent role for digitalisation at a national level. Exceptionally there are cases where the high level of competences allows internationalisation and success in a global scale but the impact on the regional scale remains mostly the norm.

Depending on the structure and needs of the region, this may mean specialising in one technology and one sector, but often a combination of different topics is more the case. In addition to specialists with sound knowledge of a technology, generalists and change managers may also be required to provide digital transformation expertise. This means that in the subsequent advice following a digital maturity assessment, the expert can evaluate the technological possibilities, knowing the current trends and market developments and provide

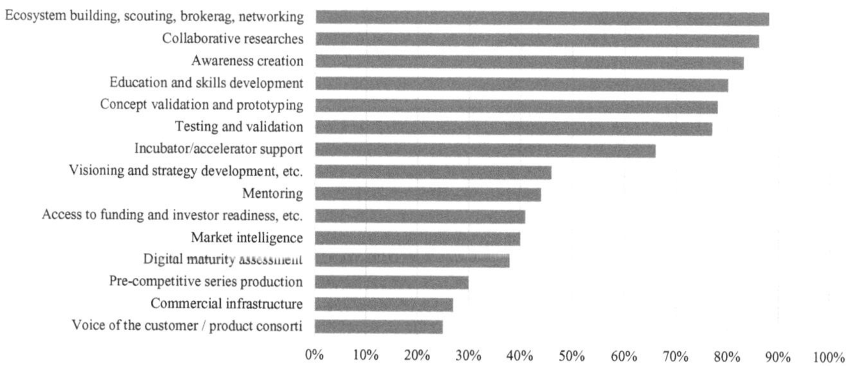

Figure 4.2 Services delivered by DIHs for all EU countries.

Source: European Investment Bank (2020).

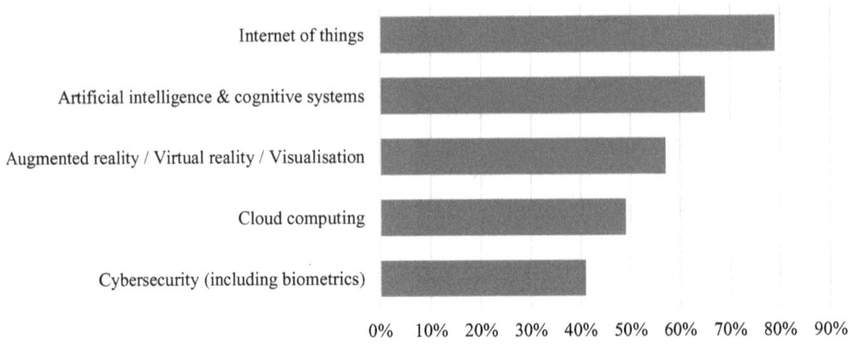

Figure 4.3 DIHs supporting selected technologies for all small-and medium-sized enterprises.

Source: European Investment Bank (2020).

access to the appropriate technical experts. The focus should always be on how best to serve the regional economy with an appropriate matrix of sectors and technologies. Figure 4.2 lists the services currently being delivered by the fully operational DIHs for all EU countries, according to the EU catalogue at the time of writing. Figure 4.3 illustrates the percentage of DIHs which support the most promising technologies for all small- and medium-sized enterprises.

Only between 2016 and 2020, more than 150 DIHs have taken part in 370 different innovation trials testing digital innovations in collaboration with DIHs. In 2020, approximately 2,000 innovative SMEs across Europe have received the EU support through the DIHs to complete their digital transformation.

Box 4.1 Digital innovation hubs, clusters, research and technology organisations (RTOs)

DIHs, clusters, and ecosystems are more than buzz words in economic development, they are engines of growth for cities and regions that accelerate innovation but there are some differences among them.

- *Digital Innovation Hubs* focus on developing innovative digital products, services, and training in a specific area of their community, taking targeted actions to help overcome key challenges in that field. Each hub operates with its own management, legal structure, and business plan and has clear, measurable objectives to deliver value to its partners.
- RTOs are often mentioned as DIHs. In many DIHs, the RTOs are one of the critical partners, but they usually do not have the capacity

to offer all the needed services to SMEs. Even though many RTOs also have network/business service capacities, their main function/mission is related to technology development (CC). Also, they are mostly networks, with departments that have a specific industry/technology orientation with related technological infrastructures/expertise. So, it can be said that an RTO is a key partner and can support many DIHs, acting as the CCs within the DIH organisation. RTOs are often an initiator of a DIH.

- *Clusters* are market-driven phenomena. Clusters emerge without the help of any specific policy, as a result either of the spontaneous accumulation of competitive advantage or by chance. Cluster/network organisations are often suggested as DIHs. As the mission of these organisations is to create (industrial) innovation networks it is not a surprise that they are highly related to the DIHs. In many cases, these types of organisations act as the orchestrator of a DIH, as they have high-quality capacities to organise the innovation ecosystem community. However, typically these clusters/networks do not have the technological infrastructure, as well as (some of the) business service expertise. Therefore, they need to partner with Competence Centres (RTOs, Universities, etc.) and in some cases other stakeholders to provide a mixed portfolio of services. This cooperation in a multi-partner entity often forms the DIH concept.

Source: Adapted from: Butter et al. (2020).

The high interest of the European Commission in DIHs has been seen over the last years in large investments for their developments. Only from Horizon 2020 programme, 500M€ has been devoted to support their development (European Commission, 2022a). It is the Commission's aim that all companies have access to a regional DIH, allowing them to access competences and to digitise their organisations, products, and services. Furthermore, in 2021, the Commission decided to create European DIH network with over 300 candidate DIHs, pan-European network of DIHs with designated DIHs from all the member states.

In August 2022, 416 fully operational DIHs, 218 in preparation, and 70 potential DIHs from H2020 were registered and listed at the EC's S3 Platform (European Commission, 2023). As presented in Figure 4.4, DIHs differ strongly in the provided technologies. The highest number of DIHs 353 being 85% of all fully operating DIHs provide the Internet of Things support, following by the AI, Big Data, and robotics (77%, 69% and 67% respectively). Cloud computing is a focus for half of the DIHs, and cybersecurity technology is supported by 44% of the DIHs.

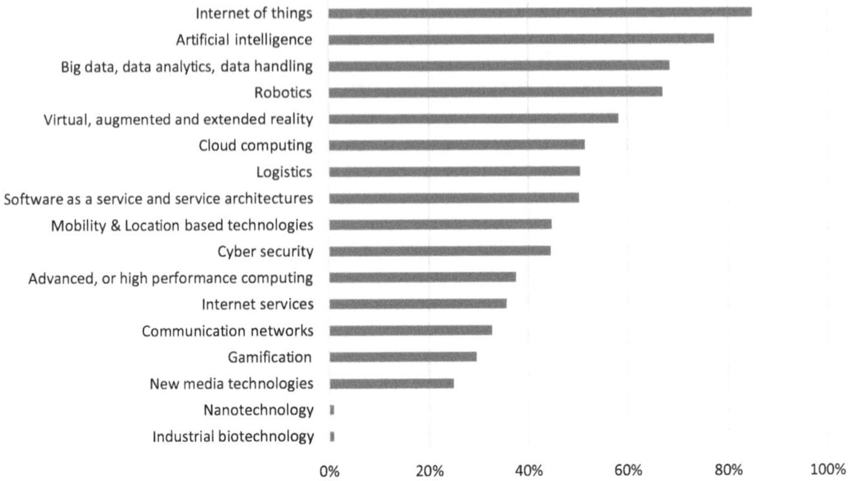

Figure 4.4 Fully operational DIHs by selected technologies they provide.

Source: Smart Specialisation Platform (European Commission, n.d.)

To provide some examples, in Italy, I – the National Confederation of Crafts and SMEs – through iICNA HUB 4.0, coordinates a network of ten DIHs, an initiative promoted by the Italian Ministry of Economic Development. The hubs accompany enterprises in transitioning to a new production model (Industry 4.0) by estimating their digital maturity, by enhancing their digital skills, by fostering experimental projects, and by exchanging best practices (Imparato, 2020).

In Norway, Digital2, Norway's national strategy for digitalising the Norwegian business sector which consists of more than 60 strategic advice and acts as a framework for how the Government should contribute to aiding companies in implementing new technology, is supporting DigitalNorway which is one of five fully operational DIHs in the country (OECD, 2021).

4.4 Digital innovations hubs' impact

The European landscape of DIHs is highly diversified and heterogeneous. There are substantial differences in the level of maturity and sophistication of DIHs across Europe. Some are fairly advanced and have a well-defined business model and clear links to the digital ecosystem, while many are still developing and have been established only in the last few years.

Most hubs have a mixed funding model, but they are mainly skewed towards public funding from European, national, or regional programmes. Private funding for DIHs is limited and it generally comes only in the form of membership fees and contributions (often in-kind) from partners (European Investment Bank, 2020).

In general, the value proposition for DIHs reflects industry needs. It might include, among other, the abilities to 'speak the language' of SMEs, understand business models and business transformation and help companies transform, and work with companies at all levels of digital maturity, including offering low-tech transfer to companies lower down the maturity curve, assess current and future skills needs and provide appropriate support, and provide funding or facilitating access to funding from external sources.

Assessing what stage, a business has reached on its digitisation journey is likely to be one of the most important services offered by DIHs. Such an assessment helps both the business and the Hub to understand the company's current position and to identify future options and needs. Typically, this would involve either a survey undertaken by Hub experts or a self-help tool that the company could apply itself. The assessment would diagnose the company's needs and readiness in relation to digital technologies, provide feedback on the level of maturity, and direct the client to further tailored help and advice within the Hub's ecosystem. This could include referrals to recognised private sector suppliers (digital IT SMEs, consultancies, etc.). For example, Mittelstand-Digital (https://www.mittelstand digital.de/MD/Navigation/DE/Service/EnglischeSeite/englische-seite.html) utilises such an assessment to place companies at one of five stages within a maturity ladder, allowing it to match the business to available services accordingly.

Although concerned with promoting digital technologies and services, DIHs should not operate only in the online space. Many of their target clients are still 'analogue' and it will be essential not only that hubs have a physical presence within the communities where these companies are situated, but also that they continuously 'scout' for opportunities within those localities. There should be a named contact point for firms to speak to. DIHs should certainly have a strong online identity, but they must also be identifiable physical entities.

Indicators to measure the impact of DIHs are many: they span from individual hub-client relationships to a hub's overall performance and the impact of the DIH ecosystem as a whole. Particular emphasis should be placed on measuring the quality and impact of collaborative links, since it is primarily the strength of these links, rather than unconnected activities, which define DIHs. Selective measurement indicators could be used to establish benchmarks and standards of services, as well as in sharing best practices (Kristiansen & Ritala, 2018).

Further impact could be measured using econometric measures, such as increased awareness, enhanced competitiveness, and assessment of digital maturity. Examples include an increase in a company's market share, creating value via new markets and business models, establishing new value chains, increasing the turnover ratio between services and products, quantifying cost reductions of services and resource optimisation due to digitisation, number of patents and other IP protections (e.g., registered designs), number of innovation projects (e.g., hackathons), and number of people trained in digital skills (Deloitte, 2018).

The economic impact of DIHs still needs to be comprehensively assessed but it has been particularly evident during the coronavirus pandemic that

DIHs have helped companies to work together to provide solutions – be it robotics for healthcare providers or new manufacturing processes for locally produced masks – thus providing an added value for the local economies.

For example, in the Lombardy region of Italy, one of the areas most affected by the outbreak, the local DIH worked with a regional industrial association, Confindustria Bergamo (https://www.confindustriabergamo.it), to tackle a shortage of surgical masks. The Italian hub led a large local initiative to help regional manufacturers pivot their business from textiles, fashion, or chemicals to making surgical masks for the public healthcare workers.

4.5 Finland as a digital leader

Finland was the first country in the world to declare that broadband access was a legal right for every citizen (Borges et al., 2017). Finland has overtaken Denmark (#1, DESI 2021) and ranked 1st in the DESI 2022 (see Figure 4.1) jumping from the second place. The DESI includes four key areas and dozens of indicators. Each country is then ranked within each of the key area categories and then DESI is the combined score. Leading the general score, Finland placed itself on the top of *Human capital* and *Integration of digital technology*, second place of *Integration of digital technology* and eight place of *Connectivity*.

Within *Human capital* key area, as presented in Table 4.1, the biggest difference between Finnish and average EU score was in share of individuals with at least basic digital skills and above basic digital skills. The proportion of employed people working as ICT specialists is above EU average by nearly 3%points (7.4% against 4.5%), ICT graduates in Finland account for 7.5% of all graduates, and the share of companies providing ICT training to their employees in Finland is almost twice the EU average. Although Finland has already reached the Digital Decade target of 80% of the population with at least basic digital skills, the Finnish Ministry of Education and Culture recently launched the new literacies programme 2020–2022 to boost the development of targeted competences in ICT and improve media literacy and programming skills (European Commission, 2022c).

Few Finnish indicators in the *Connectivity* key area score lower than EU by at least 10% points, those being shares of households with overall fixed broadband take-up, at least 100 Mbps fixed broadband take-up, fast broadband (NGA) coverage, fibre to the Premises (FTTP) coverage. Finland is a front-runner in 5G commercial services delivery, while it lags behind in the provision of VHCN, in rural areas, especially those sparsely populated. Finland aims at tackling that issue by implementing its national broadband plan and dedicated public funding.

The second strength of Finland is the *ICT integration*. The Finnish telecommunications market is very advanced. Many services and technologies have been introduced in Finland much earlier than in other countries. According to Statistics Finland (2021) among all types of industries, 16% of enterprises (10+ employees) use AI. Moreover, the share of SMEs with at least

Table 4.1 DESI 2022 indicators and scores of Finland and EU average

DESI key areas	*DESI indicators*	*DESI 2022 Finland*	*DESI 2022 EU*
Human capital	At least basic digital skills (% individuals)	79%	54%
	Above basic digital skills (% individuals)	48%	26%
	At least basic digital content creation skills (% individuals)	83%	66%
	ICT specialists (% individuals in employment aged 15–74)	7.40%	4.50%
	Female ICT specialists (% ICT specialists)	24%	19%
	Enterprises providing ICT training (% enterprises, 2020)	38%	20%
	ICT graduates (% graduates, 2020)	7.50%	3.90%
Connectivity	Overall fixed broadband take-up (% households)	61%	78%
	At least 100 Mbps fixed broadband take-up (% households)	29%	41%
	At least 1 Gbps take-up (% households)	1.45%	7.58%
	Fast broadband (NGA) coverage (% households)	75%	90%
	Fixed Very High-Capacity Network (VHCN) coverage (% households)	68%	70%
	Fibre to the Premises (FTTP) coverage (% households)	40%	50%
	5G spectrum (assigned spectrum as a % of total harmonised 5G spectrum)	99%	56%
	5G coverage (% populated areas)	72%	66%
	Mobile broadband take-up (% individuals)	96%	87%
	Broadband price index (score 0–100)	79%	73%
Integration of digital technology	SMEs with at least a basic level of digital intensity (% SMEs)	82%	55%
	Electronic information sharing (% enterprises)	48%	38%
	Social media (% enterprises)	51%	29%
	Big data (% enterprises, 2020)	22%	14%
	Cloud (% enterprises)	66%	34%
	AI (% enterprises)	16%	8%
	ICT for environmental sustainability (% enterprises having medium/high intensity of green action through ICT)	77%	66%
	e-Invoices (% enterprises, 2020)	83%	32%
	SMEs selling online (% SMEs)	23%	18%
	Selling online cross-border (% SMEs)	8%	9%
Digital public services	e-Government users (% internet users)	92%	65%
	Pre-filled forms (score 0–100)	90%	64%
	Digital public services for citizens (score 0–100)	90%	75%
	Digital public services for businesses (score 0–100)	93%	82%
	Open data (% maximum score)	86%	81%

Source: European Commission (2022c).

a basic level of digital intensity was considerably above the EU average (82% against 55%), 66% of companies use cloud solutions and 16% integrate AI technology in their operations (see Table 4.1). Finnish companies are also intensive users of social media (51% against the EU average of 29%) and of e-invoices (83% against the EU average of 32%). Online interaction between government authorities and the public is approaching the maximum with 92% of Finnish internet users using e-government services. DESI 2022 indicated that Finland is well positioned to bring 100% of key public services online and reach the Digital Decade target for 2030 ahead of schedule.

In 2021, Finland continued to implement its digital strategies, including the digital progress programme, Digivisio 2030 (https://digivisio2030.fi/en/frontpage/) and the updated strategy on AI. The country created administrative structures or continued improving their operations, financed programmes in this area and developed or launched new systems. The options for future developments were proposed in a report 'Finnish technology policy in 2020s – a global leader through technology and information' published by the Finnish Technology Advisory Board published the report (Ministry of Finance, 2022).

Box 4.2 Digitalisation in Finland's recovery and resilience plan

All EU Member States must create national recovery and resilience plans (RRPs) in order to receive funding from the EC's RRF. The RRF supports the EU in achieving the target of climate neutrality by 2050, boosts digital transition, triggers creating jobs, and supports sustainable growth in the process. The Finnish RRP is part of the Sustainable Growth Programme focusing on four key elements: green transition, digitalisation, employment and skills, and health and social services. According to the Finnish Ministry of Finance, the updated in June 2022 RRP foresees EUR 190 million for the digitalisation objective constituting bit over 10% of the Sustainable Growth Programme. The goals of the digitalisation theme of the Finnish RRP are to create a competitive operating environment for businesses and to make Finland a world-class producer of data-driven and secure services for digital societies, e.g. solutions that promote digitalisation in the transport sector (such as rail transport digitalisation within Digirail project), high-speed internet connections throughout the country, further investments in 6G networks, artificial intelligence, quantum computing, and microelectronics.

Source: European Commission (2022e).

4.6 Digital innovation hubs in Finland

The first drafts of the DIHs in Finland were based on the strong Finnish domains being transport, manufacturing, care, energy, and process industry. The drafting was initiated after the first meeting of the DEIs working group for DIHs in October 2016. In 2017, the Ministry of Economic Affairs and Employment, with the help of TEKES (the former Finnish Funding Agency for Innovation, currently called Business Finland) and the Technical Research Centre VTT, outlined the list of potential Finnish DIHs (Ministry of Economic Affairs and Employment, 2019).

Based on the ministerial recommendations and bottom-up actors after five years the EC's DIHs Catalogue now has 15 fully operational Finnish DIHs, five in preparation and one being as potential DIH from H2020. Four of the DIHs are classified as part of the European DIH network (Finnish AI Region [FAIR], Location Innovation Hub [LIH], HealthHub Finland and Robocoast EDIH Consortium) and three DIHs have a candidate European DIH status (5STAR eCorridors, SIX Manufacturing EDIH, WellLake EDIH).

Regional S3 is of utmost importance in Finland especially in the seven sub-regions of East & North Finland (ENF). These regions represent one of EU's Northern Sparsely Populated Areas which have also been viewed as a target for territorial cohesion in the regional and structural policies of the

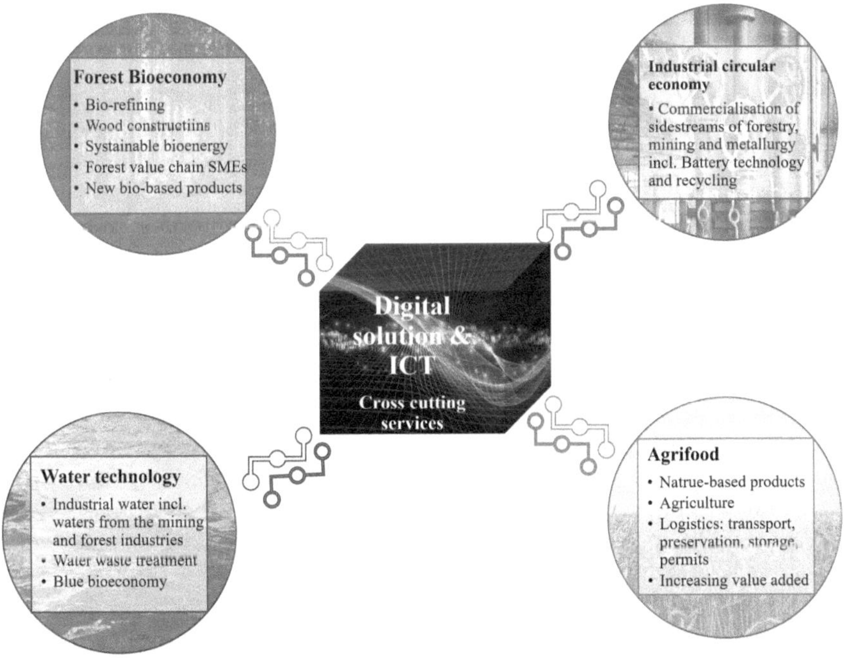

Figure 4.5 Five thematic areas for clusters in East and North Finland.

Source: ELMO project.

EU. These regions have been chosen as one of European Commission's pilot areas to develop new approaches and a S3 strategy for the period 2019–2023 has been developed.

A mapping was carried out in the ENF area during 2019 in the priority areas of the strategy in order to identify the existing competencies and networks in the regions. As a result of the mapping, five thematic areas were identified as presented in Figure 4.5: *clean technologies and low-carbon solutions, industrial circular economy, ICT and digitalisation, innovative technologies, and production processes*. The industries of the ENF area are strongly focused on the utilisation of natural resources and conditions and the ENF area is already a pioneer in the development of solutions for an industrial circular economy, one of the most crucial growth sectors in the region.

A series of networking events and training in the ENF were conducted during 2020 to facilitate cluster development and to enable cross-regional cluster networking. One of the main goals was to support better utilisation of the research, development and innovation (RDI) services offered by innovation platforms that have been systematically financed and created in the region in recent years. Creating new businesses and supporting SMEs in producing new or improved products, processes and services have been common goals.

4.7 A case study: Arctic Development Environments Cluster – the heart of Arctic Smartness Clusters

Looking closer to the ENF, Lapland is the northernmost region (NUTS3) of the country and European Union. In 2021, the regional population was a bit over 175 thousand citizens living in a sparsely populated rural area with density of less than two persons per square kilometre. At the same time, Lapland's rich natural resources have made it a favourable industrial destination blooming in forestry, mining, metallurgy, and tourism.

Lapland is one of the first Finnish regions that adopted a S3 that is centred on innovation-driven socio-economic development of territories, through innovative multi-level and multi-stakeholder governance. An interactive process of public–private cooperation is defined as an entrepreneurial discovery process that helps to identify investment priorities – i.e., entrepreneurs with scientific, technological, and engineering expertise and market knowledge jointly produce and share information on new economic activity domains in which the region excels or has the potential to excel in the future.

Lapland's S3 focuses on the sustainable utilisation and commercialisation of Arctic natural resources and conditions started in 2013 through a strategic step-by-step implementation approach. In the approach, the Regional Council of Lapland clarified the strengths, value chains, and new forms of cooperation in the Lapland region and launched the Arctic Specialisation Implementation Project. As a part of the project, 650 projects were analysed, and such analysis was used as the basis for the construction of five clusters. Clustering started in 2015 with the Arctic Smartness portfolio project (Jokelainen & Jänkälä, 2017), which works like an ecosystem, where the actors share common goals to develop Lapland.

Arctic Smartness Clusters act as engines for the regional development and are implementing new local and European initiatives and projects creating a breeding ground for growth in the regional economy. As of 2022, there are six established Arctic Smartness Clusters – Arctic Smart Rural Communities, Arctic Development Environments, Arctic Design, Arctic Safety, Smart and Sustainable Arctic Tourism, and Arctic Industry and Circular Economy. According to the data provided by Lapland University of Applied Sciences, the funding in-flow to Lapland in years 2020 and 2021 from national and international projects via the Arctic Smart Clusters exceeded EUR 22.3 Million (Table 4.2).

Table 4.2 Arctic Smartness Clusters and their aims

Arctic Smartness Clusters	*In a nutshell*
The Arctic Smart Rural Community	The cluster's main role is to prevent capital outflow from rural Lapland and to promote the region as prosperous as it offers a surplus of raw materials to a wide range of smart resource-intensive businesses. Another focus is on further processing of food and the promotion of renewable energy. This cluster, managed by ProAgria Lapland, is built upon network of 100 entrepreneurs and 200 developers: municipalities, financiers, politicians, projects (including international ones), research institutes, and business advisors
The Arctic Development Environments Cluster	The Arctic Development Environments Cluster serves as a supporting network to all Arctic Smartness Clusters by, e.g., enabling technologies to all industries and especially SMEs. This cluster, managed by Lapland University of Applied Sciences, is thoughtfully addressed further in 4.7
The Arctic Design Cluster	The cluster aims at making Lapland's businesses, products, and services nationally and internationally recognisable and competitive by utilising smart specialisation focusing on research, art, and design. The core processes are based on the knowledge and research of arctic designing including service design, product design, interaction design, and applied visual arts. The cluster is managed by the faculty of art at the University of Lapland
The Arctic Safety Cluster	The cluster aims at strengthening interregional networks and safety, both for the citizens and for the business. It is composed of the safety of tourism and everyday life and its beneficiaries are local businesses, residents, travellers, industries, and the environment. Lapland University of Applied Sciences is managing this cluster

(*Continued*)

Table 4.2 (Continued)

The Smart and Sustainable Arctic Tourism Cluster	The cluster aims at Lapland's tourism growing smartly: by 2030, the cluster wishes to increase tourism income up to EUR 1.5 billion (e.g., by developing year-round tourism). The biggest challenge and aim is to reach the growth responsibly, without compromising the safety and quality of the industry. The cluster includes a network of entrepreneurs, Destination Management Organizations, research and education institutes, development organisations, municipalities, and tourism projects managed by the Lapland Regional Council
I. The Arctic Industry and Circular Economy Cluster	The cluster supports Lapland as a frontrunner in sustainable utilisation of natural resources, sustainable industry, and circular economy. A mix of industrial expertise and commitment to sustainable development are at the core of refining natural resources in the Lapland region. The process industry actively searches for new, eco-innovative ways to modernise its processes while the management of by-product processes of industries and process optimisation is also a prioritised issue. The cluster is being managed by Digipolis

Source: arcticsmartness.eu.

The Arctic Development Environments Cluster was approved by the EC in February 2021 as Lapland's first official DIH (Arctic Smartness, 2018) with its objective to bring together the RDI environments and expert services operating separately in the region. Yet, the collaboration as part of Lapland's S3 strategy started in 2013. The aim was to form a uniform body to serve and boost Lapland's business life and business investments in product development as well as internationalisation. In contrast to other clusters from the Arctic Smartness, the Arctic Development Environments Cluster is not a thematic cluster and acts as an umbrella support to the other clusters.

The cluster produces services for the region's businesses via its 50 environments and 700 specialists. Arctic Development Environments are both physical and virtual environments providing learning opportunities and triggering innovation, such as laboratories, studios, workshops, and simulation environments. The funding is preliminary public – via the Regional Council of Lapland, Business Finland, and the EU.

The main partners in this cluster are multidisciplinary research communities from University of Lapland, Lapland University of Applied Sciences (the manager), Natural Resources Institute Finland, Geological Survey of Finland, Vocational College Lappia, and Lapland Vocational College. Yet, worth mentioning are also Artic Power – Cold climate testing, Arctic Steel, and Mining as the strong industry partners that have benefited by increased capacity and maturity of their actions and processes. The development work has been enabled via different projects, primarily financed from the European Regional Development Fund.

Box 4.3 Arctic Development Environments Cluster – service model, competences, and services

Service model in steps

- The business (client) contacts the cluster.
- The cluster prepares a requirement specification based on the client's need.
- The client receives a tender presenting the fee and schedule of the service.
- If the tender is accepted, a service contract is drawn between the client and the cluster. The fee is based on the actual costs of the service.
- A group of experts to be involved is selected, and the cooperation is coordinated by the cluster.
- The cluster assists the client with identifying and applying for suitable R&D funding.
- The cluster reports the final results to the company.

Sectors to support

- Agriculture and food
- Community, social, and personal service activities
- Construction
- Education
- Energy and utilities
- Life sciences and healthcare
- Manufacture of basic metals and fabricated metal products
- Manufacture of food products, beverages, and tobacco
- Manufacture of textiles and textile products
- Maritime and fishery
- Mining and quarrying
- Other Manufacturing
- Tourism (including restaurants and hospitality)
- Transport and logistic

Technical competences

- Additive manufacturing
- Artificial intelligence
- Cyber-physical systems
- Gamification
- Interaction technologies
- Internet of things
- Internet services

- Logistics
- Micro/nano electronics
- New media technologies
- Organic and large-area electronics
- Sensory systems
- Simulation, modelling, and digital twins
- Software as a service and service architectures
- Virtual, augmented, and extended reality

Services provided

- Awareness creation
- Collaborative Research
- Concept validation and prototyping
- Ecosystem building, scouting, brokerage, and networking
- Testing and validation
- Visioning and Strategy Development for Businesses

Source: Smart Specialisation Platform (European Commission, 2023).

The Arctic Development Environments Cluster is one of only two Finnish DIHs that offer the services up to the highest technology readiness levels (TRL9 – *Actual system proven through successful mission operations*). The cluster, operating on non-profit terms, offers several solutions and services to the clients (that represent already existing companies, mostly SMEs or micro businesses). Depending on the speed of the services and the level of expert engagement, the cluster is able to offer services free of charge provided by local students. Payment in innovation vouchers by Business Finland (accounting for EUR 5,000 of 100% aid) are one of the most common payment options by SMEs.

During the COVID-19 pandemic, the demand for the cluster's services increased. On one hand, local businesses have tried to adapt to pandemic-related restrictions or develop brand new products or services supporting distant working and remote living. An additional challenge has been to uptake the pre-pandemic level of international partners due to closure of the borders and travelling restrictions.

The evaluation of the Arctic Development Environments Cluster is ongoing. Among the challenges, the cluster faces are the identification of innovation gaps and the development of better monitoring and evaluation practises for the next programming period. The COVID-19 pandemic has had an impact on the clusters activities and has created new prioritisation. The low levels of hierarchy and low borders between organisations have helped Lapland to gain a competitive advantage on other EU clusters and have allowed the ongoing activities to be persistent and effective.

4.8 Conclusion

DIHs comprise represent a set of ecosystems characterised by high digitisation capacity building, wide advanced digital service offering, and strong linkages to European counterparts. Their importance in post-pandemic economic recovery is unquestionable. Finland has traditionally a strong cooperation culture across public and private organisations and strong digital innovation initiatives operate in the various regions across the country, including sparsely populated northern regions. In addition, Finland has Finnish strengths – numerous vibrant innovation and business ecosystems of national economic importance in which the public sector plays an important role. Digital transformation is not only about technology but requires also a deep context-specific understanding of how digital technologies can create benefit. Arctic Smartness Clusters, and especially the Arctic Development Environments Cluster, are excellent examples of how to endorse technology development but also the local competencies and know-how to solve significant economic or societal challenges in which digitisation plays a crucial role.

References

Arctic Smartness (2018). *Arctic Development Clusters, Foundations of Cooperation and Innovations*. Retrieved September 10, 2022, from: https://arcticsmartness.eu/wp-content/uploads/2018/03/arctic_development_environments.pdf.

Borges, L. A., Nilsson, K., Tunström, M., Dis, A. T., Perjo, L.; Berlina, A., Costa, S. O., Fredricsson, C., Grunfelder, J., Johnsen, I., Kristensen, I., Randall, L., Smas, L., Weber, R. (2017) White Paper on Nordic Sustainable Cities. Nordregio.

Butter, M., Karanikolova, K., Gijsbers, G., Guilloud, G. & Sanchez, B. (2020). *Defining Digital Innovation Hubs as Part of the European DIH Network (DRAFT)*. DIHNET.EU Working Paper. Available at: https://www.ip4fvg.it/wp-content/uploads/2020/06/DIHNET-Defining-the-DIH-in-its-context-FINAL.pdf.

Deloitte (2018). *Digital Maturity Model: Achieving Digital Maturity to Drive Growth* [PowerPoint Slides]. Retrieved February 21, 2023, from: https://www2.deloitte.com/content/dam/Deloitte/global/Documents/Technology-Media-Telecommunications/deloitte-digital-maturity-model.pdf.

European Commission (2023). *Smart Specialisation Platform. Digital Innovation Hubs*. Available at: https://european-digital-innovation-hubs.ec.europa.eu/edih-catalogue?f%5B0%5D=edih_soe%3Aedih&f%5B1%5D=edih_soe%3Asoe.

European Commission (2021). *Europe's Digital Decade* [Policies]. Retrieved September 10, 2022, from: https://digital-strategy.ec.europa.eu/en/policies/europes-digital-decade.

European Commission (2022a). *European Digital Innovation Hubs* [Activities]. Retrieved September 10, 2022, from: https://digital-strategy.ec.europa.eu/en/activities/edihs.

European Commission (2022b, July 28). *Digital Economy and Society Index 2022: Overall Progress But Digital Skills, SMEs and 5G Networks Lag Behind* [Press Release]. Retrieved September 10, 2022, from: https://ec.europa.eu/commission/presscorner/api/files/document/print/en/ip_22_4560/IP_22_4560_EN.pdf.

European Commission (2022c). *Digital Economy and Society Index (DESI) 2022: Finland*. Retrieved February 21, 2023, from: https://ec.europa.eu/newsroom/dae/redirection/document/88700.

European Commission (2022d). *The Digital Economy and Society Index (DESI)*. Available at: https://digital-strategy.ec.europa.eu/en/policies/desi.

European Commission (2022e). *Finland's National Recovery and Resilience Plan Latest State of Play*. Retrieved February 21, 2023, from: https://www.europarl.europa.eu/RegData/etudes/BRIE/2022/729279/EPRS_BRI(2022)729279_EN.pdf.

European Investment Bank (2020). *Financing the Digitalisation of Small and Medium-Sized Enterprises: The Enabling Role of Digital Innovation Hubs*. September 10, 2022, from: https://www.eib.org/attachments/thematic/financing_the_digitalisation_of_smes_en.pdf.

European Union (2022). *National Recovery and Resilience Plans*. Digital Skills & Jobs Platform. Retrieved September 10, 2022, from: https://digital-skills-jobs.europa.eu/en/actions/national-initiatives/national-recovery-plans.

Imparato, F. (2020, April 9). *Digital Innovation Hubs*. Interreg Europe. Retrieved September 10, 2022, from: https://www.interregeurope.eu/good-practices/digital-innovation-hubs.

Jokelainen, K. & Jänkälä, R. (2017). Älykäs erikoistuminen – miten sitä toteutetaan? Pohjois-Suomen rakennerahasto. http://www.rakennerahastot.fi/web/pohjois-suomen-suuralue/alykaserikoistuminen#.WMZm_E00OUl

Kristiansen, J.N. & Ritala, P. (2018). Measuring Radical Innovation Project Success: Typical Metrics Don't Work? *Journal of Business Strategy*, *39*(4), 34–41. https://doi.org/10.1108/JBS-09-2017-0137.

Ministry of Economic Affairs and Employment (2019). *Digital Innovation Hubs in Finland*. Publications of the Ministry of Economic Affairs and Employment 27/2019. Available at: https://julkaisut.valtioneuvosto.fi/bitstream/handle/10024/161585/TEM_2019_27_Digital_Innovation_Hubs_in_Finland.pdf?sequence=1.

Ministry of Finance (2022). *Government Resolution on Technology Policy*. Available at: https://api.hankeikkuna.fi/asiakirjat/8ac0ab12-68e7-4be5-91a5-213f572e938f/83b738af-6c18-432a-8b34-49024c5edb75/PAATOS_20220420122054.PDF.

OECD (2020). *A Roadmap towards a Common Framework for Measuring the Digital Economy, Report for the G20 Economy Task Force*. OECD Publishing. Available at: https://www.oecd.org/sti/roadmap-toward-a-common-framework-for-measuring-the-digital-economy.pdf.

OECD (2021). *Norway's Strategic Process to Capitalise on the Potential of New Technology*. Development Co-Operation TIPs (Tool Insights Practices platform). Available at: https://www.oecd.org/development-cooperation-learning/practices/dynamic/dcd-best-practices/a5c76fbf/pdf/norway-s-strategic-process-to-capitalise-on-the-potential-of-new-technology.pdf.

Statistics Finland (2021). *Use of Information Technologies by Enterprises*. Available at https://stat.fi/en/topic/digitalisation.

5 Digitalization and the impact on the labour relations[1]

Alejandro Díaz Moreno, Mª del Milagro Martín López, Myriam González Limón and Manuel Rivera Fernández

5.1 Introduction

Progress in the digital transformation process, which is largely inseparable from globalization and changes traditional economic and social organization patterns and balances, is reaching such magnitude and speed that it is currently taking a leading role in the discussions on competitiveness and economic growth in the European Union (EU). Such digital transformation has been enhanced by the impacts of the crisis caused by the COVID19.

Digital skills are not only leading to new qualification and competence requirements in all occupations but are also creating new jobs. One of the most relevant sectors is the ICT industry, where data reveal a significant increase in employment over the last decade. In spite of such increase, there is already an excess demand, with a number of vacancies in the EU28 that would rise to almost 800,000 by 2020. The OECD (2016) estimates that on average, around 25% of the jobs will experience significant changes in the competences they presently require, and some 9% will be displaced by automation of workplaces. Concerning the challenges and opportunities arising from the digital shift in employment, it is necessary to address changes in the specific characteristics of the different jobs, and ways to adjust the competences acquired by workers to the future supply and demand of labour.

Digital technologies minimize the cost of transferring ideas, knowledge, know-how and technology to anywhere in the world and reduce the cost of coordinating geographically separated complex activities. In a context of international economic liberalization and reduction of transportation costs, they allow companies to further fragment productive processes and relocate the different stages down to the task level and get the most out of international differences in costs and wages. Thus, the global economy tends to rest on long global value chains of large multinational companies, where firms and workers from all over the world compete with each other for integration (Baldwin, 2016).

This structural transformation has substantial distributive implications and poses major challenges to the economic policies of different countries. The digital economy goes beyond national jurisdictions and intensifies

DOI: 10.4324/9781003450160-8

economic interdependence among various territories, which leads to the need to reformulating and reinforcing supranational governance structures, if protectionist responses are to be avoided.

The EU is well aware of the fact that the digital shift is changing the nature of work and the structure of the labour market. EU institutions have launched various employment initiatives in the field of e-skills, education and training, but there is clear evidence of a deficit in digital skills or abilities. Moreover, the process is slow and it must be realized that there are significant differences among the member states. In 2015, the European Commission approved the Digital Single Market strategy with the aim of overcoming the fragmentation of the European Digital market, and providing a common approach to guide national strategies. However, in practice, this strategy has not been very successful, since the European Commission has proposed just a few initiatives, and they have not resulted in agreements by the Council and the Parliament to draft regulations allowing for its effective implementation (Council of the European Union, 2015). The Commission has developed the European Digital Competence Framework for Citizens (DigComp).

Digitalization of the economy has multiple implications and effects on the forms of working and organizing work, and therefore, on employment relations and on the conditions in which work is performed. Digitalization of the production of goods and services may affect, among other relevant aspects: labour relations of employees; application of employment contracts; forms of employment; terms of employment provision; exercise of management's direction and control powers; time and place where work is performed; on-the-job training; occupational health and safety; or a collective level, collective representation and bargaining instruments. Digitalization and its impact on employment relations generate new challenges resulting from changes in business models, the emergence of new forms of employment based on the online economy, and the increase in capacities brought about by the increasing connectivity. Experts believe that there will be changes in employment relations, resulting from the changes in the uniformity that was typical of the provision of subordinated work, and materialized in the fragmentation of production processes and their growing decentralization, among others. Digital technologies allow specifically, in some cases, for the replacement of employees by computers or robots in all kinds of works and tasks, either manual or intellectual, that no matter how complex they are can be expressed by programmable rules (algorithms), i.e. that are routinized, which may affect horizontally, to a greater or lesser extent, all production sectors (European Commission, 2020).

This has led to proposing the idea of a new division of labour (Levy & Murnane, 2004), between digital work and human work, where the latter would focus on performing works or tasks requiring problem-solving, intuition, creativity, persuasion, adaptation to new situations, improvisation in changing environments, sensitivity, affection and empathy, skills that are difficult to replicate by machines.

Successive industrial revolutions have caused movements in the opposite direction; although they have eliminated jobs through the destruction of certain forms of employment, they have also generated new types of employment. The digital revolution, also called the fourth industrial revolution, will produce similar effects, although it may generate imbalances leading to pay gaps between qualified and non-qualified employees, and even gender pay gaps.

Digitalization is also generating major challenges in terms of quality of employment. It reinforces the trend towards the proliferation of atypical employment relations and new forms of self-employment, which are associated with more insecure and less promising professional careers, because such workers have fewer opportunities to access training programmes, the social protection system, forms of Trade Union representation and collective bargaining processes. In addition to fostering technological innovation and its positive impacts, national digitalization strategies should include policies to minimize and balance out its negative impacts, as well as the trends towards market power concentration and increase of inequality. Governance of these policies should also focus on participation and involvement of the social partners. In terms of organization of work, digitalization will lead to greater flexibility, which will affect many aspects of the organization of work; the times and places where tasks are performed are more and more flexible, like the types of work. This may create an advantage for both employers and employees, in the form of more autonomy and productivity, a better balance between work and personal life, and cost reduction. In turn, it may also entail risks, for example, in terms of certainty of income. Moreover, flexibility requires and results in new forms of management and new types of skills. Therefore, legislation and collective agreements must take into account the need for flexibility concerning working times and workplaces.

5.2 Basic aspects of digitalization. The digital transformation process

Manufacturing processes are undergoing a digital transformation process, triggered by the advances in digital information technologies and, mainly, by the development of computers and software. The fourth industrial revolution has come about through the application of digital technologies to the industry's business models – in other words, to the production models – leading to a new concept of factory, termed "intelligent", which is dominated by the digital aspects applied to its production. "The intelligence of the new factory is the result of the convergence of information technologies; their union in a 'digital ecosystem' with other industrial technologies, and the development of new organizational processes" (Del Val, 2016, p. 4).

This digital transformation may benefit the localization process, favouring national production and industries, and open the possibility that these will recover all the value processes ("botsourcing"), which will lead to an increase in job creation. What does seem clear is that, on the one hand, new technologies, artificial intelligence, big data, the Internet of Things, 5G and robotization, among other elements, will have an impact on the labour market (employment and labour skills) and on industries, leading to a new economy in the long term.

The pandemic that we suffered in 2019–2022 forced companies and workers, as well as public and private institutions, to adopt action protocols that responded, in a nascent way, to what was imminent anyway in the not-too-distant future. While we discussed such issues as worker protection, occupational health, social dialogue in the case of the so-called digital platforms, those jobs where digitalization and big data handling were imposed – the implementation of a work system, or a system of labour relations at least, was proceeding in a necessary, almost forced, manner; based essentially on the use of technological means, on using computers outside the workplace.

This work is fundamentally oriented towards what we consider or understand to be digitalization. Leaving aside the aspects of automation or robotization, understood as the replacement of workers by machines or robots, we are referring to, and focusing fundamentally on, the impact that digitalization has on business organization. The subject of automation is analysed or defined in quantitative terms (in other words, focus is on the processes of shedding – with special emphasis – and creating jobs), while in the case of digitalization in the strict sense, the discussion is more centred on the emergence of new forms of work and therefore closely linked to the quality of employment.

This topic touches on many aspects of society: how work is being exchanged on digital platforms; how consumers are becoming producers (the so-called prosumers); how mass production is being recalibrated to local micro-production; how the capacity of under-utilized assets can be shared at a marginal cost, close to zero; how companies are reviewing their decisions on where to produce, taking into account the use of robots; how new monopolies are emerging; and, last but not least, the implications of big data for economic structures.

5.3 Changes in the labour market as a consequence of digitalization

The introduction of new technologies, i.e. the incorporation of any new developments that may affect the world of work, has often provoked opposition, and even violent opposition, from workers. It has been stated many times that digitalization can only be successful if the human element is present; in other words, if such a change enjoys favour, acceptance and support from those who represent the company's human capital. At present, it cannot be claimed that the processes of digitalization as such represent a step backwards for workers, since they only stimulate fear and generate resistance to change, in turn threatening the possibilities of progress and improvement in working conditions which, in short, affect the workers themselves. From a wider perspective, it is indisputable that since the second industrial revolution, technological progress has been a catalyst for economic welfare and improved working conditions for workers.

In the midst of the global technological revolution, in the era of digitalization, the destruction of employment will not outweigh the possible creation of new jobs. Certainly, the more skilled jobs are likely to prevail, while the less skilled jobs are likely to come under greater pressure. In this sense, there is perhaps a greater danger of generating inequalities, which is precisely what the institutions and social partners need to mitigate (Business Services Orange, 2014; Soete & Well, 2005).

In this respect, it is argued that technological innovation (Cedrola, 2017, p. 9), the hallmark of digitalization, has generated three contradictions in the world of employment. First, there is a process of competence replacement which appears to question the old skills. Second, there also seems to be an apparent contradiction between generic work and self-programmable work. Finally, there is a contradiction between the probable destruction of jobs, which require fewer professional qualifications, and the hypothetical creation of new specialized jobs needing higher qualifications.

The new technologies had to be implemented perforce and had to impact ways of working; in particular, they had to manifest themselves through the creation of new jobs based on processes such as those relating to data administration and management, digitalization in general, and technical issues. All of this resulted in the relocation of jobs, the simplification of the content of the tasks carried out by workers, and the completion of these tasks without the worker needing to travel to the workplace (that is in teleworking).

One of the most important manifestations or consequences of the whole process that we are experiencing in the field of labour relations is breaking the physical contact of workers. This refers to both contact with the workplace, in other words, with the physical space in which he or she usually worked, and with colleagues, namely other workers. We are therefore faced with a distance relationship that not only has multiple manifestations, since it is not limited to work, but also has a major effect in many ways on employees' trade union activity, and their influence on the company. As a result, everyone carries out their work with a total lack of control over their work processes, which has two effects: on the one hand, it facilitates flexibility and probably implies an improved work-life balance; and on the other hand, it puts very powerful weapons in the hands of the employer for the purpose of imposing possible disciplinary measures, or when it comes to dismissing certain workers without the need to explain the reason for their discharge, as is required at present. In this context, it is possible to talk about virtualizing labour relations.

One of the outstanding aspects of digitalization is its impact observed in the reorganization of workspaces, so that many of the hierarchies that have traditionally existed in the field of labour relations have disappeared. As a result, spaces that are more open are being taken on, not only ideally but also physically, without fixed positions, and are being gradually occupied according to different work projects.

This sense of change, even of revolution as some claim, whether or not it is disruptive, is a common feeling among most workers in today's productive economy. Digitalization, along with other developments affecting working conditions, the economic situation of workers and working life, is calling into question existing business structures, management methods, and leadership and industrial relations, as well as the scope and methods of social dialogue (European Economic and Social Committee, 2018).

5.4 Digital skills and training

Digital transformation will mean a change in the demand for professionals in Industry 4.0, a reduction in semi-qualified personnel, and an increase in the demand for highly qualified jobs, mainly linked to information technologies (Del Val Román, 2016).

Robotics, artificial intelligence, the Internet of Things, etc. will change labour markets and the skills required to perform jobs, an issue that is more far-reaching given that it could affect "working conditions, employment levels and income distribution" in the long term. Conventional employment systems and the traditional labour market are facing profound changes, although the direction, speed and scope of these changes cannot be predicted in advance (CCOO, 2017).

In addition to the need for state, regional and Community legislation to mitigate the potential negative effects that digitalization might have on labour relations, trade unions must participate in the appropriate training of workers, enabling them to acquire the skills that will equip them to carry out tasks that will arise in the future, in the new era of technological and digital development. Therefore, through collective bargaining, trade union action has an important and fundamental role in ensuring that jobs are adapted, and workers are trained. In this way, digitalization can become an improvement, rather than simply a destruction of jobs by replacing workers with machines or robots.

Training has to take account of technological advances, so that the aim is to give the worker sufficient skills to adapt to the successive changes which may occur, and which affect the performance of their work. For this reason, it is essential that the digitalization process also includes a process of continuous training for workers.

A fundamental aspect to which social dialogue must refer is certainly training and the acquisition by workers of the necessary skills and competences, according to each sector of activity. The European Economic and Social Committee pointed out, as early as 2014, the need to contribute to the training of workers. This contribution was intended to guarantee access to the necessary support for those workers whose jobs are likely to undergo greater change or transformation as a result of digitalization, without excluding self-employed workers and to encourage the option of so-called STEM disciplines, i.e. training specific workers in IT and artificial intelligence (European Economic and Social Committee, 2014). So, one of the key points for tackling the consequences of digitalization is to strengthen the capacities of workers, including independent workers, through the creation of specific vocational training programmes, guaranteeing access to higher education and continuous training where appropriate (Consejo Económico y Social, 2016).

There is a need to strengthen digital skills, both generic and specific, specialized and complementary. Furthermore, a strategy needs to be designed aimed at eliminating or reducing the inequalities or imbalances that may exist between the demand and supply of professionals prepared for the new technologies (CCOO, 2019). For this reason, trade unions must cooperate and collaborate with companies and educational institutions in order to plan future study programmes that will satisfy the potential concerns of the industry.

Here in Spain, the majority unions have proposed strategies to try to avoid a degradation in the quality of employment, caused precisely by digitalization. They highlight especially the importance of improving professional qualifications, based on the establishment of training characterized by interdisciplinarity and variety. In other words, more complex and more heterogeneous training being at the same time transversal and allowing for the re-qualification and retraining of workers.

The public sector also has a crucial responsibility to modernize public education and to build the necessary skills, as well as to help create a quality business environment. The gender perspective should be a central element of all digital initiatives, in order to promote the full integration of women in the digital economy, with a view to reducing the gender pay gap and promoting work-life balance.

5.5 Collective bargaining and social dialogue in the digital transformation

Social dialogue, as an "open process of permanent negotiation, which is made possible through formulas for monitoring the results obtained, and which generates a set of social practices of exchange that are incorporated into a cultural heritage of both companies and workers' representatives", provides "the institutional capacities needed to navigate the future of labour transitions" Baylos (2017, p. 6).

Digitalization of the economy is a social process that, undoubtedly, is still under construction, although it has accelerated recently. This process, which is extremely complex, must be governed and led by the stakeholders, i.e. by all those who make up the social dialogue, both public administrations of all areas and sizes, and the social partners, employers and trade unions, so that the risks of social exclusion and fragmentation can be avoided and mitigated as much as possible.

The role of social dialogue is not to oppose these transitions, but rather to steer them in the best possible direction in order to reap the full benefits: to achieve growth, the promotion of innovation and skills, quality jobs, and sustainable and solidarity-based financing of social protection.

Similarly, the report on trade unions faced with technological challenges (Fundación Cotec & Eticas Foundation, 2018, p. 10) states that their role must be strengthened,

> their strategies for future bargaining and collective agreements, as well as their role in defining the technological agenda, must be rethought... The impact of this phenomenon on the forms of collective organization is profound, and undermines the foundations of modern trade unionism, which makes it essential to rethink both practices and strategies.

This digital transformation, or new revolution, has affected, and is affecting, the world of work in a structural way. It not only affects employment, both in a quantitative and qualitative sense, but also implies a modification in structuring the labour relationship, not in a singular way, but to a collective or general extent. Hence, trade union activity itself, whether in the field of social dialogue, or in the closer context of collective bargaining, is trying to adapt to this new reality.

Digitalization implies a new means of understanding the forms of working and of organizing work and therefore necessarily affects the complex world of labour relations. As a consequence, the basic institutions on which current labour law is based will be affected, from the very concept of the employment contract, which will also be impacted by the appearance of new contract formulas, to the business faculties or powers of direction and control, including salaries and access to social benefits. They will be influenced especially in relation to the collective level: in other words, the instruments of representation and collective bargaining (Álvarez Cuesta, 2019).

The problems of the current collective bargaining framework in maintaining forms of group protection, mainly caused by outsourcing and mass outsourcing, are evident. In particular, organizational fragmentation, vague company and sector boundaries, as well as individualization, are the main problems faced by the current collective bargaining framework and its actors.

Technological transformation leads to distancing from the collective, described by Mercader Uguina as a "type of disintegration that translates into a clear disintegration of unions" (Mercader Uguina, 2017, p. 174). In short, we are faced with the question of whether, as a result of digitalization, the current framework of collective bargaining is adequate and sufficient to carry out effective collective protection of workers' interests.

Therefore, the first thing that should be stressed is that collective bargaining, and social dialogue in general, has not played a leading role in establishing or testing solutions to the risks of digitalization, and the potential for abuse that it presents to companies and business organizations.

Regarding this point, although responsibility must be shared among all the social agents, we should focus on trade union activity, which has probably not been sufficiently zealous and vigilant in the face of what appeared to be a less immediate future.

Digitalization necessarily gives rise to a new way of conceptualizing the labour relationship, and labour relations in the plural, since it will bring about new mechanisms and processes; in short, new figures. References are made to a true deconstruction of the labour relationship; in other words, changing the physiognomy of the labour relations existing today, although maintaining to a certain extent the current schemes.

These practices contribute to informalization or casualization, and polarization of the labour market (Drahokoupil & Jepsen, 2017). The latter will occur between those workers who enjoy a certain degree of stability and protection, and others who develop activities as independent workers, either on platforms or outside them. With regard to the growing casualization of work, this implies increased risk and uncertainty for the worker, distancing him or her from sufficient wages and possible projection and stability. As a consequence of the two previous effects, the labour relationship has become increasingly individualized, to the extent that the expansion of digitalization entails the fragmentation and division of the work process, and its mass outsourcing to groups of self-employed workers, freelancers, etc. (Molina & Pastor, 2018).

Digitalization can accelerate and accentuate individualization in employment relations, while eroding the capacity of current collective bargaining frameworks and trade unions to provide protection to workers. Moreover, it necessitates a rethink of the basic categories of labour law, which are built around the idea of the dependent "employee".

In the first of these aspects, the increase in outsourcing and subcontracting of activities to self employed or independent workers is indisputable. The shift to "on demand" – in other words, casualized – workplaces puts undue pressure on workers who face a serious lack of certainty about their future income and employment that greatly benefits employers.

This effect can be further reinforced when subcontracting is combined with offshoring. Undoubtedly, the increase in working from home, or at least outside the workplace, is not favourable for the development of day-to-day trade union work.

The second major change associated with subcontracting is the reorganization of work content. This can be associated with the breakdown of work into different tasks, which are then performed by different workers, sometimes in different parts of the world.

Digitalization, understood in a broad sense, determines the existence of a different relationship between trade unions and workers, changing not only the form of this relationship but also its very nature. Digitalization physically distances unions from workers, whether they are members or not, and this means that the union itself, its power, ends up being weakened. In addition to the concept of teleworking, which is already well established among us, a corresponding term should be coined: tele-unionism.

Individualization, fragmentation and the absence of employment and/or contractual relations imply a reduction in the capacity of trade unions to represent and protect workers. In fact, not only is it difficult to determine bargaining units, but working for different platforms would, in principle, make it difficult for workers to be covered by a collective agreement (Todolí Signes, 2015).

Individualism, disaffection and desertion from protecting collective rights: we observe a strongly "volatile" workforce, with distinct interests, difficult to reconcile with unitary and shared objectives. It is an indisputable fact that the relocation of a worker that involves virtual work, or work outside the workplace, causes him or her to become detached, and at the same time isolated, from other colleagues; and in addition, where appropriate, from the company's trade union representation.

> How can we organize workers in the company when the company itself is diluted, as a result of the processes of fragmentation that they carry out? How can we organize nomadic workers who change workplaces? How can we organize workers on digital platforms who have no workplace or company?
>
> (Gutiérrez & Pueyo, 2017, p. 231)

These forms of work (casual work, crowdworking, collaborative work, etc.) are deficient from the point of view of collective representation and negotiation (Eurofound, 2015).

As there are only particular interests, it is logical that membership of trade union organizations in Spain should be even lower, as well as the interest in holding positions in employee representation. In this situation, it is difficult to convince workers that collective bargaining is a suitable method for solving their specific problems, let alone the possibility of collective action to exert pressure for maintaining or exercising certain rights.

For these reasons, major problems are encountered in adopting/introducing regulations, unified to some degree, for workers who lack precisely the qualities or characteristics of employees. The diversity and fragmentation of this group makes it difficult to provide regulation that is unspecific, but at least adequate to their needs. The diversity we are talking about translates not only into the plurality of activities or jobs they carry out but also into the objectives or purposes pursued. Thus, there are workers who combine self-employment with another salaried job they already have, to supplement their income or simply to hedge against growing unemployment in Spain (Molina & Pastor, 2018).

Representation of collective interests is also under threat, as structures of worker representation and social dialogue are largely absent in the world of on-demand work and collective labour. However, some proposals and experiments are creating new internal structures within the trade unions, aimed at attracting economically dependent self-employed workers, as they are called in Spain, and providing this formula of collective assistance, i.e. treating them collectively as a class of workers with the same rights as employed workers (Degryse, 2016).

An example of this is platform work which not only leads to a reduction in bargaining power but practically excludes this possibility. All these cases when the worker is alone – in other words, when the worker is unprotected, isolated from collective support – generate an imbalance between the powers of the worker and the employer. Today, we can see how, despite a very unfavourable environment, in some cases, these workers and trade unions have organized themselves to encourage collective action.

Although the courts have finally recognized many platform workers as salaried employees, the specific nature of this work requires that existing labour legislation be updated. The specificity of platform work requires new special labour regulations.

In Spain, the government has chosen to regulate teleworking through legislation, specifically through the Law 10/2021 of 9 July on remote work, that seeks to mitigate abuse or inconveniences that may arise from deregulation. In particular, the aim is to prevent companies from passing on production costs to workers without offering any kind of compensation.

The aim is to ensure that teleworking does not lead to a decrease in wage benefits, or a loss or weakening of labour rights. This is based on the basic premise that teleworking should be an option that is accepted by workers voluntarily, and under no circumstances can it be imposed by the company. It would therefore be a working modality which would depend on the worker's own wishes, and which would be reversible; in other words, the possibility would always remain open for the worker to revoke his or her consent and return to a face-to-face activity.

Among the most important issues arising from teleworking are those relating to the exercise of collective rights. This brings us precisely to the role of trade unions in the future framework of labour relations. In addition, we will address the question of equal treatment, not only with regard to gender and wage or salary gaps but also very especially with regard to promotion and professional training.

Digitalization linked to the performance of work outside the company raises enormous doubts regarding employer control of workers' private lives, either in a direct and invasive way, or in an indirect way, depriving the worker of privacy even during hours outside the workplace.

5.7 Digitalization and quality of employment. New forms of employment linkage

The incorporation of new technologies into the world of work, or the digitalization of employment, requires a dynamic and flexible labour law, capable of being adapted to successive innovations of this type. This labour law should permit and guarantee, as established in art. 38 of the Spanish Constitution (1978), the company's planning and defence of productivity.

At the same time, the law carries out its traditional function of protecting the worker. In this sense, our rules must allow the integration of new technologies into the company with the aim of increasing and optimizing its productivity. However, the implementation of new technologies brings with it the responsibility of the employer towards his staff. This is what has become known as a "technologically responsible company" (Mercader Uguina, 2017). Thus, our Spanish legislature recognizes the right of the worker "to promotion and vocational training at work, including training aimed at adapting to changes in the workplace, as well as the development of training plans intended to promote increased employability" [art. 4.2(b), Worker's Statute Law]. Furthermore, Article 23.1(d) of the Worker's Statute Law provides for the specific right of workers to training necessary for their adaptation to changes in the workplace. On the one hand, it stresses that training is the company's responsibility, "without prejudice to the possibility of obtaining financing intended for the training purposes"; and, on the other hand, that "the time allocated to training shall in all cases be considered effective working time". In short, in today's global world, workers need the competence of learning to learn or lifelong learning, understood as the continuous development of knowledge and skills that people are offered, subsequent to formal education, throughout their lives.

The legislature is making giant strides in the case of Spain, with such statutes as the recent Law 10/2021 of July 9 on remote work which has established the latest legal regulations for distance working in Spain. In addition, Organic law 3/2018 on the protection of personal data and the guarantee of digital rights responds to the processing of personal data and, more importantly, to the use of certain electronic or computer-based devices in the workplace, and contains a relatively detailed regulation directly applicable to the employment contract, deployed under the general heading of "guarantee of digital rights" (Articles 87 to 91, Organic Law 3/2018).

Digitalization and working time: The impact of new technologies is evident in a model of labour relations in which it is increasingly difficult to determine when the working day begins, and when it ends. The world of work, in this new era of digitalization, is immersed in the search for flexibility policies concerning the working day, called "flexiworking". This is a new way of working in which each employee can manage his or her schedule and work according to his or her needs. The aim is to find a simpler, more efficient, and more flexible way of working. The situation described would undoubtedly allow the worker to make work compatible with other types of personal or family occupations or aspirations. But, at the same time, new technologies can generate new ties and servitudes in the performance of wage-earning work. We should consider, above all, the worker's connection through digital means with the company's management and decision-making bodies. There is only one step from flexibility of working time according to production to the permanent availability of the worker, as the main tool of distance work. Technology eliminates the coordinates of time and place and blurs the boundaries between work and rest, to the point of perpetual connection.

However, the use of electronic media in the workplace is undoubtedly linked to greater availability of the worker for company business. Within this framework, we run the risk of identifying ourselves with the permanently connected professional who consequently constantly works. The presence of new technologies in the field of labour, expanding the possibilities of permanent and uncontrolled connectivity, also leads to legal uncertainty about which regulations are applicable to these new situations. Therefore, to maintain an unchanged number of hours worked, the existence of effective regulations is necessary, establishing the right to digital disconnection (in Spain, the Organic Law 3/2018 of 5 December on the protection of personal data and the guarantee of digital rights and the Law 10/2021 of 9 July on remote work introduce for the first time the right to digital disconnection in the sphere of employment).

The new digital platforms: The issue that has undoubtedly received the most attention is the situation of workers who provide their professional services through digital platforms. The platforms do not consider themselves as employers, nor do they consider the professionals who provide their services as employees. This situation does not fit in with either self-employment or paid employment. Therefore, authoritative voices have proposed the creation of a new intermediate figure called the "independent worker".

This type of worker would have the majority of the employed worker's recognized labour rights, since the organization of work through digital platforms is considered, in most cases, a de facto relationship of subordination and labour dependence. The various legal rulings lacking a unitary solution do not help to clarify the issue.[2]

But, apart from the legal recognition that employment relationships generated on digital platforms deserve, the working conditions of the professionals who provide their services through these platforms are undoubtedly characterized by (1) low remuneration which depends on the number of services provided; (2) confusion about access to social security benefits; (3) risks to occupational health and safety, identified, for example, with permanent availability; and (4) the unilateral establishment of working conditions by the platform, which may even make remuneration, or stability of the service itself, dependent on surveys, in which the work carried out by the professional is rated; these are prepared by the platform itself. For all these reasons, measures need to be introduced that promote decent work, in all the aspects mentioned (salary, social security, working conditions, occupational health), for professionals who work in this field.

Teleworking, A new path in labour relations in Spain: The pandemic that we have suffered has decisively promoted a specific form of work: teleworking. Telework is one of the facets of companies' digitalization (the most visible one at present), and even though all physical work cannot be converted to teleworking via telematics, certain characteristics, modes and ways of working online are going to be transferred to the majority of services provided, merging (which was already happening previously) physical and remote work. Telework is currently not covered by any international statistical standards. Countries have used slightly different operational definitions, which are typically based on two different components (Eurofound & ILO, 2017, p. 5):

I The work is fully or partly carried out at an alternative location other than the default place of work. This criterion is based on the previous definition of remote work.
II The use of personal electronic devices such as a computer, tablet or telephone (mobile or landline) to perform the work: The use of personal electronic devices needs to be an essential part of carrying out specific job-related tasks without being directly in contact with other persons.

This phenomenon historically carried little weight in the organization and work culture of most companies in Spain but has achieved a sudden and intense growth due to the need to maintain economic activity and guarantee social distance during the pandemic.

As of 9 July 2021, the Law 10/2021 on remote work has introduced new regulations on telework in Spain, applicable to any work performed in the worker's home, for at least 30% of the working day during a reference period of three months, or an equivalent percentage depending on the duration of the employment contract (Article 13 of the Workers' Statute).

The Spanish law addresses many essential questions. (1) The statute introduces payment and compensation by the company of expenses generated by this type of work as a specific right of workers, as well as the company's obligation to provide its employees with all the means, equipment and tools necessary for performing their work. This is a matter for collective bargaining. (2) The requirement for a printed form of the distance working contract, and its minimum contents (Article 6 of the Law 10/2021 of 9 July on remote work). (3) The possibility of unilateral withdrawal of the worker from remote working model, in accordance with the voluntary nature of remote work (Article 5 of the Law 10/2021 of 9 July on remote work). (4) The refusal of the worker to work remotely may not be a cause for the termination of the employment relationship, nor for the modification of his working conditions. (5) The new regulations on remote work bring the rights of the workers affected into line with those of workers in an ordinary employment relationship. (6) The right to digital disconnection regulated in Article 18 of the Law 10/2021 of 9 July on remote work, and the business duty to guarantee such disconnection. This right is also associated with the right of workers to have the company keep an appropriate record of their working hours.

The right to disconnect: In Spain, the right to digital disconnection arises from the Organic Law 3/2018 of 5 December on the protection of personal data and the guarantee of digital rights, which introduced for the first time the right to digital disconnection in the sphere of employment. More recently, Article 18 of the Law 10/2021 of 9 July on remote work emphasizes special relevance of the right in the case of distance workers. Specifically, the first paragraph of Article 88 of the Organic Law 3/2018 indicates that workers have the right to digital disconnection in order to guarantee, outside the legally or conventionally established working time, respect for their rest time, leave and holidays, as well as their personal and family privacy (this is also confirmed by Article 18 of the Law 10/2021 of 9 July on remote work). The legislature intends to control misuse of electronic media outside working hours, and provides, in the second point of the aforementioned Article 88 of the Organic Law 3/2018, that the modalities of exercising this right will take into account the nature and purpose of the labour relationship, promoting the right to work-life balance, referring to collective bargaining or, where appropriate, to the individual contract, the power to regulate the scope and conditions of exercising this right to disconnection. The third point of the article, and this is relevant, includes the obligation of the company to develop an internal policy (after consulting employee representatives, if they exist in the company in question, including those who hold management positions) which regulates the modalities of exercising the right to disconnection and training in the use of technological means, preventing the risk of "computer fatigue", with a special reference to those cases in which work is carried out remotely.

This business obligation is strict, and its breach will be sanctioned. Any company that provides a mobile device, or that simply demands in one way or another availability by email or telephone from its employees, will have to carry out this control policy. The employer's duty is to

> ... ensure that the disconnection is limited to the use of technological means of business communication and work during rest periods, as well as to respect the maximum duration of the working day and any limits and precautions regarding the working day that are provided for in the applicable legal or conventional regulations.
>
> (Article 18 of the Law 10/2021 of 9 July on remote work)

In any case, there must be a working schedule established by the parties, so that, outside this schedule, the worker has the right to interrupt communication with the company and co-workers, regardless of the form of remote working that has been agreed. Thus, the right of the remote worker to disconnect implies a duty of the employer to limit his or her ability to send communications to workers during rest periods. However, this right is not absolute and there is room for extraordinary "re-connection". Thus, the 1st Additional Provision of the Law 10/2021 of 9 July on remote work states in its 2nd section that "Collective agreements or arrangements may regulate (...) possible extraordinary circumstances modifying the right to disconnection".

Notes

1 "This work is the result of a Project carried with the title "The impact of digitalization of the economy on the skills and professional qualifications and labour relations" (Call for Proposals: Improving expertise in the field of industrial relations (VP/2018/004), Sub-programme II, within the budget heading 04.03.01.08). The Project has been financed by the European Commission DG Employment, Social, Affairs & Inclusion.

2 According to the European Commission, a digital platform is the provider of the underlying service, that is, with active and direct intervention in the organization and provision of the service, and not a simple technology company, when it is the one that: (1) determines the final price what the customer must pay; (2) sets the conditions and terms that determine the contractual relationship between the provider and the client; and (3) possesses the key assets or resources for the provision of the service. This has been expressly confirmed by the CJUE in relation to the Uber platform in its judgments of December 20, 2017 (Court of Justice of the European Union, 2017, p. 217) (Elite Taxi case against Uber) and April 10, 2018 (Court of Justice of the European Union, 2018, p. 70) (Uber case against Nabil Bensalem), characterizing it as a transport company and not as a simple intermediary, since the company exerts a decisive influence on the conditions of the services provided by its drivers. However, the fact that the platform is considered the company providing the underlying service does not automatically convert those who personally carry out the activity into employed workers.

References

Álvarez Cuesta, H. (2019). El diálogo social y la negociación colectiva como herramienta para lograr una transición digital justa. *Revista de Relaciones Laborales* (42), 13–49. https://doi.org/10.1387/lan-harremanak.21204.

Baldwin, R. (2016). *The Great Convergence. Information Technology and the New Globalization.* Cambridge: Harvard University Press.

Baylos, A. (2017). El futuro del trabajo que queremos. In *Conferencia Nacional Tripartita, 28 de marzo de 2017* (vol. 2, pp. 487–502). Palacio de Zurbano, Madrid: Iniciativa del Centenario de la OIT (1919–2019), Ministerio de Trabajo y Seguridad Social. ISBN: 978-84-8417-522-3.

Business Services Orange (2014). *Les nouveaux modes de travail a l´ere du digital: enjeux et opportunités, exemples et enseigne-ments*, April, 2014. Retrieved 1 June 2022, from: https://www.orange-business.com/fr/blogs/usages-dentreprise/mobilite/etude-les-nouveaux-modes-de-travail-l-ere-du-digital.

CCOO (2017). *La digitalización y la industria 4.0. Impacto industrial y laboral.* Secretaría de Estrategias Industriales. Retrieved 1 June 2022, from: https://industria.ccoo.es/4290fc51a3697f785ba14fce86528e10000060.pdf.

CCOO (2019). *Reforzar la participación sindical para una transición justa a la digitalización.* Secretaría de Juventud y Nuevas Realidades del Trabajo. Retrieved 1 June 2022, from: https://www.ccoo.es/d5e6c5a69d6f8c6c15911196fd633915000001.pdf.

Cedrola Spremolla, G. (2017). El trabajo en la era digital: Reflexiones sobre el impacto de la digitalización en el trabajo, la regulación laboral y las relaciones laborales. *Revista Internacional y Comparada de Relaciones Laborales y Derecho del Empleo*, 5(1), 8–37.

Court of Justice of the European Union, Judgment C-434/15, Asociacion Profesional Elite Taxi v Uber Systems Spain SL, 20 December 2017.

Court of Justice of the European Union, Judgment C-320/16, Nabil Bensalem v. Uber France SAS, 10 April 2018.

Communication from the Commission to the European Parliament, the Council, the European Economic and Social Committee and the Committee of the Regions a European Agenda for the Collaborative Economy, COM (2016) 356, 2 of Juneof 2016. Available at: https://eur-lex.europa.eu/legal-content/EN/TXT/PDF/?uri=CELEX:52016DC0356.

Consejo Económico y Social (2016). Resolución del CES sobre la digitalización: "hacia un trabajo digital justo". Adoptada en el Comité Ejecutivo el 8-9 de junio 2016. Retrieved 1 June 2022, from: https://www.ccoo.es/21d4392f1c3a0985ca39f00 50cd3a773000001.pdf

Constitución Española, approved by national referendum on December 6, 1978, Boletín Oficial del Estado, 29 December 1978, núm. 311.

Council of the European Union (2015). Brussels, 6 May. (8672/15). COM (2015) 192 final. Communication from the Commission to the European Parliament, the Council, the European Economic and Social Committee and the Committee of the Regios. "A Digital Single Market Strategy for Europe". Retrieved 1 June 2022, from: https://data.consilium.europa.eu/doc/document/ST-8672-2015-INIT/en/pdf.

Degryse, C. (2016). Digitalisation of the Economy and Its Impact on Labour Markets (February 10, 2016). ETUI Research Paper – Working Paper 2016.02. http://doi.org/10.2139/ssrn.2730550.

Del Val Román, J.L. (2016). Industria 4.0: La transformación digital de la industria. In *Conferencia de Decanos y Directores de Ingeniería Informática*. Retrieved 1 June 2022, from: http://coddii.org/wp-content/uploads/2016/11/Informe-CODDII-Industria-4.pdf.

Drahokoupil, J. & Jepsen, M. (2017). The digital economy and its implications for labour. *Transfer: European Review of Labour and Research*, 23(2), 103–107. https://doi.org/10.1177/1024258917701380.

Estatuto de los trabajadores, ET, (Workers Statute Law), Royal Legislative Decree 2/2015, of October 23, which approves the consolidated text of the Workers' Statute Law. Official State Bulletin (BOE) núm. 255, 24 October 2015.

Eurofound (2015). New Forms of Employment. Publications Office of the European Union. Retrieved 1 June 2022, from: https://www.ioe-emp.org/fileadmin/ioe_documents/publications/Policy%20Areas/future_of_Work/EN/_2015-12-04__New_Forms_of_Employment_Eurofound.pdf.

Eurofound & ILO (2017). Working Anytime, Anywhere: The Effects on the World of Work. Publications Office of the European Union the International Labour Office. Retrieved 1 June 2022, from: https://www.eurofound.europa.eu/sites/default/files/ef_publication/field_ef_document/ef1658en.pdf.

European Commission (2020). The Digital Economy and Society Index (DESI). Available at: https://digital-strategy.ec.europa.eu/en/library/digital-economy-and-society-index-desi-2020.

European Economic and Social Committee (2018). 40TH EESC PLENARY SESSION, 23.1.2019-24.1.2019, Opinion of the Opinion of the European Economic and Social Committee on 'Social dialogue for innovation in digital economy' (own-initiative opinion) (2019/C 159/01) Rapporteur: Jukka AHTELA.

European Economic and Social Committee (2014). Opinion of the European Economic and Social Committee on 'The digital society: access, education, training, employment, tools for equality' (own-initiative opinion), (2014/C 451/04), Rapporteur: Isabel Caño Aguilar.

Fundación Cotec & Eticas Foundation (2018). Los sindicatos antes los retos tecnológicos. Dinámicas y buenas prácticas. Available at: https://cotec.es/proyecto/los-sindicatos-ante-los-retos-tecnologicos/4bb8fa92-cc19-4c2d-98ae-f940148d5662.

Gutiérrez, C. & Pueyo, J. (2017). Todo lo sólido se desvanece en el aire. Precariedad y nuevas realidades del trabajo: una perspectiva sindical. *Gaceta sindical: reflexión y debate*, 29, 225–234.

Law 10/2021, of July 9, on remote work, Official State Bulletin (BOE), núm. 164, 10 July of 2021.

Levy, F. & Murnane, R.J. (2004). *The New Division of Labor. How Computers Are Creating the Next Job Market*. Princeton University Press. ISBN: 0691124027.

Mercader Uguina, J.R. (2017). *El futuro del trabajo en la era de la digitalización y la robótica*. Tirant lo Blanch. ISBN: 9788491437574.

Molina, Ó. & Pastor, A. (2018). La Digitalización, Relaciones Laborales y Derecho del Trabajo. In F. Miguélez (ed.), *La revolución digital en España. Impacto y Retos sobre el Mercado de Trabajo y el Bienestar* (pp. 311–342). Universitar Autónoma de Barcelona. Avaliable at: https://ddd.uab.cat/record/190328.

OECD (2016). *Automation and Independent Work in a Digital Economy*. OECD Publications. Retrieved 1 June 2022, from: https://www.oecd.org/els/emp/Policy%20brief%20-%20Automation%20and%20Independent%20Work%20in%20a%20Digital%20Economy.pdf.

Organic Law 3/2018, of December 5, Protection of personal data and guarantee of digital rights, Official State Bulletin (BOE) núm. 294, de 6 of December, 2018.

Signes, A.T. (2015). El impacto de la "Uber Economy" en las relaciones laborales: los efectos de las plataformas virtuales en el contrato de trabajo. *IUSLabor*, IUSLabor 3/2015, 1-25. Available at SSRN: https://ssrn.com/abstract=2705538.

Soete, L. & ter Well, B. (2005). *The Economy of the Digital Society*. Edward Elgar Publishing. ISBN: 978-1-84376-774-9.

6 Digitalization and digital skills development patterns. Evidence for European countries

Helena Anacka and Ewa Lechman

6.1 Introduction

Societies and economies are not digitally neutral. Technological progress is a disruptive process that alters social and economic structures, stimulating the emergence of a new *status quo*. Technology and technological change do not just bring change or inventions to the economy and society; they enrich and shape socio-economic systems, raising their responsiveness and adaptability to further technological development. This demonstrates the interrelatedness of society, economy and technology, driving home the point that none of these elements exists in isolation.

Digital technologies are claimed General Purpose Technologies; hence, they generate path-breaking innovations and are recognized as fundamental factors in long-run technological progress and deep-going structural and qualitative shifts in economies and societies (Sahal, 1981; Bresnahan, 2010; Coccia, 2017). As argued by Rosenberg and Trajtenberg (2004), digital technologies are 'epochal innovations' as they demonstrate the capacity to radically reshape the contours of the world economies, ways of doing business, and enforce the emergence of new industries, services *et alia*.

Digital technologies (ICT) are widely acknowledged as the critical drivers for knowledge and information acquiring, labour and capital productivity, social, political and economic empowerment (Graham, 2019). Digital technologies, due to strong network effects (Katz & Shapiro, 1985) that they generate, enable the emergence of various networks reshaping the way businesses are run, as well as trading and consumption patterns, economic and social behaviours, social norms and attitudes (Graham & Dutton, 2019). The network economy emerges in the economy that is driven by digital technologies. Henceforth, tracing and understanding of relationships existing between society wide adoption and usage of digital technologies and economic development deserve special attention. Not only because this deepens our knowledge on how economies work but also from a perspective of state policy that shapes the institutional and economic environment and is of seminal importance in this case (Gilbert, 2020).

Moreover, digital technologies (information and communication technologies, ICT) greatly affect socio-economic transformation (van Deursen

DOI: 10.4324/9781003450160-9

et al., 2021; Zhou et al., 2021) which is traceable in the context of, inter alia, growing demand for digital skills, which in turn affect labour market (Elia et al., 2020; Aissaoui, 2021; Falck et al., 2021). From the 1980s onwards, the proportion of high-skill jobs in the market is increasing in the majority of industrialized economies, giving evidence for a long-term shift in employment, while routine-based jobs tend to diminish due to automation and technological replacement in a long run (Autor et al., 2020). According to Acemoglu and Restrepo (2022), skill premia are related to the skills gap in a way that the skill premium is reduced if the skills supply rises while the technologies set is constant. However, in a long run, a higher supply of skills accelerates technological shifts and raises a demand for skills, which increases skill premia and their relative demand with time (Nogueira & Afonso, 2018). Finally, highly digitalized businesses tend to grow faster than the others, while both offshoring and digitalization are the main drivers of asymmetric employment dynamics and job polarization, observed in Europe over the last decade (Biagi & Falk, 2017). Principally, internet skills and IT infrastructure are complementary and mutually they allow for more efficient ICT use (van Deursen et al., 2021). Due to the 'IT value paradox', ICT must be extensively used in value chains before becoming capable of generating any significant benefits (Hsu, 2013). Moreover, countries and businesses with higher digital intensity perform better in learning and ICT employment, which in turn leads to higher returns on digital investment (Biagi & Falk, 2017). On the other hand, cross-country results demonstrate a differentiated impact of Technology–Organization–Environment factors, explaining uneven innovation diffusion in the EU countries, which is associated with country-specific conditions (Zhou et al., 2021).

This research focuses on digitalization and digital skills development, and this picture is supported by some empirical evidence regarding European economies. For the clarity of the research, we have identified three detailed research goals:

1. Identification of digitalization trajectories in European countries;
2. Identification of digital skills development patterns in European countries;
3. Examination of digitalization and digital skills inequalities across countries in Europe.

Our empirical sample comprises 28 European economies, and the time span of the analysis is set for the period between 1980 and 2022. All statistical data on digitalization and digital skills are to be extracted from ITU and Eurostat.

6.2 Background

Over the last decades, since the 1970s onward, we witness worldwide, unprecedented in terms of speed and geographic coverage, dynamic diffusion of new information and communication technologies (ICT). Information and communications technologies are pervasive, disruptive and cutting-edge technologies leading to profound shifts and transformations in societies and economies. ICT enable a rapid spread of information and knowledge and facilitate interpersonal communication among geographically isolated agents. Due to its disruptiveness and pervasiveness, ICT produce cross-cutting effects in all sectors of the economy and bring long-term productivity gains. ICT as General Purpose Technologies (Bresnahan & Trajtenberg, 1995) are 'prime-movers' of the economy; they produce positive network externalities and open up new opportunities. In Helpman and Trajtenberg (1996), we read 'GPTs[1] appear [...] there is a spell of growth, with rising output, real wages, and profits' (Ibid., p. 4). The process of dynamic diffusion of ICT is not limited to the high-income and well-developed economies, but it is also reported even in the most economically backward countries. ICT are now being fast distributed across low-income economies, which never before have widely adopted 'old' technological solutions, and this predominantly was a consequence of infrastructural and geographical barriers, lack of financial resources or lack of knowledge of the use of these technologies. The latter caused deep technological and institutional deficiencies constituting a great hindrance to entering a pattern of stable economic growth and development. The in-depth analysis of the diffusion process of ICT reveals a number of their unique features. These characteristics significantly distinguish the process of ICT diffusion from the diffusion of 'old' technologies and make it of special importance when considering its impact on long-term social and economic growth and development. First, broad access to and use of ICT stimulates the development of social networks, generating several economic advantages, like, for instance, economies of scale (Economides, 1996), and providing solid foundations for economic growth. Second, wireless networks, offered under ICT, enable direct connections among society members, facilitating information and knowledge flows, regardless of the physical location of the agents, diminishing their economic and technological marginalization. Cairncross (2001) announces the emergence of the 'death of distance', demonstrating how due to the use of ICT the geographic distance is no longer a barrier for various types of economic activities. Broad adoption of ICT enables fast flows of knowledge and information, which become easily acquirable to all society members who previously suffered constant technological marginalization and information poverty.

Importantly, one of the prime positive effects generated by strong network effects fostering fast ICT diffusion should be that initially 'technologically peripheral' economies are enabled to technologically catch up with developed countries, so that the existing gaps eventually diminish. This technological catching up is also labelled 'technology convergence' that inevitably leads to the 'digital (technology) gaps' narrowing and to the gradual eradication of different forms of exclusion from access to and use of ICT. Technically speaking, convergence occurs if average annual growth rates are inversely correlated with the initial *per capita* income. A straightforward implication of undisturbed convergence is that – in a long-term perspective – cross-country disparities should inevitably be eradicated. If this is not the case, countries instead experience divergence and the gap between 'rich' and 'poor' enlarges.

The rapid spread of digital technologies is closely associated with the emergence and growing importance of digital skills. In an extensive literature on digital skills, this concept is referred to using different terms, for example: *ICT skills*, *digital skills*, *internet skills*, *digital literacy*, *e-skills*, *digital competencies*, *computer skills*, *computer use*, *internet literacy* and *media literacy*(van Laar et al., 2020). According to the literature, internet skills are highly determined by education, by gender, by age, by a household or family; also by human capital, by income, by residency, by mother's and father's education, by frequency of use, by internet access and years of internet experience; while traditional literacy, formal skills, digital support, social networks, internet access quality and employment status also influence internet skills, but to a lesser extent according to the literature (van Laar et al., 2020).

It is important to distinguish between basic media literacy – or technical ability to perform basic ICT tasks – and more advanced and creative ICT skills components, and to analyse their applications and measurement. Digital literacy can be defined as an ability to write, read and understand content online while performing basic ITC manipulations, or as elementary practical and cognitive skills enabling understanding and usage of digital information via ICT means (Chan et al., 2017; Spante et al., 2018). Additionally, the *Critical Digital Literacies* concept, proposed by Ávila and Pandya (2013), focuses on an ability to critically assess, process and produce digital content, i.e. to evaluate and develop digital content.

On the other hand, internet skills often involve a broader range of elements, according to the literature. For example, Van Deursen et al. (2016) identified internet skills through a conglomerate of *social, creative, technical and critical skills* that include 'operational skills' or basic technical skills, 'social skills' or social media skills for online social interactions, 'information navigation skills' or operative skills to handle online content, and 'creative skills' or content creation skills essential for online content production and distribution (Helsper & Eynon, 2013; Van Deursen et al., 2016). Additionally, depending on the advancement level and type of skills application, internet skills can be defined as *Content-related internet skills*, including Strategic internet skills and Information internet skills, and *Medium-related internet skills* including Formal internet skills and Operational internet skills (Deursen & van Dijk, 2010).

Digital competencies can be described as a set of Information skills, Content-creation skills, Problem-solving skills, Communication skills and Digital safety skills. Linares and Romero (2016) define digital competency as a key skill enabling development of other essential skills, such as numerical, linguistic, ability to learn, as well as multicultural consciousness. The authors understand digital competency as critical, effective and creative computer usage essential to achieve, e.g., job-related objectives (Linares & Romero, 2016).

A large body of literature focuses on the concept of digital divide and its impact on economic development (DiMaggio et al., 2004; van Dijk, 2005; Scheerder et al., 2017; Hidalgo et al., 2020). According to Aissaoui (2021), The digital divide – or a socio-economic gap in access to and usage of ICT on the individual, business, regional and country levels – may be interpreted as ICT performance divide, digital use divide and ICT access divide (Aissaoui, 2021). The digital divide is thus present on different levels, for example:

- First-level digital divide or inequality in access to ICT devices and hardware,
- Second-level digital divide may appear in digital skills and effective usage gaps,
- Third-level digital divide could be measured as discrepancies in ICT-related performance, and offline outcomes (Aissaoui, 2021).

Several studies confirm the digital divide in terms of hardware access and broadband access (Van Deursen & Van Dijk, 2018), while mobile internet access is seen as a way to close this digital gap in regions with underdeveloped ICT fixed-line infrastructure (Srinuan et al., 2012). Further research results confirm that ICT usage and broadband access have a significantly positive effect on economic growth (Lechman, 2017). On the other hand, various empirical results confirm a 'skill-biased technological change' hypothesis, saying that second- and third-level digital divide are present in wage inequalities, in tasks-automation or job-prospects inequalities (Cirillo et al., 2021).

To conclude, while 21st-century digital skills or ICT-related abilities to use ICT to solve problems, to create and effectively communicate, to learn, critically analyse and master the use of technological means may be interpreted from different perspectives (e.g. technological, social, creative, applied, formal or access-driven), they are of critical importance for driving the digital economy, employability and innovation. Productive (within-sectoral) and structural (between-sectoral) employment transformation in Europe shows technology-space linkages and a general shift towards non-routine, high-value-added jobs in the tertiary sector; meaning that ICT skills can become a significant determinant of relative advantages, polarizations and employment transformations that need further thorough and comprehensive investigation.

6.3 Empirical underpinnings

6.3.1 Data

Our research covers 28 European countries, and the time span for the analysis is set for 1980 to 2021. As for ICT, we use three types of indicators approximating a country's general level of digitalization. First, we use mobile cellular telephony (MCS) penetration rates showing the share of a country's population having access to and using mobile cellular telephony infrastructure. Next, we have chosen an indicator approximating infrastructural development as regards digital technologies: active mobile-broadband subscriptions (AMS). The indicator of active mobile-broadband subscriptions refers to the sum of standard mobile-broadband and dedicated mobile-broadband subscriptions to the public internet. The third chosen ICT-related indicator demonstrates the use of networks – internet users (IU) – and shows the 'proportion of individuals who used internet from any location in the last three months'. Importantly, the time series available for these three indicators are different in each case. MCS data is available for the period 1980–2021, while IU aand AMS data – for 1990–2021 and 2007–2021, respectively.

Additionally, we examine three basic digital skills indicators that are provided by Eurostat. Specifically, we use three selected measures corresponding to individuals' levels of digital skills,[2] and these are as follows: individuals with basic or above basic information and data literacy skills; individuals with online information and communication skills; and individuals with basic or above basic overall digital skills. The data on digital skills in its current form is presented for the year 2021.

6.3.2 Methods

To verify the ICT diffusion patterns and to check whether in sample countries gaps are diminishing or rather growing, we rely on several analytical techniques. First, we rely on logistic equation that allows tracing the S-shaped pattern approximating the process of digital technologies diffusion. The S-shaped pattern is generated by the sigmoid asymptotic function, widely used to approximate the growth of given variables that is time-dependent. The S-shaped curve is generated by the logistic function (Kudryashov, 2013), which in its generalized form is expressed as

$$N(Z) = \frac{exp\,Z}{1 + exp\,Z} = \frac{1}{1 + exp^{-Z}} \tag{6.1}$$

under the assumption that the number of new technology adopters – N – is determined by more than one explanatory variables captured in Z, while

$$Z = \alpha + \beta X \tag{6.2}$$

The simplified form of Eq. (6.1) is the logistic function generating S-shaped trajectories including the time variable (t). The latter originates from the exponential growth model (Meyer et al., 1999) formalized as

$$\frac{dY_x(t)}{dt} = \alpha Y_x(t) \tag{6.3}$$

where $Y(t)$ explains the level of x, t denotes time and the parameter α is the growth rate. By introducing e^3 to Eq. (6.3), it can be rewritten as:

$$Y_x(t) = \beta e^{\alpha t} \tag{6.4}$$

To solve the problem of 'infinite growth', the 'resistance' parameter (Cramer, 2003; Kwasnicki, 2013) is added to Eq. (6.4), which introduces the limit of growth. The adjusted version of Eq. (6.4) follows the logistic differential function:

$$\frac{dY(t)}{dt} = \alpha Y(t)\left(1 - \frac{Y(t)}{\kappa}\right) \tag{6.5}$$

where the additional parameter κ shows the 'limit of growth', the upper asymptote limiting the potentially infinite growth of Y. Put differently, parameter κ may be labelled the 'slowing parameter' or the 'negative feedback', which in effect generates the sigmoid trajectory. The logistic differential equation, Eq. (6.5), can be expressed as the logistic growth function:

$$N_x(t) = \frac{\kappa}{1 + e^{-\alpha(t-\beta)}} \tag{6.6}$$

where $N_x(t)$ stands for the value of variable x in time period t. The logistic growth function, by definition, is always taking non-negative values, thus $N_x(t) > 0$.

The terms in Eq. (6.6) represent (Lechman, 2015) as follows:

- κ – upper asymptote determining the limit of growth ($N(t) \rightarrow \kappa$), also labelled 'carrying capacity' or 'saturation';
- α – growth rate determining the speed (rate) of diffusion;
- β – midpoint, which specifies the exact time (T_m) when the logistic pattern reaches 0.5.

In order to examine how cross-countries distribution of ICT and other tested variables are changing, we use the non-parametric density estimator – kernel density estimator. Kernel density curves, generated by non-parametric estimation, are used to draw the probability density function having a general form

$$f(x) = \frac{d}{dx}F(x) \tag{6.7}$$

where F(x) shows continuous distribution of variable X. To estimate kernel density function f(x), its discrete derivative is adopted and then the non-parametric estimator has a general form as follows:

$$f'(x) = \frac{1}{nh}\sum_{i=1}^{n} k\left(\frac{X_i - x}{h}\right) \tag{6.8}$$

where k(u) stands for the kernel function satisfying the condition of $\int_{-\infty}^{\infty} k(u)du = 1$. In our study, we adopt an Epanechnikov kernel:

$$\frac{3}{4}\left(1-u^2\right)\Big/\left(|u|<1\right) \tag{6.9}$$

Finally, to determine cross-country inequalities and divides, we use the Gini coefficient (Dorfman, 1979; Milanovic, 1997) that represents the inequality of, e.g., income distribution or any other variable. For a given population attributed to values y_i, I = 1, ..., n, if $(y_i \leq y_{i+1})$, the general formula of Gini coefficient is as follows:

$$\frac{1}{n}\left(n+1-2\frac{\sum_{i=1}^{n}(n+1-i)y_i}{\sum_{i=1}^{n}y_i}\right) \tag{6.10}$$

The values of Gini coefficient range from 0 to 1, where 0 reflects perfect equality and 1 – perfect inequality.

6.4 Digital technologies and digital skills development trajectories and inequalities

The empirical evidence summarized below was collected to draw a general picture of the development of digital technologies across 28 European economies between 1980 and 2021. The picture telling about the ICT diffusion trajectories complements a brief analysis of digital gaps evolution, and digital skills state of development.

Figure 6.1 shows country-wise ICT diffusion patterns, for three macro-ICT indicators: mobile cellular telephony subscribers, active mobile-broadband subscribers and IU. These selected indicators perfectly show changes in access to and use of digital technologies in Europe, since the very initial years that certain technological solutions have started being absorbed by societies. The visualization of digital technologies diffusion patterns is then enriched by the logistic growth estimates – see Table 6.1 that shows specific features of the ICT diffusion process, including the most significant intrinsic growth rate.[4] Next, Figures 6.2 and 6.3 demonstrate changes regarding digital gap and digital skills development, respectively.

Considering jointly the country-wise graphs summarized in Figure 6.1 and logistic growth estimates in Table 6.1, several interesting conclusions can be drawn. Apparently, from the 1980 and the first introduction of mobile telephony to the general public, the assimilation of this digital means of communication started to spread fast across countries in Europe. A brief analysis of the country-wise diffusion pattern with regard to MCS shows

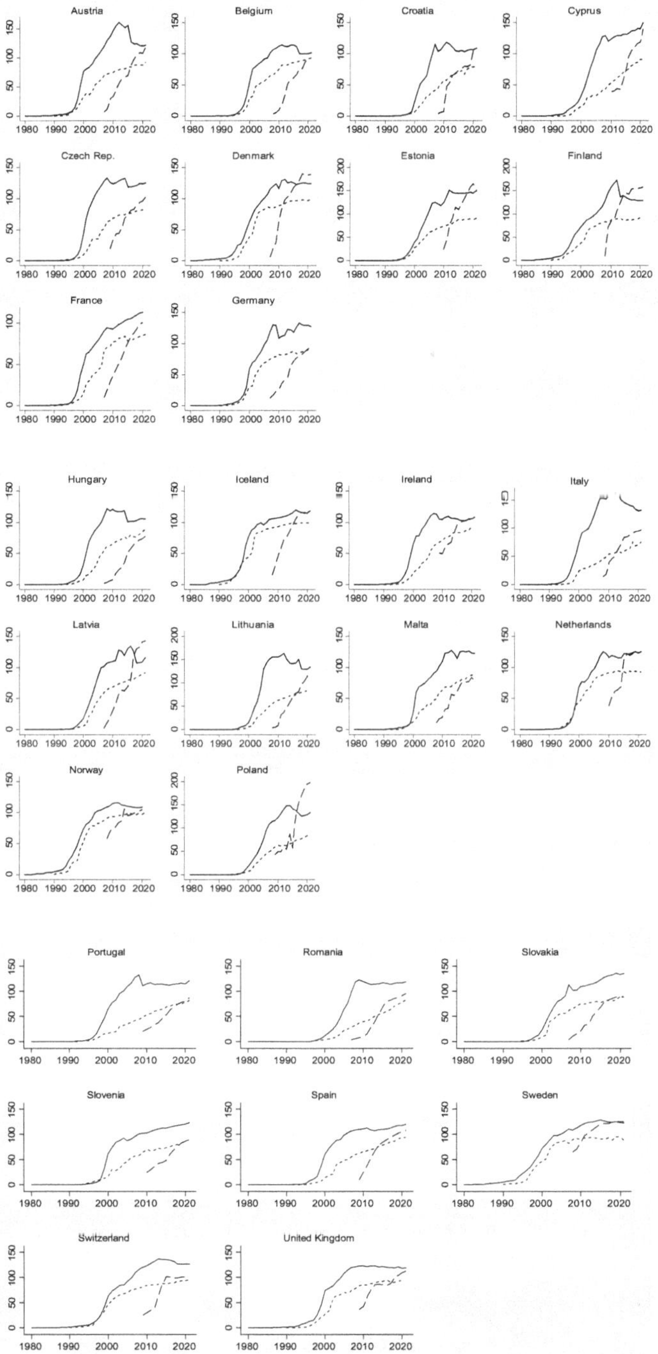

Figure 6.1 ICT diffusion trajectories. Mobile cellular telephony, active mobile subscribers and IU. 1980–2021.

Table 6.1 ICT development pattern estimates. Mobile cellular telephony and IU. European countries. 1980–2021

	Mobile cellular telephony				Internet users			
Country	Upper ceiling (κ)	Intrinsic growth rate (α)	Midpoint (β)	Root MSE	Upper ceiling (κ)	Intrinsic growth rate (α)	Midpoint (β)	Root MSE
Austria	137.5	0.41	2,000.8	10.9	86.4	0.31	2,002.6	3.25
Belgium	105.8	0.57	2,000.3	4.99	87.9	0.31	2,003.2	4.46
Croatia	108.9	0.54	2,002.6	4.54	77.9	0.28	2,006.6	2.91
Cyprus	134.9	0.45	2,002.5	3.98	98.1	0.19	2,008.9	3.63
Czech Republic	124.7	0.71	2,001	3.56	79.9	0.35	2,004.9	2.48
Denmark	125.7	0.35	2,000.3	2.62	94.3	0.48	2,000.7	3.47
Estonia	144.5	0.41	2,002.6	4.65	87.01	0.32	2,002.9	3.54
Finland	140.3	0.31	2,000.3	10.5	89.3	0.38	2,000.4	2.66
France	103.5	0.38	2,001.1	5.01	83.7	0.36	2,004.2	3.08
Germany	124.1	0.43	2,001.3	6.03	85.6	0.44	2,001.8	2.67
Hungary	110.6	0.62	2,001.5	5.29	79.9	0.37	2,005.4	2.81
Iceland	111.4	0.49	1,998.9	4.34	97.5	0.41	1,999.8	3.77
Ireland	106.6	0.61	1,999.6	3.4	87.1	0.31	2,004.8	2.35
Italy	147.1	0.45	2,000.5	8.12	69.7	0.23	2,005.1	4.51
Latvia	118.9	0.52	2,003.4	5.3	82.3	0.39	2,004.8	4.12
Lithuania	147.1	0.82	2,003.1	7.78	79.5	0.33	2,005.8	3.62
Malta	123.4	0.35	2,003.1	6.98	86.3	0.25	2,006.1	3.29
Netherlands	120.5	0.45	2,000.6	5.27	92.2	0.41	2,000.6	2.39
Norway	111.3	0.38	1,998.7	2.22	95.2	0.44	1,999.8	3.1
Poland	135.6	0.47	2,004.3	4.77	77.1	0.31	2,005.6	3.87
Portugal	116.5	0.57	1,999.9	4.45	81.6	0.22	2,006.9	2.61
Romania	117.7	0.62	2,004.5	3.78	89	0.21	2,011.6	3.22
Slovakia	125.5	0.39	2,003.2	6.01	81	0.42	2,003.4	5
Slovenia	109.2	0.61	2,000.4	6.97	81.5	0.28	2,004.3	3.59
Spain	111.4	0.55	2,000.3	3.93	87.5	0.28	2,005.3	4.87
Sweden	123.7	0.32	1,999.6	3.03	91.7	0.47	1,999.7	3.19
Switzerland	130.8	0.34	2,001.4	5.56	88.2	0.39	2,000.4	4.17
United Kingdom	120.9	0.49	2,000.1	3.5	90.1	0.41	2,001.8	3.99

Source: Authors' estimates.

Note: Logistic growth model applied; nonlinear least square estimator adopted; raw data used.

that this process follows a fairly similar trajectory in each country. Initially, the process of assimilation is slow since this path-breaking invention is not really broadly recognized. However, strong network effects emerge then and the number of users grows exponentially, inevitably leading to the stabilization phase during which societies are fully saturated with this type of technological solution. What also attracts attention are extremely high intrinsic growth rates (see Table 6.1) estimated for the process of diffusion of mobile telephony.

According to logistic growth model estimates, the intrinsic growth rate – in our sample – ranges from 0.31 in Finland to 0.82 in Lithuania, which suggests average 31% and 82% annual rates of increase in the number of mobile telephony subscribers in respective countries. Interestingly, Finland, along with Sweden and Norway, belongs to the group of core innovators where the mobile technologies were first invented and implemented among society members. The specific feature of these core innovating countries is that the process of assimilation of technological innovations is relatively slow there, compared to other economies that simply imitate and introduce ready-made technological solutions. If we look at our sample of countries, we see that approximately twice as high intrinsic growth rates (compared to Finland) are reported for, e.g., Czech Republic (0.71), Hungary (0.62), Portugal (0.57) or Romania (0.62). Another interesting feature of the MCS diffusion process noted among our 28 countries is the relatively short time span for achieving the midpoint along the diffusion trajectory.

The midpoint (β) shows the specific period (here – the year) during which saturation reaches 50% in a certain environment. In Table 6.1, we see summarized estimated β-parameters for each country in a time span from the year 1998 in Norway and Iceland to 2004 in Poland and Romania. These results show high homogeneity of MCS diffusion paths in European economies, as the assimilation of mobile telephony proceeds quite analogously and simultaneously across countries. In the case of mobile telephony, the process of rapid diffusion and hence growing number of its users gave birth to another interesting process – technological substitution, which in this instance led to gradually diminishing role of fixed-line telephony infrastructure in societal communications. Mobile telephony fast gained a massive part of the telecommunication market, and today the role of traditional (fixed-line) telephony is absolutely marginal.

Quite similar concluding remarks can be made, if we consider the diffusion of active mobile-broadband networks and – consequently – changes in the percentage of society using internet applications and services. For the AMS variable, data is not available until 2007 as this is the initial year during which that type of technological solutions began to be widely accessible. Hence, the time series are relatively short in this case, but what can be seen in country-wise charts (see Figure 6.1) is that the increase in its usage is extremely fast in Europe. In only 12 years, in almost all 28 European countries, the saturation rates exceeded 100%, meaning that almost all society members have access to this type of digital solution. The rapid diffusion and fast-growing access to mobile-broadband resulted in universal access to internet applications. As for the IU indicator, our data covers the period beginning in 1990; we need to note that during early years, access to internet services was facilitated mostly by the fixed-line – not mobile – infrastructure. Initially, societies could access internet services using fixed-line narrowband networks that were then gradually substituted by fixed-line broadband, and today – a huge proportion of connection is facilitated by mobile networks (although their throughput is still lower than that of fixed-line broadband). Logistic growth estimates for IU (see Table 6.1) – analogously to what we have concluded for MCS – support the hypothesis on fast increasing number of IU in Europe. Estimated – for the period 1990–2021 – intrinsic growth rates (α) show how fast the number of IU was growing annually. Starting from 19% per annum in Cyprus, to 47% per annum in Sweden and 48% in Denmark. As for the estimated country-specific midpoints (β), they cover the period from the year 1999 in Iceland, Norway and Sweden, to 2008 in Cyprus and even 2011 in Romania. Here, in the case of IU indicator, we see relatively greater differences in achieving midpoints, which might be a direct consequence of poor development of hardware infrastructure in some countries that was the necessary condition for internet access during early years of its implementation.

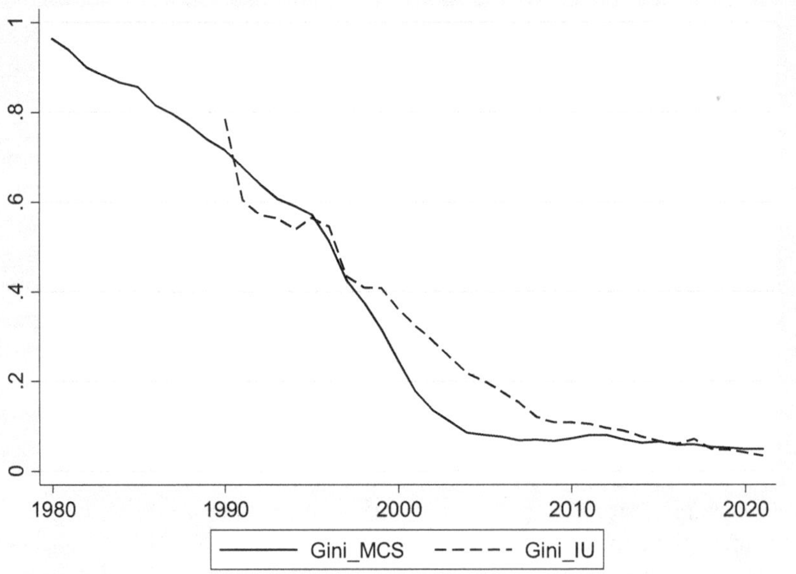

Figure 6.2 Changes in ICT-related inequalities. Gini indices values. Mobile cellular telephony and IU. 1980–2021.

Such fast and unequivocal diffusion of digital technologies inevitably leads to gradual eradication of digital gaps and inequalities. Figure 6.2 illustrates changes in cross-country inequalities regarding mobile telephony adoption and IU. The evidence clearly demonstrates how massive drops – both in terms of MCS and IU – in cross-country inequalities took place between 1980 and 2021. In the case of MCS, the 1980 Gini coefficient was 0.96 which suggested 'perfect' inequality among examined economies. However, this extreme inequality was rapidly and steadily dropping over subsequent years, reaching 0.51 in 1996, then 0.11 in 2003, and from 2004, the Gini coefficient was below 0.1, to drop to 0.049 in 2021. Analogous trends in cross-country inequalities are observable for the IU variable. During the period 1990–2021, the gaps in this regard greatly diminished. In 1990, the Gini coefficient was 0.785, indicating massive inequalities among European economies; however, in 2021, it dropped to 0.035 indicating hardly any inequalities in this respect.

Extensive diffusion and society-wide assimilation of digital solutions result – after all – in the emergence of digital skills. Those skills, as stated above, constitute unique attributes of individuals that make them able – or not – to effectively use ICT tools and software, both for professional and for personal purposes. Still, digital skills development is not automatically associated with the technological distribution, which is visible in the data related to basic and above basic information and data literacy skills, overall digital skills and online information and communication skills (see Figures 6.3 and 1A). For example, online communication skills most frequently fall within the range from 0 to 5 on the 0–10 scale (Figure 6.3), suggesting that the overall level of communication e-skills still crawls in Europe and those competencies are to be further developed in the coming years. On the other hand, results for the informational data literacy skills range between 75% and 99% in the absolute majority of European countries. Similarly, overall digital skills range from 50% to 80% in almost all European economies in 2021. This leads to a conclusion that a majority of the European countries have improved statistics related to the basic digital skills and increased their overall competitiveness while gradually catching up with the leading economies.

To summarize, the distribution of digital skills across European economies (Figure 1A of the Appendix part) demonstrates significant disparities when it comes to individual e-skills levels. These results bring evidence of the strong variation in different digital competencies, and rather mixed outcomes regarding the distribution of advanced digital skills across Europe. Additional evidence comes from Figure 6.3 results ranking European countries in order of computer skills, where mean values and whiskers demonstrate significant runaways and disparities in maximum and minimum distribution across European countries. According to the analysed data, Romania, Bulgaria and Greece are lagging behind when it comes to overall digital skills, while Denmark, the Netherlands and Luxembourg are the leaders of the studied sample. These results confirm previous studies of Bejaković and Mrnjavac (2020) or Bontadini et al. (2022) on diverse distribution of digital skills across European economies.

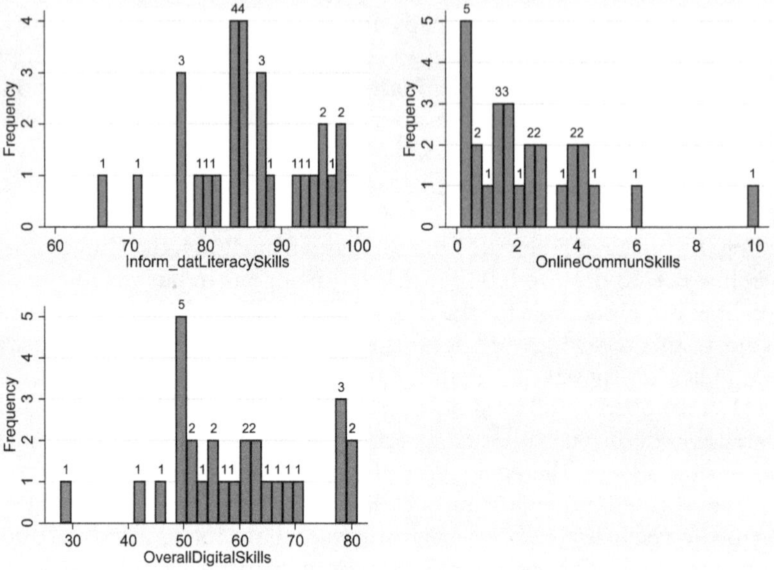

Figure 6.3 Individuals with basic or above basic information and data literacy skills; individuals with online information and communication skills, and individuals with basic or above basic overall digital skills. Year 2021.

6.5 Final remarks

This research has identified core digital trajectories in the European economies related to the digital development patterns. In the examined sample, digital technologies penetration and usage significantly expanded, leading to European market saturation over the tested period of 1980–2021. The diffusion rate of mobile cellular telephony and IU numbers demonstrate high intrinsic growth rates reaching the midpoint around 2002. Due to strong network effects, European economies managed to reach technological saturation and an impressive decrease in technological penetration disproportions, getting to a symbolic 0.05 inequality rate in 2021.

While less technologically developed European countries catch up with Europe's digital leaders by achieving an impressive growth rate, differences are still evident when it comes to the online communication and advanced digital skills. Therefore, digital skills development patterns are rather diverse, and they do not automatically arise from the technological penetration itself. In order to address those inequalities, European countries need further investment, e.g., in research and development, education, as well as policies on continuous upskilling and re-skilling (Jagannathan et al., 2019). Relative advantage in terms of technological innovations and digital lead is only possible when all three levels of the digital divide are appropriately addressed.

To conclude, we identified digital skills development patterns and examined digital skills inequalities across European economies. The results not only confirm a significant and positive impact of digital skills on labour productivity but also expose disparities in digital skills among European economies, revealing technological leaders, moderately advanced adopters of technology and laggers in terms of digital performance and use. The next step is to further investigate those disparities and their impact on labour productivity and growth across the examined countries.

Notes

1 GPTs – General Purpose Technologies.
2 [ISOC_SK_DSKL_I21__custom_6251082].
3 Base of natural logarithms.
4 The logistic growth estimates were made exclusively for the MCS and IU variables. The AMS variable demonstrates extremely rapid growths over short periods of time, which leads to significant overestimates of the model parameters.

References

Acemoglu, D., & Restrepo, P. (2022). Demographics and automation. *The Review of Economic Studies*, 89(1), 1–44. https://doi.org/10.1093/restud/rdab031.

Aissaoui, N. (2021). The digital divide: a literature review and some directions for future research in light of COVID-19. *Global Knowledge, Memory and Communication*, 71(8/9), 686–708. https://doi.org/10.1108/GKMC-06-2020-0075.

Autor, D., Mindell, D., & Reynolds, E. (2020). *The Work of the Future: Building Better Jobs in an Age of Intelligent Machines*. Boston: MIT. Retrieved 1 March 2023, from: https://workofthefuture.mit.edu/wp-content/uploads/2021/01/2020-Final-Report4.pdf.

Ávila, J., & Pandya, J.Z. (2013). *Critical Digital Literacies as Social Praxis: Intersections and Challenges*. New York: Peter Lang. ISBN: 9781433116940.

Biagi, F., & Falk, M. (2017). The impact of ICT and e-commerce on employment in Europe. *Journal of Policy Modeling*, 39(1), 1–18. https://doi.org/10.1016/j.jpolmod.2016.12.004.

Bejaković, P., & Mrnjavac, Ž. (2020). The importance of digital literacy on the labour market. *Employee Relations*, 42(4), 921–932. https://doi.org/10.1108/ER-07-2019-0274.

Bontadini, F., Evangelista, R., Meliciani, V., & Savona, M. (2022). Patterns of integration in global value chains and the changing structure of employment in Europe. *Industrial and Corporate Change*, 31(3), 811–837. https://doi.org/10.1093/icc/dtab076.

Bresnahan, T. (2010). General purpose technologies. In B. Hall & N. Rosenberg (eds.), *Handbook of the Economics of Innovation* (pp. 761–791). North-Holland. https://doi.org/10.1016/S0169-7218(10)02002-2.

Bresnahan, T.F., & Trajtenberg, M. (1995). General purpose technologies 'Engines of growth'? *Journal of Econometrics*, 65(1), 83–108. https://doi.org/10.1016/0304-4076(94)01598-T.

Cairncross, F. (2001). *The Death of Distance 2.0*. Texere Publishing. ISBN: 158799089X.

Chan, B.S., Churchill, D., & Chiu, T.K. (2017). Digital literacy learning in higher education through digital storytelling approach. *Journal of International Education Research*, 13(1), 1–16. https://doi.org/10.19030/jier.v13i1.9907.

Cirillo, V., Evangelista, R., Guarascio, D., & Sostero, M. (2021). Digitalization, routineness and employment: an exploration on Italian task-based data. *Research Policy*, 50(7). https://doi.org/10.1016/j.respol.2020.104079.

Coccia, M. (2017). Sources of technological innovation: radical and incremental innovation problem-driven to support competitive advantage of firms. *Technology Analysis & Strategic Management*, 29(9), 1048–1061. https://doi.org/10.1080/09537325.2016.1268682.

Cramer, J.S. (2003). *Logit Models from Economics and Other Fields*. Cambridge University Press. https://doi.org/10.1017/CBO9780511615412.

Dorfman, R. (1979). A formula for the Gini coefficient. *The Review of Economics and Statistics*, 61(1), 146–149. https://doi.org/10.2307/1924845.

Deursen, A.V., & Van Dijk, J.A. (2010). Measuring internet skills. *International Journal of Human-Computer Interaction*, 26(10), 891–916. https://doi.org/10.1080/10447318.2010.496338.

DiMaggio, P.J., Hargittai, E., Celeste, C., & Shafer, S.J. (2004). From unequal access to differentiated use: a literature review and agenda for research on digital inequality. In K. Neckerman (ed.), *Social Inequality* (pp. 355–400). Russell Sage Foundation. ISBN: 0871546205.

Economides, N. (1996). The economics of networks. *International Journal of Industrial Organization*, 14(6), 673–699. https://doi.org/10.1016/0167-7187(96)01015-6.

Falck, O., Heimisch-Roecker, A., & Wiederhold, S. (2021). Returns to ICT skills. *Research Policy*, 50(7). https://doi.org/10.1016/j.respol.2020.104064.

Gilbert, R.J. (2020). *Innovation Matters: Competition Policy for the High-Technology Economy*. MIT Press. ISBN: 0262044048.

Graham, M. (ed.) (2019). *Digital Economies at Global Margins*. MIT Press. ISBN: 0262535890.

Graham, M., & Dutton, W.H. (eds.) (2019). *Society and the Internet: How Networks of Information and Communication Are Changing Our Lives*. Oxford University Press. ISBN: 019884350X.

Helpman, E., & Trajtenberg, M. (1996). Diffusion of general purpose technologies. *National Bureau of Economic Research Working Paper*, 5773. https://doi.org/10.3386/w5773.

Helsper, E.J., & Eynon, R. (2013). Distinct skill pathways to digital engagement. *European Journal of Communication*, 28(6), 696-713. https://doi.org/10.1177/0267323113499113.

Hidalgo, A., Gabaly, S., Alonso, G., & Uruena, A. (2020). The digital divide in light of sustainable development: an approach through advanced machine learning techniques. *Technological Forecastiong and Scial Change*, 150. https://doi.org/10.1016/j.techfore.2019.119754.

Hsu, P.F. (2013). Commodity or competitive advantage? Analysis of the ERP value paradox. *Electronic Commerce Research and Applications*, 12(6), 412–424. https://doi.org/10.1016/j.elerap.2013.06.004.

Jagannathan, S., Ra, S., & Maclean, R. (2019). Dominant recent trends impacting on jobs and labor markets-an overview. *International Journal of Training Research*, 17(1), 1–11. https://doi.org/10.1080/14480220.2019.1641292.

Katz, M.L., & Shapiro, C. (1985). Network externalities, competition, and compatibility. *The American Economic Review*, 75(3), 424–440. https://www.jstor.org/stable/1814809.

Kudryashov, N.A. (2013). Polynomials in logistic function and solitary waves of nonlinear differential equations. *Applied Mathematics and Computation*, 219(17), 9245–9253. https://doi.org/10.1016/j.amc.2013.03.032.

Kwasnicki, W. (2013). Logistic growth of the global economy and competitiveness of nations. *Technological Forecasting and Social Change*, 80(1), 50–76. https://doi.org/10.1016/j.techfore.2012.07.007.

Lechman, E. (2015). *ICT Diffusion in Developing Countries: Towards a New Concept of Technological Takeoff*. Springer. https://doi.org/10.1007/978-3-319-18254-4.

Lechman, E. (2017). *The Diffusion of Information and Communication Technologies*. Routledge. ISBN: 9780367889579.

Linares, S.M., & Romero, A.C.D. (2016). Developing a multidimensional checklist for evaluating language-learning websites coherent with the communicative approach: a path for the knowing-how-to-do enhancement. *Interdisciplinary Journal of E Learning and Learning Objects*, 12, 57–93. https://eric.ed.gov/?id=EJ1098991.

Meyer, P. (1994). Bi-logistic growth. *Technological Forecasting and Social Change*, 47(1), 89–102. https://doi.org/10.1016/0040-1625(94)90042-6.

Milanovic, B. (1997). A simple way to calculate the Gini coefficient, and some implications. *Economics Letters*, 56(1), 45–49. https://doi.org/10.1016/S0165-1765(97)00101-8.

Nogueira, M.C., & Afonso, Ó. (2018). Intra-country wage inequality in the OECD countries. *Panoeconomicus*, 65(3), 339–362. https://doi.org/10.2298/PAN1803339N.

Rosenberg, N., & Trajtenberg, M. (2004). A general-purpose technology at work: the Corliss steam engine in the late-nineteenth-century United States. *The Journal of Economic History*, 64(1), 61–99. https://www.jstor.org/stable/3874942.

Sahal, D. (1981). *Patterns of Technological Innovation*. Addison-Wesley. ISBN: 0201066300.

Scheerder, A., van Deursen, A., & van Dijk, J. (2017). Determinants of internet skills, use and outcomes. A systematic review of the second- and third-level digital divide. *Telematics and Informatics*, 34(8), 1607–1624. https://doi.org/10.1016/j.tele.2017.07.007.

Spante, M., Hashemi, S.S., Lundin, M., & Algers, A. (2018). Digital competence and digital literacy in higher education research: systematic review of concept use. *Cogent Education*, 5(1), 1519143. https://doi.org/10.1080/2331186X.2018.1519143.

Srinuan, C., Srinuan, P., & Bohlin, E. (2012). An analysis of mobile internet access in Thailand: implications for bridging the digital divide. *Telematics and Informatics*, 29(3), 254–262. https://doi.org/10.1016/j.tele.2011.10.003.

Van Deursen, A.J., Helsper, E.J., & Eynon, R. (2016). Development and validation of the Internet Skills Scale (ISS). *Information, Communication & Society*, 19(6), 804–823. https://doi.org/10.1080/1369118X.2015.1078834.

Van Deursen, A.J., & van Dijk, J.A. (2018). The first-level digital divide shifts from inequalities in physical access to inequalities in material access. *New Media and Society*, 21(2), 354–375. https://doi.org/10.1177/1461444818797.

van Deursen, A.J., van der Zeeuw, A., de Boer, P., Jansen, G., & van Rompay, T. (2021). Digital inequalities in the Internet of Things: differences in attitudes, material access, skills, and usage. *Information, Communication & Society*, 24(2), 258–276. https://doi.org/10.1080/1369118X.2019.1646777.

van Dijk, J.A. (2005). *The Deepening Divide: Inequality in the Information Society*. Sage Publications. https://doi.org/10.4135/9781452229812.

Van Laar, E., van Deursen, A.J., van Dijk, J.A., & de Haan, J. (2020). Determinants of 21st-century skills and 21st-century digital skills for workers: a systematic literature review. *Sage Open*, 10(1). https://doi.org/10.1177/2158244019900176.

Zhou, L., Wang, L., & Breedlove, J. (2021). Impact of digital technology on optimizing organizational and social dynamics of the sport industry in China. In J. Zhang et al. (eds.), *International Sport Business Management: Issues and New Ideas* (pp. 145–168). Routledge. ISBN: 9780367740504.

Appendix

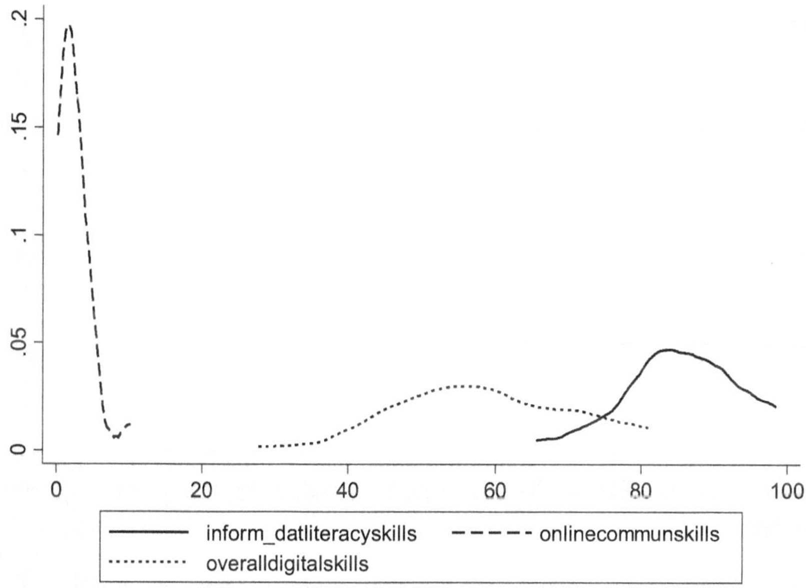

Figure 6.A1 Digital skills cross-country distribution. Year 2021.

Source: Authors` elaboration.

7 Virtual reality in legal education. Challenges and possibilities to transform normative knowledge

Amalia Verdu Sanmartin and Johanna Niemi

7.1 Introduction

The digital economy is changing the economic, political, and societal landscape. In Chapter 3, Mateusz Biernacki, Agata Luśtyk, and Rafał Wisła explain how digital economy creates a dynamic combination of various dimensions,

> such as economic aspects (changes in the nature of resources, production factors and economic processes), the area of technology (technological progress viewed from a macroeconomic perspective vs. technological innovation viewed from a microeconomic perspective), regulatory measures (challenges facing regulators, new risks affecting the institutional order) and sociological phenomena (changes in social functioning principles, attitudes towards work and human relations).

The conventional way of perceiving these dimensions involves a linear one-to-one linkage, with the third dimension usually omitted. However, several scholars representing various disciplines argue that the dimensions constituting our world are entangled and have an embedded relational nature. Donna Haraway (1997) and Humberto Maturana (2000) reveal the relational nature of humans, non-humans, technologies, and the environment in a becoming process of knowledge and meaning. These entanglements matter and foreseeing their implications requires understanding their embeddedness.

To understand the complex holistic relationship of these realms, we should explore the convergence of advancements in epistemologies, technologies, and society (Cloatre, 2015). The relational implies a comprehensive approach. Legal challenges posed by the digital economy are difficult to solve with current legal tools and require more complex thinking. Latest theoretical trends, such as new materialism (Dolphijn & van der Tuin, 2012), actor-network theory (Latour, 1996), post-human, and decolonial approaches, underline the need to analyse phenomena as intra-actions (Barad, 2007) of different dimensions, thus encouraging interdisciplinary analysis. The focus is on materiality, deeply challenging normative knowledge, and on rethinking

DOI: 10.4324/9781003450160-10

the world from a perspective questioning binary Western thought. These latest ethic-onto-epistemological approaches serve to rethink legal education in a digital era and to address the human and non-human from a relational perspective in teaching (Revelles Benavente & Cielemecka, 2016).

Digitalization poses a new challenge to legal professionals, to society, to education, and, thus, to knowledge. When it comes to legal research, many lawyers are still using methods that were popular in the past. This means that they dedicate a lot of time to looking through case law, which can be time-consuming and often inefficient. AI-based software can help to improve the efficiency and accuracy of legal research, and therefore, it is important not only to explore its potential uses but also to train law students in its application. Some observers recommend law students to learn coding or programming. While this may be an advisable option for some, we believe that the transformation of the legal profession goes deeper than this, since future jobs will require skills in designing feasible digital systems and regulations that also consider the requirements of law and justice. Law faculties have traditionally trained lawyers to solve problems known before digitalization, but technology is rapidly transforming the world and creating new legal challenges and relations. While some researchers attend conferences on different intersections of law and the digital, there has yet to be enough fundamental analysis of how the latter affects epistemology and the law faculty curriculum. Digital technologies have a profound impact on education, with their novel approaches such as e-learning, mobile learning, and learning analytics (Zhu et al., 2016). The rising digital society requires new legal skills, besides social interaction between lawyers, IT, and social scientists (Mähönen et al., 2021).[1] How should we train law students for these new demands that also involve new modes of thinking?

In this chapter, we explore the intersection between the digital, education, and law to grasp how they challenge each other while coming together in a continuous becoming process affecting the substance of law, the legal profession, and education. Using diffractive reading (Barad, 2014; Hill, 2017; Merten, 2021), this chapter examines a variety of epistemologies focusing on how legal education should embrace the digital as an avenue of training future legal professionals. Furthermore, technology is examined for its potential to foster awareness of the relational embeddedness of the world and encourage people "to think anew, through remaking the world materially and relationally" (Hickey-Moody & Page, 2015, p. 1). Particular emphasis is placed on virtual reality (VR) and its possibilities for altering perceptions about legal dogmatic image of thought. While not addressing new legal challenges posed by that technology, this chapter offers insights into the intra-actions between the non-human and human and the physical and non-physical world.

The authors organize the chapter so that Part 2 introduces VR, Part 3 discusses how VR transforms the classroom into a smart learning environment, and Part 4 explores the possibilities of using VR in legal education. We consider how the use of VR in legal education can help to teach students to re-create the physical and legal world, challenge law's immateriality, learn and traverse critical thinking, and develop new ways of thinking that will allow them to understand the digital transformation challenges and their repercussions in law. In this chapter, we propose an initial understanding of VR capability promoting experiential thinking in legal education. In doing so, we are aware of the need to make a critical analysis of the many ethical issues that must be addressed before VR is fully implemented.

7.2 What is virtual reality?

7.2.1 Tracing back real virtuality

VR is not new. For more than 50 years, scientists and engineers have been working on achieving immersive experiences which are known as extended reality (XR), VR, and augmented reality (AR).[2] In the 1950s, the filmmaker Morton Heilig and Hugo Gernsbac were credited with inventing the multisensorial theatre experience known as Sensorama (Sherman & Craig, 2003), and *Teleyeglasses*, respectively. These head-mounted devices were similar to a glass-formed portable TV and facilitated an immersive experience via dual and stereoscopic TV image. In 1965, Ivan Sutherland published his article "The ultimate display" introducing the *Sword of Damocles* (Sutherland, 1965). Sutherland together with David Evans would go on to write software for creating virtual worlds with 3D images and stored data. In 1966, Thomas A. Furness's flight simulator would become a major development for VR.

Tony Zimmerman's (data gloves) and Jaron Lanier's (data program) collaboration in the 1980s provided foundational elements for VR development, as put by Michael Heim (2011). Simultaneously, Myron Krueger created a device for art interaction (Kreuger, 1993). The development of the gaming industry started during the same period. The latest breakthrough came in 2012 with the headset device OCULUS by Palmer Luckey. Meta bought OCULUS in 2014, which, besides the improvement of fast connections allowing 3D computer-based images, moved VR technologies forward (Harris, 2019). With 5G now, 6G connectivity and the mass commercialization of VR glasses soon, the technology is spreading beyond the gaming industry to other realms. Such glasses as The Oculus, Valve, HTC, and Microsoft are flooding the consumer market not only for gaming but also for professional and educational use. The metaverse is growing, and tech companies are investing heavily in this area as evidenced by the upcoming entry of Apple in the metaverse with the planned release of a headset combining AR and VR.

7.2.2 Virtual reality today

There is much controversy surrounding the definition of VR. Over the past decade, several authors have provided various definitions, some emphasizing the use of a headset for interaction or immersion in an artificial world, others combining different elements. Fuchs, one of the many scholars working on the VR definition, explains that the definition differs depending on the purpose and the functional or technical elements of VR (Fuchs et al., 2011). Others, like Burdea and Coiffet (2003), define VR as a combination of interaction, immersion, and imagination. Sherman and Craig (2018) define VR as the combination of a virtual world, sensory feedback, immersion, and interaction. The different definitions show the three main paradigms that form what is understood as VR: realism, immersion, and interaction (Tori et al., 2006).

In a combination of these approaches, the definitions refer to a person using a head-mounted display connected to a computer that creates an immersive simulated experience. Burdea and Coiffet's (2003) approach indicates the relation in VR to non-human elements such as the avatar and the metaverse. Avatars act as virtual representations of humans who interact with each other within the 3D metaverse. This simulated environment appears to be real when experienced through a device, producing an immersive experience that merges the physical and the virtual world (Sparkes, 2021). VR is also a platform that can be used for professional, cultural, social, and economic activities (Kye et al., 2021).

The human is immersed and interacting in a non-physical/non-human environment. The experience is a sense of presence, of actually "being there", in the world of VR or AR (Barfield, 2016). The type of this human/non-human interaction with and within the 3D environment is what divides VR into distinct categories: non-immersive, semi-immersive, full immersive, or a mixture of them. *Non-Immersive VR* is often not viewed as VR due to users remaining conscious of their surroundings. Interaction takes place via a computer screen without using any other devices and commonly entails 360 videos for either business use or professional instruction. *Semi-Immersive VR* provides users with a partial immersive experience in a cube-shaped space that consists of four screen sets: three screens for the walls and one for the floor. This experience requires a device designed for tracking the user's movements. *Fully Immersive VR*, such as created by Oculus headsets, is considered to be full VR. However, this is not full immersion in terms of providing skin and olfactory sensations. There are ongoing efforts to develop materials for sensory stimulation and simulation engaging these two senses. Despite this limitation, users of the current full-immersion VR still experience a sense of immersion in the artificial environment and being out of the physical world. Therefore, immersive VR involves diverse types of immersion, as noted by Björk and Holopainen who divide the immersive experience into sensory-motoric, cognitive, and emotional and add a fourth one termed spatial immersion referring to such VR immersion in which the simulated computer-based environment is perceptually convincingr (Holopainen & Björk, 2003).

VR has evolved into AR using computer-generated perceptual information to provide an immersive experience on its own or in combination with VR.

AR does not replace the world entirely; it supplements computer-generated perceptual items of information and interacts with them. AR requires the use of special glasses like VR, and it can be combined with VR to create mixed reality (MR). The difference between this and other digital interconnections lies in the emotions experienced by the user (Dieck et al., 2021).

7.3 VR as a tool of Smart Education: the relationship between education and the digital

Now, the digital realm has become an active content creator and is causing educational methods to move from the first timid steps into online education with tools, such as Moodle, to interactive digital tools and gaming. The emergence of smart education compels us to rethink our approaches to learning and knowledge creation, as it engages universities and research institutes in new paradigms of teaching and learning by intertwining teaching/learning with digital technologies.

New concepts pop up in relation to smart education, such as smart pedagogy, smart environment, and smart learning (Meng et al., 2020). Zhu, Sun and Riezebos (2016) suggest that smart education is a shift from traditional teacher-centred pedagogies towards more learner-centred methods, making use of adaptive and interactive technologies. Coccoli et al (2014). say that it is "education in a smart environment supported by smart technologies, making use of smart tools and smart devices" (2014, p. 1008). Additionally, Lee et al. (2014) underline the potential applications of intelligent technologies aimed to support online collaborative activities and create an active learning environment in which emerging technology tools promote knowledge sharing between learners.

Research has shown that the relationship between devices and technology requires the development of smart pedagogies, that create a smart learning environment for smart learners (Zhu et al., 2016), and education adaptive to students' needs (Bajaj & Sharma, 2018). Smart education appears as a novel approach in which digital intertwines with education and knowledge. The research shows that smart education in combination with smart pedagogies improves high-order thinking skills (Julius et al., 2018). However, this integration of technology and learning is not sufficiently implemented in legal education (Rabadi & Salem, 2018).

Smart education is now incorporating VR, as shown by the EDUCAUSE Horizon Report (2020), with very positive results. Kavanagh et al. (2017) conducted a systematic review that revealed four main applications of VR when used in the educational setting: simulation, training, accessing limited resources, and distance learning. By utilizing immersive VR, students are able to interact more effectively with knowledge, and those living in remote locations with limited access to education can also benefit from its use. However, the relationship between technology and education requires specific frameworks due to potential ethical concerns (Zhu et al., 2016; Meng et al., 2020;

Fischer et al., 2021). Cai et al. (2021) propose a blended approach which would maintain self-efficacy and individuality while addressing pedagogical aims of high-order skills and deep learning alongside community knowledge building and transformation in smart education contexts (Cai et al., 2021).

7.4 Technology, law, and education: from a linear one-to-one connection to becoming together

7.4.1 One-to-one relationships

In the last 20 years, digital technologies have rapidly progressed and spurred a lively interdisciplinary debate. Richard Susskind (1996) predicted that lawyers would communicate via email which, though revolutionary at the time, has since become commonplace. On top of all these changes, the production of knowledge and the acquisition of information are leaving traditional sites; the Internet and digital technologies are enabling self-learning and new knowledge.

The relation between law and technology is shaped by a one-to-one binary discourse about the constraining and fostering role of each other in this mutual relation. The result is usually the production of norms, principles, standards, and new legislation, ignoring the nature of knowledge technology. The legal response to technologies was first focusing on the problems of privacy and data, such as the implications of Big Data and AI for privacy, anti-discrimination, due processing, and the rule of law, and resulted in the adoption of "digital" regulation which emphasizes processes of writing that resemble drafting a legal text (Lezaun, 2012, p. 38). The latest growing use of AI shifts the focus towards its ethical implications and the question how it may alter the practice of law.

In the legal realm, digital tools have a poor image and are blamed due to their negative effects. However, the effects of using digital tools may merely be reflections of the existing discriminatory and biased practices in society. Since technology deals with real data, the outcome is merely a reflection of the society we live in and only results in exposing the normative flaws that sustain discriminatory and biased legal practices (Whittaker, 2019). The ethical implications of digital technologies led to the emergence of trendy AI ethics which is a rebirth of the concerns and critiques already expressed by feminist, gender, critical, race, colonial, and decolonial theories, among many others, over the last decades. But still, the solution offered at the EU level is more new legislation (European Commission, 2022).

Richard and Daniel Susskind (2022) explored the one-to-one relation between the legal sector and technologies, forecasting an increase in the demand for digital dispute resolution, replacing traditional courts with online resolution systems. LegalTech tools are currently being implemented to scrutinize court verdicts,[3] and to review case material (e.g. Westlaw Edge). Fears are voiced that algorithms and machines will replace the work of legal professionals such as lawyers, juries, and judges; however, a general change and transformation of legal jobs and services reveals interesting prospects for individuals working in the legal sector rather than a decline in jobs. Therefore, law faculties must begin a curricular transformation to prepare law students to thrive in 21st-century society. With the millennial generation of digital native students engaging in new ways of learning (Manuel, 2002), different skills are required than those prior to digitalization. Consequently, legal professionals must learn new tools and skills in order to adapt to evolving legal problems and gain the knowledge needed for success.

In 1936, Fred Rodell said "There are two things wrong with legal writing. One is style; the other is content" (Rodell, 1936), asserting that the traditional style and content of legal writing were not in sync with society and professional needs. Despite these issues, legal education continued to rely upon the written text as indubitable truth and focus on the legal style. With the emergence of online education offering online courses, intensified by the Covid-19 pandemic, technology has been introduced into law faculties in the form of Mass Online Courses, Moodle courses, and teaching with Zoom, Teams, Skype, etc., yet this has not necessarily resulted in pedagogical innovation. Alimisis states in his comments on robotics education that current uses of technology are simply reinforcing old ways of teaching and learning. She critically argues, "most uses of technologies in schools today do not support 21st-century learning skills" (2013, p. 66). Interactive teaching methods such as flipped classrooms and simulations have been left to stagnate. Amidst this digital knowledge era, much remains unchanged within law faculties, predominantly due to an ongoing reliance on "legal writing style".

Legal education in the European context has been characterized as banking education, according to Paulo Freire (1974). Deleuze (1994) further explains that this banking education fails to promote critical and creative thinking and reinforces dogmatic thinking. Banking education relies on the belief that thinking means representational repeating, reinforcing, and reifying dogmatic thought. However, as Gandorfer and Ayub (2021) argue, "Thought is relational, non-representational, and collaborative" (2021, p. 2). There is urgency for integrating the ethics of thought in the co-creation and transmission of knowledge to achieve "both sense-making and sensing in the making" (Gandorfer & Ayub, 2021, p. 1). Higher education has a political dimension (Barrier et al., 2019), and Diana Laurillard described teaching in higher education as fundamentally being "a rhetorical activity, persuading students to change the way they experience the world through an understanding of the insights of others" (Laurillard, 2013, p. 23).

The problem of the rhetorical teaching/learning method in law, as revealed by pedagogical approaches, is the difficulty in achieving deep learning, which prevents the acquisition of higher order skills such as critically examining texts or making connections with other ideas and knowledge (van Dongen & Kirschner, 2020; Wang et al., 2022). A power relationship between academic, experiential, and everyday knowledge underlies banking education.

Written texts and norms "impose" this hierarchy, curbing thoughtful enquiry and supressing the importance of experience-based insight and relations in producing knowledge. Alfred Whitehead recognized this hierarchical method of legal thought when he said: "In all systematic thought, there is a tinge of pedantry. There is a putting aside of notions, of experiences, and of suggestions, with the prim excuse that of course we are not thinking of such things" (1938, p. 2). With no interaction between such modes of thought like sensing or feeling (Manning, 2009), a dogmatic image remains fixed. The dogmatic image of thought should be replaced in order to recognize the violence implicit in representational thinking. Legal systems are presented as independent from social, cultural, political, economic, and especially digital systems. Additionally, law is traditionally viewed as an established and authoritative symbolic representation of truth. Students during legal studies learn to refer to the world using this legal representation which leads to the reification of symbols.

Students are still largely experiencing legal education as "learning by heart", despite the implementation of several projects aimed to introduce new methods such as flipped classrooms, game-based learning (GBL), and problem-based learning (PBL) (Knight & Wood, 2005; Kapralos et al., 2015). These methods have produced positive results in integrating experiential knowledge and stimulating active student involvement, yet they are usually restricted within traditional environments not encouraging to transgress the disciplinary boundaries of thought. Therefore, alongside lectures, the modern Socratic method is still a preferred teaching style in legal education. This method enables a dialogue among the students, advancing critical and creative thinking aimed to discover solutions for the world's legal problems. However, there is the risk of reifying legal symbols and norms, since dialogues are often limited to the definition of concepts from a positivist perspective. In this way, students become familiar with predetermined court-made interpretations and are not encouraged to search for creative alternative solutions. Hence, the application of knowledge becomes a narrow exercise of discerning a pre-settled matter. The modern Socratic method as used in current legal education ends up in a right and normative reconstruction of the normative truth and, thus, teaching students to think like a lawyer, which entails learning how the world is and should be experienced. The modern Socratic method is infused with the very same pedantic truth earlier exposed by Whitehead (1938), promoting normative representational thought.

Recognizing the relationship between education, technology, and society, as well as understanding their relational rather than representational nature, is critical for improving students' understanding of the role and effects of law (Maharg, 2016). There is an inner relational quality within the system and in-between the systems. Investigations into the "Knowledge Practices" that are present within and between these systems can help to achieve this aim by highlighting their co-production through contingent entanglements (Weidemaier & Gulati, 2013). Despite the relational nature of thinking/acting, the digital influence on education is limited to a one-to-one relation, thus placing emphasis on the acquisition of IT skills and the sourcing and handling of information now freely available in a vast amount online. Through incorporation into blended teaching curricula, VR can become a transformative technology capable of heightening attention to non-representational knowledge involving situated learning (Maharg, 2001, 2016). Many studies indicate the effectiveness of VR in education across a myriad of disciplines including medicine (surgery training) (Nassar et al., 2021) and law, in the form of legal case management simulations and visualizations of legal actions (Baksi, 2016). VR has the potential for providing a new form of access to knowledge previously disconnected from education. It can foster collaboration across disciplines and represent complex connections, aiding in the connective understanding of laws and the legal process. VR enables students to experience law concepts in a way that is both realistic and interactive. This allows them to better understand the way the law works and its context. Additionally, robots can be used to create online tutorials for students – making learning easier than ever before.

Students' experience of living in VR as well as in the physical world necessitates a re-evaluation of the relationship between materiality, relationality, and representation in both worlds. Knowledge acts as the catalyst for investigating this entanglement between technology, education, law, and VR which enables us to go beyond a mere simulation and explore the hidden interactions influencing knowledge. The growing ubiquity of digital aspects in other parts of life brings up further questions with regard to law, VR, and humanity.

7.4.2 Becoming together

Mobile learning and e-learning are the precursors of crossing the temporal and spatial boundaries in teaching/learning (Looi et al., 2009). Previous research on smart education revealed that effective teaching/learning strategies can improve thinking skills (Julius et al., 2018). Zhou's smart education framework (Zhu et al., 2016) includes such vital elements as teaching presence, technological presence, and the learner's presence. Within this framework, a focus on the construction of knowledge enables us to understand how knowledge reproduces, and what are the possibilities for transformation (Berry & Fagerjord, 2017). Rethinking this relationality from a new materialist perspective exposes the power relations embedded in the binaries pervading the transmission of normative knowledge, like: teaching vs learning, teacher vs student, nature vs culture, physical vs non-physical, and human vs non-human. The becoming-together approach highlights the role of what is sensible but not represented or, as Deleuze words it, what is between the actual and the virtual (Deleuze, 1994).

A diffractive reading (Barad, 2014; Bozalek & Zembylas, 2017; Merten, 2021) of pedagogical and critical approaches in education, alongside digital technologies and law, allows us to analyse and understand the becoming together of all these dimensions. This task stems from realizing that, when thinking as a lawyer, representational and critical thinking alone are insufficient for future legal professionals in the technology-mediated 21st century. The modern approach to the relationship between these elements leads to the transmission of legal knowledge within a modern framework with some touches of the postmodern, which in a blended world seems inadequate. The postmodern element contracts to fit within the boundaries set by the modern framework.

Modern boundaries are challenged by the non-human elements and their entanglement with human subjects. However, the modern framework rejects these entanglements and reproduces itself through text-based academic and legal knowledge and through the fixity characteristic of the written text. This fixity attaches to written texts, privileging them in legal education, and marginalizing messages that are not written. Nonetheless, the actual/virtual becomes materialized when the digital comes in. The non-human is entangled with the human, producing new phenomena; however, the transformative possibilities brought in by the non-human evaporate due to the insistence on complying with the modern principles embedded in the deeper layers of law and education. The erosion of the boundaries between law and other practices requires engaging with the materiality of meaning in the transmission of knowledge. This would entail openness to reimagining knowledge ontologies to understand the doing of theory and the effect of the presupposed (Barad, 2007). Reimagining law and visualizing the power/knowledge co-constitution, the entanglement with the digital creates the opportunity to explore the embeddedness of bodies, nature, space, and time in the material-semiotic entanglement of law before entering the process of thinking as a lawyer. The digital realms reconfigure the modern boundaries, offering a crack from which we can reimagine and rethink knowledge while experiencing the entanglement between the physical and non-physical. Post-human, postmodern, and new materialist pedagogies of inclusion and collaboration offer a breakthrough, replacing representational thinking and binaries. Gilbert (2005) further solidified this opinion by verifying that traditional locations for gaining knowledge are expanding further onto such platforms as the Internet.

Laurillard (2013, p. 27) has explained that academic knowledge is reliant on symbolic representation "or any symbol system that can represent a description of the world and requires interpretation": legal knowledge relies on the text and language for interpretation within a specified legal framework delimited by inherited implicit assumptions. Successful learning is possible only if it is related to the given context of action. Through VR, the distinction between knowledge and object is questioned, as well as that of written representation and law. VR leads to a new mentality concerning the body, emotions, and how they go hand in hand with theory, while maintaining a focus on the words used in legal practice – uncovering any unseen undefined issues within language. The body and emotions are entangled when putting theory, the text into practice, revealing the silences and absences of the text alongside the materiality of the words. The experiential turn is entangled with the linguistic turn, opening the possibility to understand the agency of the intra-actions, the "other" matter in the construction of knowledge. Knowledge as the intersection point of law, technology, and education is, from a new materialist perspective, embedded and becomes another intra-acting element. This understanding creates another node where technology, law, and education meet which consequently changes academic views of everyday knowledge.

Constructivist theories of learning seem to underpin Bloom's taxonomy of knowledge and learning in university pedagogics, where students are viewed as active participants in the learning process. Educators recognize that the transfer of knowledge is not solely responsible for educating the student; rather, students actively seek, accumulate, critique, and construct knowledge (Anderson, 2005). Anderson (1991, 2010) also notes that higher levels of learning require an ability to reflectively critique both subject matter and the process applied. Nonetheless, it is believed that in legal education, students must initially learn the content of law before being able to critically assess it. Constructivist elements tend to be found at the Master's level, at which courses with a critical approach are often elective additions to the mandatory curriculum. However, courses framed as critical approaches to law form part of wider shifts in education, where learning outcomes and goals focus on skills, and teachers are seen as facilitators rather than lecturers (Lemaître, 2018). Notwithstanding these shifts, the teacher is the primary active agent leading the learning process and defining the learning outcomes, as regards both content and skills, yet forgetting the constructive elements.

Constructivist pedagogy and VR advocate a radical shift towards a system in which students are seen as active participants in the construction of knowledge and as actors responsible for their own learning. In a smart education framework, constructivist pedagogies are explored in VR to overcome the limitations encountered by traditional teaching and promote deeper learning. The goal of research on smart education is to develop methodologies and frameworks assisting in purposeful planning of courses that include the effective use of technology from the beginning of study. To utilize the full potential of VR, the students should be seen as active participants in knowledge production early on. It is important to acknowledge their agency within the world (Lemley & Volokh, 2018; Jian et al., 2019; Mohamad et al., 2020; Cho et al., 2021).

Post-human and new materialisms pedagogies seem to deconstruct the power hierarchies implicit in the Western binary thinking (Baofu, 2011; Gough, 2013; Kosofsky Sedgwick, 2003; Sherbine, 2015; Revelles Benavente & Cielemecka, 2016; Carstens, 2019; Egea et al., 2020). Thus, the first binary to break is that of teacher/student. Students are actively encouraged to work together in the metaverse, with the aim of facilitating peer interaction and ultimately producing a collaborative environment in which both academic and experiential knowledge is shared by all parties involved. Teachers' hierarchical position diminishes as students share their digital skills and situated knowledge with their teacher. Informal knowledge is entangled with academic knowledge (Prensky, 2007). The role of the teacher shifts towards that of facilitator, while students practice and transform academic knowledge as they engage with each other. Passive reception of information is transformed into learning by being, rather than doing, and this shows how academic and experiential learning intra-act in creating and transforming knowledge. Students provide their individual experiential knowledge integrating it with others' and academic knowledge (Lee& Reeves, 2017). VR can activate silent voices and perspectives, encouraging visual learners or shy students to become more participative and motivated (Herrera et al., 2018).[4] Research indicates that immersive and non-immersive VR can improve student focus, engagement, and interest in the subject of study. Simulations have shown that students become bolder when given a role, often overcoming their shyness. However, the lack of authenticity minimizes the effectiveness of simulation learning (Daly & Higgins, 2011). Through immersive VR, not only are students provided with an engaging learning experience but also with an environment that is highly interactive and realistic. This lends itself to enabling a deeper understanding of complex concepts and providing learners with more comprehensive knowledge. These simulations are often controlled and interactive, allowing students to interact with the environment and experience the relevant scientific concepts in a simulated environment. Furthermore, VR can be used to provide students with a virtual tour of a location or process, immersing them in a realistic environment. The integrated use of technology is a not just a mediated tool; but it also allows us to reflect on how the virtual, the non-human in general, is embedded in and transforms law-making (Lezaun, 2012; Cloatre, 2015).

The deployment of power/knowledge of law through legal education is a journey from imparting knowledge to enabling student's learning. In both stages, there is an ontological transmission of academic knowledge. However, the disembodied nature of thinking in, of, and about law prevents individuals from visualizing material entanglements and the ontological-epistemological nature of this knowledge (Barad, 2007). In teaching law, it is essential to comprehend how the meaning behind law shapes laws and how such laws will in turn continue to shape society. Thus, questioning what law does and will do becomes vital when making sense of why certain laws are presupposed in certain ways. Reflection on such questions with law students may sound utopian, but utopias are possible in a digital environment giving the opportunity to understand becoming processes and invisible relational entanglements.

The Research Handbook on the Law of Virtual and Augmented Reality (Barfield & Blitz, 2018) elucidates the immanent obstacle that accompanies the confluence of the physical and the virtual world. Current legal theory belongs to the physical world and needs reinterpretation or rethinking to address the virtual world. The union of the online universe and the tangible plane equivalates to the amalgamation of the human and the non-human; we can be ourselves or our avatars. Therefore, the established legislation on injuries, amenities, crimes, responsibilities, adjudication, etc. may encounter many future challenges in the virtual world.

When engineering a VR environment for legal education, we can develop principles that will support attaining an intuitiveness of the intrinsic mechanics of the law and "what the law does". For this purpose, the design principles of a VR law course may focus on:

1 Knowledge production and transformation: experiential and academic knowledge entanglement. This allows us to understand the shift in knowledge production and the future challenges.
2 Interdisciplinarity of knowledge: The simulated environment enables practicing how to solve problems and situations with others and in collaboration with students with different experiential and academic knowledge.
3 Theoretical perspective entanglement with practice: to play and understand intersectionality, situated knowledges, experiences, and identities.

These principles help to achieve deep learning and heightened attention to the ethics of thought using the *matterphoric* (Gandorfer, 2020) possibilities offered by the virtual realm. The entanglement of the digital/physical elements in a simulated environment enables an understanding of the links between experiential and academic knowledge from a multidisciplinary perspective. This results from context-based learning (CBL)[5] and crowd learning[6] that promote deeper learning through exposure to other users, students, and learners that goes beyond GBL due to its realistic challenges experienced through body, senses, emotions, and feelings (Rose, 2012; Kalisz, 2016; Plass et al., 2020). The role of the body in the act of thinking is widely acknowledged, yet rarely considered in the academic world. Embodiment and situatedness rarely cross the line that divides academic and experiential knowledge. "Thinking like a lawyer" requires detaching oneself from personal experiences, making neutral analysis and interpretations of various situations. Avatar technology enables students to explore different identities, backgrounds, and layers of intersectionality, and their effects on others. Through engaging education, technology, and students' multiplicity, tools are provided to promote intrinsic motivation while highlighting individuals' connection with the group. A 3D simulated environment creates a space where to comprehend the interconnectedness of the world. Students integrate themselves with this non-physical domain in order to solve interdisciplinary problems by experiencing rather than speculating or reading an authoritative text. Furthermore, digital entanglement with law and education highlights embodiment by bringing into focus the act of thinking that is often neglected. The digital entanglement with law and education allows bringing in embodiment and situatedness while experiencing its implications in the very act of thinking. Simulation is a key factor within VR which enables all senses to become engaged in an experiential learning event, thus opening diverse ways of learning and implementing practical experiences. This demonstrates the role that the body plays regarding understanding, interpreting, and deciding issues at hand; emotions and feelings are also employed in order to deepen the understanding of the knowledge-production processes associated with bodily engagement. The incorporation of digital technologies allows us to work with tools that can be adapted to different learning experiences while promoting collaboration.[7] VR offers experience-based teaching/learning that encourages engaging with the issue in question rather than assimilating and memorizing: it helps to experience it.

7.5 Conclusion

With technology advancements, the legal world has begun to embrace the concept of smart education. Smart education has opened up new possibilities for the transformation of knowledge and the building of a better future for society.

VR usage in education has both positive and negative implications. Nevertheless, digital technology is an ever-increasing presence in modern society, and it is important to research and experience its role at the intersection of education and knowledge. If students wish to stay ahead of the challenges posed by a quickly changing society, it is essential for them to become familiar with advances in technology as well as comprehend how societies evolve. Furthermore, understanding the collaborative creation of knowledge can help students to recognize potential issues, before a legal recourse becomes necessary. Analysis of the potential implications carried by VR technology suggests that it may help to teach legal reasoning and develop problem-solving skills, enabling students to explore theory in practical terms and recognize the interrelation between different legal fields. Further study into this technology is necessary in order to predict potential policy changes, new laws, and educational benefits: to anticipate problems rather than merely react by drafting new legislation which is usually outdated by the time it is enacted.

VR encourages students to explore theoretical materiality of the intertwining physical and non-physical, human and non-human realms, which present not only new legal challenges but also transformative opportunities. VR can be used to assist in teaching students to re-create the physical and legal world as well as challenge the foundations of law, to promote diverse ways of thinking and of understanding digital landscapes from an onto-epistemological perspective. Encouraging them to analyse how virtual worlds shape their experiences, identities, and bodies is undoubtedly a good starting point for understanding, learning, practicing, and experimenting with embodied thinking within the realm of law. Simulations in a VR environment focus on the role of matter and its importance in introducing embodied teaching/learning in a non-human environment. The real and virtual entanglement creates a utopian setting in which the boundary between subject and object becomes less distinct. VR simulation supplements the written word and exposes the role of spacetimemattering. VR simulations are more than tools to be used for learning; they facilitate an understanding of how law can be transformed by bringing together all aspects of the past, present, and potential future. Students can experience knowledge and challenge ontological binaries. Contesting the human/non-human binary encourages legal professionals to become creators, problem solvers, and thinkers rather than law users and practitioners. Thus, it is critical to equip lawyers with the skills necessary for meeting upcoming challenges and to avoid relying solely upon legal education models from a pre-digital era. Through VR simulations, students have the opportunity to explore alternative approaches to practice while also creating innovative thought processes. This ability gives them agency in reimagining knowledge and transforming education in law as they recognize their potential as active individuals.

Moreover, through the use of matter in immersive VR simulations, students can develop a deeper understanding of the legal environment and its complexities. These simulations go beyond the letter of the law which can often be difficult to comprehend and limited in its application. VR simulations allow students to gain physical and emotional experience of handling a case. Other disciplines than law, such as medicine, already test VR in teaching/learning. Nevertheless, the integration of VR into educational environments is difficult because it entails structural changes and implications. Therefore, it may be advisable to proceed gradually and start integrating VR technology as part of blended education. Testing blended education with VR will also give us enough data and experience to initiate the transition to a future teaching/learning style suitable for present-day students. This testing will also provide safe conditions for integrating non-mainstream ways of thinking. Transformative thinking is possible when we dare give room for other modes of thought.

Notes

1 In "KARVI The evaluation of higher education in law", 2021, an assessment of the Finnish legal education, the employers called for better skills in interaction and communication. They also underlined that lawyers should be forward-looking, not only focused on finding and analyzing problems. See https://karvi.fi/en/general-upper-secondary-education/.
2 XR comprises VR, AR, MR, and haptic reality.
3 See e.g. Lawgeex (2022) that automates contract reviewing process: https://www.lawgeex.com/.
4 There is evidence that the empathic response obtained by a 360 video is more effective than reading case studies. The results of studies on VR impact on student engagement in the learning process show that in more than 60% of cases, students have increased attention, and interest in the subject. Teachers see this technology as the best option for personalized differentiated learning.
5 Context-based learning is an instructional approach that involves students understanding the context of a situation or subject in order to acquire knowledge of

a given topic. This type of learning encourages learners to explore their environment for potential learning opportunities and actively seek out resources pertinent to the material being studied. The use of contextual clues helps learners build connections between new concepts encountered during instruction, allowing them to make meaningful associations with existing information they have previously acquired in addition to attaching practical value beyond mere memorization and rote retention of facts.

6 Crowd learning can be used to create collaborative learning experiences, foster peer learning, support online learning, and facilitate knowledge sharing. Its innovative online educational model harnesses the collective power of members in a community to facilitate learning and knowledge sharing. By having participants from diverse backgrounds collaborate on projects and lessons, crowd learning leverages the strengths of each while eliminating traditional educational hierarchies, such as teachers or experts leading classrooms. This approach allows learners to gain access to resources, perspectives, and methods not typically found within their own circle or sphere of influence which enables deeper understanding and appreciation of various subject matter areas.

7 Adaptive learning refers to technologies that dynamically adjust to the level or type of course content based on an individual's abilities or skill attainment, in ways that accelerate a learner's performance with both automated and instructor interventions.

References

Alimisis, D. (2013). Educational Robotics: Open Questions and New Challenges. *Themes in Science & Technology Education* 6(1), 63–71. Available at: https://files.eric.ed.gov/fulltext/EJ1130924.pdf.

Anderson, L.W. (1991). *Increasing Teacher Effectiveness. Fundamentals of Educational Planning*, 39. ISBN: 92-803-1140-9.

Anderson, L.W. (2005). Objectives, Evaluation, and the Improvement of Education. *Studies in Educational Evaluation* 31(2–3), 102–13. https://doi.org/10.1016/J.STUEDUC.2005.05.004.

Anderson, L.W. (2010). Curricular Alignment: A Re-Examination. *Theory into Practice* 41(4), 255–60. https://doi.org/10.1207/S15430421TIP4104_9.

Bajaj, R. & Sharma, V. (2018). Smart Education with Artificial Intelligence Based Determination of Learning Styles. *Procedia Computer Science* 132, 834–42. https://doi.org/10.1016/J.PROCS.2018.05.095.

Baksi, C. (2016). Virtual Reality Helps Students to Master Criminal Law. *The Times*. Accessed September 18, 2022. https://www.thetimes.co.uk/article/2b86edf0-9074-11e6-91d4-91c7eaaf09d6.

Baofu, P. (2011). *The Future of Post-Human Education : A Preface to a New Theory of Teaching and Learning*. Cambridge International Science Publishing. ISBN: 1907343245.

Barad, K. (2007). *Meeting the Universe Halfway*. Duke University Press. ISBN: 978-0-8223-3917-5.

Barad, K. (2014). Diffracting Diffraction: Cutting Together-Apart. *Parallax* 20(3), 168–87. https://doi.org/10.1080/13534645.2014.927623.

Barfield, W. (2016). Musings on Presence Twenty-Five Years after "Being There". *PRESENCE: Teleoperators and Virtual Environments* 25(2), 148–50. https://doi.org/10.1162/PRES_a_00252.

Barfield, W. & Blitz, M.J. (Eds.) (2018). *Research Handbook on the Law of Virtual and Augmented Reality*. Edward Elgar. https://www.e-elgar.com/shop/gbp/research-handbook-on-the-law-of-virtual-and-augmented-reality-9781786438584.html.

Barrier, J., Quéré, O. & Vanneuville, R. (2019). The Making of Curriculum in Higher Education, Power, Knowledge, and Teaching Practices. *Revue d'Anthropologie des Connaissances* 13(1). http://journals.openedition.org/rac/465.

Berry, D.M. & Fagerjord, A. (2017). *Digital Humanities: Knowledge and Critique in a Digital Age*. Polity. ISBN: 978-0-745-69765-9.

Bozalek, V. & Zembylas, M. (2017). Diffraction or Reflection? Sketching the Contours of Two Methodologies in Educational Research. *International Journal of Qualitative Studies in Education* 30(2), 111–27. https://doi.org/10.1080/09518398.2016.1201166.

Burdea, G.C. & Coiffet, P. (2003). *Virtual Reality Technology*. Wiley India. ISBN: 978-0-471-36089-6.

Cai, Y., van Joolingen, W. & Veermans, K. (Eds.) (2021). *Virtual and Augmented Reality, Simulation and Serious Games for Education*. Springer. https://doi.org/10.1007/978-981-16-1361-6.

Carstens, D. (2019). New Materialist Perspectives for Pedagogies in Times of Movement, Crisis and Change. *Alternation – Interdisciplinary Journal for the Study of the Arts and Humanities in Southern Africa* 26(2). https://doi.org/10.29086/2519-5476/2019/v26n2a7.

Cho, J., Jung, T., Macleod, K. & Swenson, A. (2021). Using Virtual Reality as a Form of Simulation in the Context of Legal Education. In M.C. Dieck, T.H. Jung & S.M.C. Loureiro (Eds.), *Augmented Reality and Virtual Reality* (pp. 141–54). Springer. https://doi.org/10.1007/978-3-030-68086-2_11.

Cloatre, E. (2015). *Knowledge, Technology and Law*. Routledge. ISBN: 9781138665354.

Coccoli, M., Guercio, A. Maresca, P. & Stanganelli, L. (2014). Smarter Universities: A Vision for the Fast Changing Digital Era. *Journal of Visual Languages & Computing* 25(6), 1003–11. https://doi.org/10.1016/J.JVLC.2014.09.007.

Daly, Y. & Higgins, N. (2011). The Place and Efficacy of Simulations in Legal Education: A Preliminary Examination. *AISHE-J* 3(2). Avaliable at: https://ojs.aishe.org/index.php/aishe-j/article/view/58/41.

Deleuze, G. (1994). *Difference and Repetition*. Columbia University Press. ISBN: 0231081596.

Dieck, M. C., Dieck, D. T. & Jung, T. (2021). Exploring Usability and Gratifications for Virtual Reality Applications at Festivals. *Event Management* 25(6), 585–99. https://doi.org/10.3727/152599521X16106577965152

Dolphijn, R. & van der Tuin, I. (2012). *New Materialism: Interviews & Cartographies*. Open Humanities Press. Available at: http://openhumanitiespress.org/books/download/Dolphijn-van-der-Tuin_2013_New-Materialism.pdf.

Egea, A., Amorós, M., Sánchez-Margalef, F. & Vilafranca, I. (2020). *La Pedagogía Ante El Reto Del Poshumanismo* [Paper presentation]. Educación 2020-2022: retos, tendencias y compromisos. Universidad de Barcelona, España. Accessed May 17, 2022. https://dialnet.unirioja.es/servlet/articulo?codigo=7662229.

EDUCAUSE. (2020). 2020 EDUCAUSE Horizon Report: Teaching and Learning Edition. *EDUCAUSE Publications*. Available at: https://library.educause.edu/resources/2020/3/2020-educause-horizon-report-teaching-and-learning-edition.

European Commission. (2022). *The Digital Services Act Package*. Accessed September 15, 2022. https://digital-strategy.ec.europa.eu/en/policies/digital-services-act-package.

Fischer, H., Arnold, M., Philippe, S., Dyrna, J. & Jung, S. (2021). VR-Based Learning and Teaching. A Framework for Implementation of Virtual Reality in Formal Education. *INTED2021 Proceedings* 1, 3304–14. https://doi.org/10.21125/INTED.2021.0694.

Freire, P. (1974). *Education for Critical Consciousness*. Sheed and Ward.

Fuchs, P., Moreau, G. & Pascal, G. (Eds.) (2011). *Virtual Reality: Concepts and Technologies*. Routledge. ISBN: 9780415684712.

Gandorfer, D. (2020). *Matterphorics: On the Laws of Theory*. Princeton University Doctoral Dissertation. https://dataspace.princeton.edu/handle/88435/dsp01pv63g3200.

Gandorfer, D. & Ayub, Z. (2021). Introduction: Matterphorical. *Theory & Event* 24(1), 2–13. https://muse.jhu.edu/article/780765.

Gilbert, J. (2005). *Catching the Knowledge Wave? The Knowledge Society and the Future of Education*. NZCER Press. ISBN: 978-1-877398-04-9.

Gough, N. (2013). RhizomANTically Becoming-Cyborg: Performing Posthuman Pedagogies. *Educational Philosophy and Theory* 36(3), 253–65. https://doi.org/10.1111/J.1469-5812.2004.00066.X.

Haraway, D. J. (1997). *Modest_Witness@Second_Millennium. FemaleMan_Meets_OncoMouse Feminism and Technoscience*. Routledge. ISBN: 0-415 90386-6.

Harris, B.J. (2019). *The History of the Future: Oculus, Facebook and the Revolution That Swept Virtual Reality*. Day Street Books. ISBN: 0062455966.

Heim, M. (2011). *The Metaphysics of Virtual Reality*. Oxford University Press. https://doi.org/10.1093/acprof:oso/9780195092585.001.0001.

Herrera, F., Bailenson, J., Weisz, E., Ogle, E. & Zak, J. (2018). Building Long-Term Empathy: A Large-Scale Comparison of Traditional and Virtual Reality Perspective-Taking. *PLOS ONE* 13(10). https://doi.org/10.1371/JOURNAL.PONE.0204494.

Hickey-Moody, A. & Page, T. (2015). Introduction. In A Hickey-Moody & T. Page (Eds.), *Arts, Pedagogy and Cultural Resistance: New Materialisms*. Rowman & Littlefield International. ISBN: 978-1-7834-8486-7.

Hill, C.M. (2017). More-than-Reflective Practice: Becoming a Diffractive Practitioner. *Teacher Learning and Professional Development* 2(1), 1–17. Available at: https://journals.sfu.ca/tlpd/index.php/tlpd/article/view/28/pdf.

Holopainen, J. & Björk, S. (2003). *Game Design Patterns* [Paper presentation]. Digital Games Research Conference, University of Utrecht, The Netherlands. Accessed September 15, 2022. http://www.digra.org/wp-content/uploads/digital-library/05163.15303.pdf.

Jian, K., Nai, P. & Yu, T. (2019). Simulation Application of Virtual Reality Technology in Legal Education. *Journal of Physics: Conference Series* 1419(1). https://doi.org/10.1088/1742-6596/1419/1/012046.

Julius, E., Mun, S.H., Abdullah, A.H., Mokhtar, M. & Suhairom, N. (2018). Using Digital Smart Board to Overcome Higher Order Thinking Skills Learning Difficulties in Data Handling among Primary School Students. *International Journal of Interactive Mobile Technologies* 12(7), 43–59. https://doi.org/10.3991/IJIM.V12I7.9644.

Kalisz, D.E. (2016). Crowd Learning: Innovative Harnessing the Knowledge and Potential of People. In S. Tiwari & L. Nafees (Eds.), *Innovative Management Education Pedagogies for Preparing Next-Generation Leaders* (pp. 55–74). IGI Global. https://doi.org/10.4018/978-1-4666-9691-4.ch004.

Kapralos, B., Kapralos, B., Fisher, S., Clarkson, J. & van Oostveen, R. (2015). A Course on Serious Game Design and Development Using an Online Problem-Based Learning Approach. *Interactive Technology and Smart Education* 12(2), 116–36. https://doi.org/10.1108/ITSE-10-2014-0033.

Kavanagh, S., Luxton-Reilly, A., Wuensche, B. & Plimmer, B. (2017). A Systematic Review of Virtual Reality in Education. *Themes in Science and Technology Education* 10(2), 85–119.

Knight, J.K. & Wood, W.B. (2005). Teaching More by Lecturing Less. *Cell Biology Education* 4(4), 298–310. https://doi.org/10.1187/05-06-0082.

Kosofsky Sedgwick, E. (2003). *Touching Feeling: Affect, Pedagogy, Performativity*. Duke University Press. ISBN: 978-0-8223-3015-8.

Kreuger, M.W. (1993). The Artistic Origins of "Virtual Reality". Accessed September 15, 2022. https://digitalartarchive.siggraph.org/wp-content/uploads/2018/01/1993_kruger.pdf.

Kye, B., Han, N., Kim, E., Park, Y. & Jo, S. (2021). Educational Applications of Metaverse: Possibilities and Limitations. *Journal of Educational Evaluation for Health Professions* 18. https://doi.org/10.3352/JEEHP.2021.18.32.

Latour, B. (1996). On Actor-Network Theory: A Few Clarifications. *Soziale Welt* 47(4), 369–81. https://www.jstor.org/stable/40878163.

Laurillard, D. (2013). *Rethinking University Teaching: A Conversational Framework for the Effective Use of Learning Technologies*. Routledge. https://doi.org/10.4324/9781315012940.

Lawgeex. (2022). https://www.lawgeex.com/.

Lee, J., Zo, H. & Lee, H. (2014). Smart Learning Adoption in Employees and HRD Managers. *British Journal of Educational Technology* 45(6), 1082–96. https://doi.org/10.1111/BJET.12210.

Lemaître, D. (2018). L'innovation Pédagogique En Question: Analyse Des Discours de Praticiens. *Ripes* 34(1). https://doi.org/10.4000/RIPES.1262.

Lemley, M. & Volokh, E. (2018). Law, Virtual Reality, and Augmented Reality. *University of Pennsylvania Law Review* 166(5), 1051–138. Available at: https://scholarship.law.upenn.edu/penn_law_review/vol166/iss5/1.

Lezaun, J. (2012). The Pragmatic Sanction of Materials: Notes for an Ethnography of Legal Substances. *Journal of Law and Society* 39(1), 20–38. https://doi.org/10.1111/J.1467-6478.2012.00568.X.

Looi, C.-K., Seow, P. & Wong, L.-H. (2009). Leveraging Mobile Technology for Sustainable Seamless Learning: A Research Agenda. *British Journal of Educational Technology* 41(2), 154–69. https://doi.org/10.1111/j.1467-8535.2008.00912.x.

Maharg, P. (2001). Negotiating the Web: Legal Skills Learning in a Virtual Community. *International Review of Law, Computers & Technology* 15(3), 345–60. https://doi.org/10.1080/13600860220108139.

Maharg, P. (2016). *Transforming Legal Education : Learning and Teaching the Law in the Early Twenty-First Century*. Routledge. ISBN: 9781138248274.

Mähönen, J., Airaksinen, M., Korte, A., Mattsson, A., Mielityinen, S., Niemi, J., Paso, M., Rantanen, J., Moitus, S., Partanen, L. & Huusko, M. (2021).

Oikeustieteellisen alan korkeakoulutuksen arviointi. *Karvi.* https://karvi.fi/wp-content/uploads/2021/11/KARVI_2221.pdf.

Manning, P.K. (2009). Reflections on 'Two Concepts of Rules'. *Journal of Classical Sociology* 4, 429–49. https://doi.org/10.1177/1468795X09344451.

Manuel, K. (2002). Teaching Information Literacy to Generation. *Journal of Library Administration* 36(1–2), 195–217. https://doi.org/10.1300/J111V36N01_12.

Maturana, H. (2000). The Nature of the Laws of Nature. *System Research and Behavioral Science* 17(5), 459–68. https://doi.org/10.1002/1099-1743(200009/10)17:5<459::AID-SRES371>3.0.CO;2-I

Meng, Q., Jia, J. & Zhang, Z. (2020). A Framework of Smart Pedagogy Based on the Facilitating of High Order Thinking Skills. *Interactive Technology and Smart Education* 17(3), 251–66. https://doi.org/10.1108/ITSE-11-2019-0076.

Merten, K. (Ed.) (2021). *Diffractive Reading: New Materialism, Theory, Critique.* Rowman & Littlefield Publishers. ISBN: 978-1-78661-396-7.

Mohamad, A.M., Salleh, A., Nor, M. & Yusuff, Y. (2020). *Impacts of Augmented Reality in Legal Studies: Students' Reflections* [Paper presentation]. 2020 7th International Conference on Information Technology Trends, ITT 2020, Abu Dhabi, United Arab Emirates. https://doi.org/10.1109/ITT51279.2020.9320872.

Nassar, A.K., Al-Manaseer, F., Knowlton, L.M. & Tuma, F. (2021). Virtual Reality (VR) as a Simulation Modality for Technical Skills Acquisition. *Annals of Medicine and Surgery* 71. https://doi.org/10.1016/J.AMSU.2021.102945.

Plass, J.L., Mayer, R.E. & Homer, B.D. (Eds.) (2020). *Handbook of Game-Based Learning.* MIT Press. ISBN: 9780262043380.

Prensky, M. (2007). *Digital Game-Based Learning.* Paragon House. ISBN: 1557788634.

Rabadi, W. & Salem, R. (2018). The Level of High-Order Thinking and Its Relation to Quality of Life among Students at Ajloun University College. *International Education Studies* 11(6). https://doi.org/10.5539/ies.v11n6p8.

Lee, S. J. & Reeves T. C. (2017). Edgar Dale and the Cone of Experience. In R.E. West & K.D.N. Christensen (Eds.), *Foundations of Learning and Instructional Design Technology* (pp. 1–477). EDT books. https://doi.org/10.59668/3.

Revelles Benavente, B. & Cielemecka, O. (2016). (Feminist) New Materialist Pedagogies. *New Materialism.* Available at: https://newmaterialism.eu/almanac/f/feminist-new-materialist-pedagogies.html.

Rodell, F. (1936). Goodbye to Law Reviews. *Virginia Law Review* 38, 1936–37.

Rose, D.E. (2012). Context-Based Learning. In N.M. Seel (Ed.), *Encyclopedia of the Sciences of Learning.* Springer. https://doi.org/10.1007/978-1-4419-1428-6_1872.

Sherbine, K. (2015). Making, Matter and Pedagogy. *Practice, Pedagogy, Resistance: A New Materialism* 37(5), 785–97. https://doi.org/10.1080/01596306.2015.1075732.

Sherman, W.R. & Craig, A.B. (2003). *Understanding Virtual Reality: Interface, Application, and Design. Understanding Virtual Reality: Interface, Application, and Design.* Elsevier Inc. https://doi.org/10.1162/105474603322391668.

Sherman, W.R. & Craig, A.B. (2018). *Understanding Virtual Reality: Interface, Application, and Design.* Morgan Kaufmann. https://doi.org/10.1016/C2013-0-18583-2.

Sparkes, M. (2021). What Is a Metaverse. *New Scientist* 251(3348), 18. https://doi.org/10.1016/S0262-4079(21)01450-0.

Susskind, R.E. (1996). *The Future of Law: Facing the Challenges of Information Technology.* Clarendon Press. ISBN: 0198764960.

Susskind, R.E. & Susskind, D. (2022). *The Future of the Professions: How Technology Will Transform the Work of Human Experts.* Oxford University Press. ISBN: 0198841892.

Sutherland, I.E. (1965). The Ultimate Display. Accessed at: http://worrydream.com/refs/Sutherland%20-%20The%20Ultimate%20Display.pdf.

Tori, R., Kirner, C. & Siscoutto, R. (2006). *Fundamentos e Tecnologia de Realidade Virtual e Aumentada.* SBC. Available at: https://pcs.usp.br/interlab/wp-content/uploads/sites/21/2018/01/Fundamentos_e_Tecnologia_de_Realidade_Virtual_e_Aumentada-v22-11-06.pdf.

van Dongen, E. & Kirschner, F. (2020). Blended Learning in Legal Education Using Scalable Learning to Improve Student Learning. *Law and Mathod.* https://doi.org/10.5553/REM/.000048.

Wang, S., Griffiths, R., Christensen, C., D'Angelo, C. & Condon, K. (2022). An Evaluation of a First-of-Its-Kind Hybrid Law Degree Program. *Journal of Computing in Higher Education* 34(2), 517–44. https://doi.org/10.1007/s12528-022-09308-3.

Weidemaier, W.M.C. & Gulati, G.M. (2013). Collateral Knowledge: Legal Reasoning in the Global Financial Markets Annelise Riles (Chicago: University of Chicago Press, 2011). [Book Review] *PoLAR: Political and Legal Anthropology Review* 36(1), 190–92. https://doi.org/10.1111/PLAR.12017.

Whittaker, J. P. (2019). *Tech Giants, Artificial Intelligence, and the Future of Journalism.* Routledge.

Whitehead, A.N. (1938). *Modes of Thought.* Collier-Macmillan Canada. ISBN: 9780029352106.

Zhu, Z.T., Yu, M.H. & Riezebos, P. (2016). A Research Framework of Smart Education. *Smart Learning Environments* 3(1), 1–17. https://doi.org/10.1186/s40561-016-0026-2.

Zhu, Z.T., Sun, Y. & Riezebos, P. (2016). Introducing the Smart Education Framework: Core Elements for Successful Learning in a Digital World. *International Journal of Smart Technology and Learning* 1(1), 53. https://doi.org/10.1504/IJSMARTTL.2016.078159.

8 The patent system and the problem of innovation diffusion in the digital economy

Małgorzata Niklewicz-Pijaczyńska

8.1 Introduction

Controversies surrounding the functioning of patent systems over the years not only do not lose their strength but also make the answer to the question regarding the legitimacy of their continued maintenance particularly difficult. This is because the environment for which they were originally designed has recently evolved. Different areas of technical knowledge have emerged, new players have appeared in the market and the importance of intangible property and its protection has been radically re-evaluated. Additionally, digitalization processes are rapidly accelerating and intensifying, and digital technology is becoming a new dimension in the functioning of enterprises, public institutions and consumers. The Internet-based digital economy accelerates the datafication process, creates network relationships and enhances personalization. Thus, it completely re-evaluates the course of the innovation process.

As H. Varian rightly observes,

> Now what we see is a period where you have Internet components, where you have software, protocols, languages, and capabilities to combine these component parts in ways that create totally new innovations. The great thing about the current period is that component parts are all bits. That means you never run out of them. You can reproduce them, you can duplicate them, you can spread them around the world, and you can have thousands and tens of thousands of innovators combining or recombining the same component parts to create new innovation. So there's no shortage. There are no inventory delays. It's a situation where the components are available for everyone, and so we get this tremendous burst of innovation that we're seeing.
>
> (Varian, 2009)

However, based on a dynamic and virtually uncontrolled flow of integrated data, radical verification of business models and automation of work with the use of artificial intelligence, the digital economy is forced on many levels to confront the values of patent systems, which are based on extremely

DOI: 10.4324/9781003450160-11

different principles – attachment to traditional models of innovation, inviolability of the rights possessed by the creator and tight protection of intellectual property. As a consequence, patent regulation, rather than enhancing the diffusion of innovation necessary for the development of the digital economy, in fact often slows it down. Thus, the question arises: What is the role of patent systems in the new economic reality with the diffusion of innovation as one of its most important components?

The aim of this article is twofold: (1) to describe the areas in which the contemporary patent systems operate that are problematic from the perspective of innovation diffusion processes and (2) to indicate a new function that can be implemented to provide an important tool for supporting the development of the digital economy.

Considering its implementation, a critical analysis of the economic and legal source literature was carried out. The conclusions drawn in this article show that the patent systems, with the information function implemented, show a significant potential for a wide spectrum of application in the process of innovation diffusion. However, in order for this role to be performed in an optimal way, it is necessary to urgently verify the applicable patent rules and thoroughly improve the IT infrastructure so that they respond to the challenges of the digital economy to a greater extent than before.

8.2 Controversies around the functioning of patent systems

In order to understand the reasons for introducing patent systems, it is necessary to go back to their origins. It is believed that the roots of patent systems can be found already in antiquity, but their structures were finally shaped in the 19th century. The oldest known patent privilege dates to 1234, while the documented origins of the patent law are found in the Venetian Act passed in 1474 that also lays down modern rules which include territorial and temporal limitation of protection, and the rule of disclosing the essence of an invention in exchange for the acquisition of certain rights. According to the guidelines of the Venetian Act, the inventor received a document known as *litterae patentes* an open letter confirming special powers granted to its holder by the ruler. Patent privileges, similar to Venetian open letters, were also granted in Bohemia, Silesia, Meissen, Saxony and Hungary (Krasser & Bernhard, 2008). It is worth noting that the oldest patent privileges were distinguished from their later forms by the fact that they did not entail a monopoly on use, but only a claim for payment for the use by a third party of an object covered by protection. The later evolution of patent law was determined, on the one hand, by the rapid development of natural and technical sciences and, on the other hand, by the dynamics of inventive activity, mainly in Great Britain, and the 19th-century intensification of trade contacts.

From the historical perspective, there are three main stages in the long-term development of patent law: a period of privileges, then national laws and finally internationalization as well as efforts to strengthen patent convergence more and more clearly present in the international trend. Today, three international sources of regulation can be identified in this area: World Intellectual Property Organization (WIPO) agreements, regional agreements affecting supranational patent protection systems and the TRIPS (Agreement on Trade-Related Aspects of Intellectual Property Rights). They establish the fundamental principle of the system: the exclusive use of benefits from an invention granted to its creator, within a strictly defined territorial and temporal scope (Niklewicz-Pijaczyńska, 2019).

The establishment of patent systems was questionable from the very beginning, as shown by Thomas Jefferson's statement that patents caused society more shame than good, and that ideas should be treated as natural public goods whose transfer does not cause their loss by the original creator (Standing, 2021). However, the 19th-century patent abolitionism is considered the first organized movement to undermine the sense of their existence. Its representatives were of the opinion that patent protection, as a factor limiting the development of free trade and competition, should not be reformed or strengthened, but definitely abolished. An article published in 1851 argued that patent "excites fraud, stimulates men to run after schemes that may enable them to levy a tax on the public, begets disputes and quarrels betwixt inventors, provokes endless lawsuits [and] bestows rewards on the wrong persons" (Biga, 2017), and some parties obtain patents as wide as possible only to withhold inventions or to appropriate the effects of inventions made by others. It was emphasized that it was only the expiry of J. Watt's patent on the steam engine in 1785 that dynamized the Industrial Revolution. It was also argued that almost all of the most important technological advances, from mechanical spinning machines to railroads, from steamers to gas lighting, appeared despite the lack of patent protection (Biga, 2017). It is these accusations raised in the public debate that contributed to the deliberate opting out by subsequent countries from the granting of exclusive rights by their legislators – Switzerland, the Netherlands and Germany. In 1863, the Congress of German Economists, and a year later also the German chambers of commerce, recognized that patents were detrimental to general welfare. In 1828, the English press began to publish a series of letters whose author proposed the thesis that patent protection was based on the interests of a particular group which consisted of state officials (Vindicator, 1830, cited in Newton & Partington, 1830). There were also emotionally charged accusations – "a deviation from common sense, common honesty, and the common sense of social good". Instead of exclusive rights, it was proposed to introduce alternative compensation systems, e.g., in the form of scholarships granted from public funds or private capital. S. Kinsella makes a strong summary of the arguments against patent systems, pointing out that they are an example of an attempt to morally justify plunder, which is the deprivation of the right to free use of property for the common good. He also argues that comparing utility by calculating the difference between the costs and the benefits of patent protection is unfounded as these cannot always be estimated on the basis of market value. Moreover, there is no clear evidence that patents really encourage research efforts, and the benefits obtained thanks to them outweigh the costs of maintaining an institutional system of their protection (Kinsella, 2001).

Currently, discussions on the protection of inventions are closely related to attempts to define the role they play in innovative processes and in the process of economic growth (Audretsch, 1995). The allegations against patent systems focus on the following problematic aspects:

a exclusive rights lead to monopolization of the market,
b the ownership of ideas cannot be exclusive,
c patent exclusivity has no moral justification,
d the patent system does not perform an incentive function.

(Niklewicz-Pijaczyńska, 2019)

One more objection discussed in this publication should be added to those mentioned above. The patent system blocks the creation, implementation and, consequently, the diffusion of innovation.

8.3 The innovation diffusion process and its stages

Modern societies experience what is known as "future shock" described by Toffler in the 1970s (Toffler, 1998). This state is characterized, e.g., by a rapid acceleration of economic processes that is conditioned by the creation and then diffusion of innovation. Innovation diffusion is a complex process that requires certain conditions to be met, e.g., direct or indirect interaction with process participants, taking into account links with third parties and being ready to quickly absorb new knowledge. These aspects of the innovation diffusion process are emphasized in two economic trends: evolutionary and neo-Schumpeterian, in which this process results from an interactive and collective network process, personal and institutional connections evolving over time (Oslo Manual, 2018). Diffusion means not only the acquisition of knowledge and technologies, but also the further process of their use as a basis for subsequent activities; through modification also providing the original innovator with feedback (Firlej & Żmija, 2014). It takes place at various levels; therefore, it may be inter-organizational, inter-state or intra-organizational. According to the Oslo Manual, innovation diffusion is the way in which innovation is disseminated through market and non-market channels, contacts with consumers and presence in various countries, regions, sectors, markets and companies (Oslo Manual, 2018). Therefore, according to Rogers, it is a process whereby innovation is communicated, through time-defined channels, to individual members of the social system. However, this is a specific type of communication where the message is about new ideas (Rogers, 2003).

The French sociologist J. G. Tarde is considered to be the precursor of research initiated in the 19th century on the process of innovation diffusion.

He was searching for an answer to the question of what influences the spread of new solutions and what is its dynamics (Rogers, 2003). Research on its duration was carried out by Z. Griliches and E. Mansfield, who confirmed its logistic distribution course, and by G. F. Ray, opting rather for linearity of the process (Ray, 1969). Currently, the problem of diffusion of innovations is addressed primarily in the geographical context, while their dissemination constitutes the foundations of the convergence theory and the polarized development theory. The theoretical development of the problem of innovation diffusion in the geographical context was undertaken in works by T. Hägerstrand and L.A. Brown (Wendt, 2010). Using this approach, the innovation diffusion is also discussed in the works of F. Perroux (industry research), A. Hirschman (spatial studies) and in the theory of cumulative causation by G. Myrdal (Niklewicz-Pijaczyńska, 2019).

Two research perspectives can be distinguished here. The first one focuses on the determinants of individual diffusion processes and their time path. Such an approach is presented, among others, by Z. Griliches and E. Mansfield in the epidemic model as well as by S. Davis. The other perspective "pays special attention to the paths for the transmission of new knowledge and the adaptation of new technologies or products on a macroeconomic scale, and their impact on the productivity of production processes or consumer welfare" (Niklewicz-Pijaczyńska, 2019). In this area, research is carried out, among others, by M. Trajtenberg, A. Jaffe, R. Henderson (1993) and W. Keller (2001). However, while economists primarily study the relationship between the costs of acquiring new technologies and the strategic benefits obtained due to their acquisition (Oslo Manual, 2018), the sociological perspective is adopted to analyze the potential of enterprises for absorbing new knowledge and using it (e.g., convergence of new knowledge with the current pattern of operation and the degree of its complexity). It is noted in the source literature that the course of the diffusion process may vary depending on external and internal factors. The first ones include the economic situation, the scope of invention protection, the infrastructure owned, the status of competition and the innovation policy pursued by the government. The internal factors identified include the economic calculation indicating the potential profitability of innovation, the degree of its technical complexity and the amount of expenditure necessary for its implementation. In the popular model of innovation diffusion by E.M. Rogers, this process depends on such features of innovation as:

a relative convenience compared to already used solutions;
b compatibility with existing norms, values and experience;
c complexity;
d divisibility, i.e., the possibility of its gradual adaptation;
e accessibility.

(Rogers, 2003)

8.4 Patent systems and the diffusion of innovation in the digital economy

In Chapter 1, Judyta Lubacha et al. described the phenomenon of digital economy and development of the research in that area. The concept of digital economy was used in the literature on the subject in the mid-1990s, in the study of the digital economy. Rethinking Promise and Peril in the Age of Networked Intelligence by D. Tapscott (1995). According to its author, societies are entering the era of network intelligence, in which machines and people communicate with each other through technology. Tapscott has identified the main features of the digital economy, such as knowledge as an intangible good, digitalization, virtualization, integration, convergence, innovation, immediacy, globalization and incompatibility (despite the expected unification, the differences in income and opportunities for people with and without relevant competences are increasing). E. Brynjolfsson and B. Kahin in their book Understanding the Digital Economy: Data, Tools and Research note that this is the last and still largely unrealized transformation of all sectors in the economy due to computer digitization of information (Brynjolfsson et al., 2018). In the formulation proposed by the Organisation for Economic Co-operation and Development (OECD) in 2012, it was assumed that "the digital economy enables and executes the trade of goods and services through electronic commerce on the Internet" (7 European Public Service Union, 2015). A similar concept can be found in the approach of the European Commission from 2013 – this is "the economy based on digital technologies (sometimes referred to as the internet economy)" (Parker et al., 2016).

Therefore, the initial definitions identified the digital economy with the Internet economy. However, this is not the right approach: the digital economy is a broader concept, as it means the implementation of economic processes using electronic means of data exchange, for which the Internet is the basic tool. The digital economy is the result of technological development and the convergence of data processing methods, means of communication and knowledge accumulation (Radomska, 2019). The digital economy is defined as a broad spectrum of economic, social and cultural activities supported by the Internet as well as related information and communication technologies (OECD, 2018). For the purposes of this study, the digital economy will be understood as economic activity resulting from billions of daily online connections between people, companies, devices, data and processes, the backbone of which is hyperconnectivity, meaning the growing interconnection of people, organizations and machines, enabled by the Internet, mobile technologies and the Internet of Things (Dahlman et al., 2016). The digital economy so understood is characterized by:

the exceptional importance of intangible goods – such as algorithms, software, big data repositories, patents, copyrights, business models, organizational opportunities, social capital, knowledge, competences, skills and strategic linkages;

- mass use of data (especially personal data);
- the popularity of platforms as a business model;
- difficulties with assessing which link in the production chain contributes to the final value of a given good;
- technologies and processes based on advanced information and communication solutions reducing the need for routine tasks and changing the location, organization and content of intellectual work.

(Śledziewska &Włoch, 2020)

Consequently, if we look at the diffusion of innovation as a process of spreading an idea realized through communication – from its source, through imitators, to the end user – in this sense, the patent system becomes an integral part of the digital economy responsible for its network operation. This role is important at the stage of both creation and diffusion of innovation. This is for two reasons. First, through the adopted rules, it actually stimulates or slows down the circulation of innovation (regarding time, the scope and geographical area of application). Second, it archives huge amounts of data and materialized technical knowledge used in the three classic phases constituting the process of creating inventions, namely, in basic research – scientific publications (case studies, articles, monographs); in applied research – scientific and technical publications, descriptions of inventions, technical and economic analyses, methodological studies and reports; in implementation works – information on the development trends of techniques and technologies, e.g., standards, patents, comparative analyses and technical documentation. The collected source materials and specific technical solutions made available through patent systems are considered to represent technical standards reflecting the state of the art; therefore, access to them is a condition for the proper functioning of competition in the area of creating and using a specific technology (Niklewicz-Pijaczyńska, 2019) and sets the course of the innovation diffusion process. Thus, the patent system has in this context an extremely strong advantage. Its databases form a huge collection of advanced, content-verified technical knowledge constituting the basis for current and future solutions, often revolutionizing the market. In a world where knowledge becomes a currency, they are among the innovation sources of an external open nature, i.e., those that do not require the purchase of technology or intellectual property rights or direct interaction with the source.

In addition, the detailed information contained in the collections of patent documentation also covers various sensitive areas such as the field of technology to which the invention belongs, the potential value of a new solution, identification of entities involved in the process of creating new technologies and reconstructing the history of the application or the legal status of the invention (Niklewicz-Pijaczyńska, 2019). Such documentation requires a standardized bibliographic description of its content, and the data it contains is collected according to the purposes and typology characteristic of a given classification. The WIPO recommends Standard ST.9 for the bibliographic description of a patent document (WIPO, 2013). The description of the invention is an obligatory element of the patent documentation (reflecting its essence in such a way that a specialist in a given field can recreate it), along with patent claims containing a set of technical features necessary to define the subject of the invention, an abbreviation of the description consisting of concise information specifying the subject and characteristic technical features of the solution and technical drawings, if they are necessary for its understanding.

As a result, patent systems, acting as a kind of intermediary in the transmission of information, significantly affect the course and intensity of innovation diffusion. This understanding of the information function has been repeatedly verified by scholars from various research fields. For example, J. Jeon, C. Lee and Y. Park (2011) demonstrate that patent information makes it easier to properly identify and select collaborators for the implementation of joint research and development projects. Empirical research conducted by H. Ernst confirms that the availability of data contained in patent databases enables entities to control and determine potential research directions and technological development paths (Ernst, 2003). The research by C. Haeussler, D. Harhoff and E. Mueller (2014), concentrated on venture capital in the biotechnology industry, shows that patent databases are one of the most important sources of knowledge used by investors. A. Jaffe, M. Fogarty and B. Banks (1998), using patent documentation, conducted their 1998 research on the impact of federal labs on commercial patents. J. Lanjouw, A. Pakes and J. Putnam (1998) analyzed the paid protection time and the countries in which it was granted. Based on that analysis, they verified the value of patent rights. In turn, D. Johnson (2002) analyzed the usefulness of the OECD – Technology Concordance indicator as a tool that enables researchers to transform data based on International Patent Classification (IPC) into a number of patents by economic sector. D. Popp (2005) in his publication drew attention to the usefulness of patent information for measuring technological changes in environmental models. Z. Acs and D. Audretsch (1989), assuming that the exclusive protection is a reward for expensive research and development works, recognize patent data as an indicator of innovative activity reflecting technological advancement in an area of research.

Research papers on the use of patent data for measuring the diffusion of technical knowledge and technology have been published, among others, by A. Jaffe, D. Coe, E. Helpman, J. Lanjouw, A. Pakes, J. Putnam, C. Jones, J. Williams, P. Stoneman and B. Verspagen (Niklewicz-Pijaczyńska, 2019). And though so far "the developed [...] measurement methodologies emphasize various aspects of the diffusion process; and the task of improving the measurement of the knowledge and technology diffusion is far from being complete", the tools based on patent data are currently most used in this area. They are also applied in conducting research using patent information to measure the progress of science, technology, innovative activity and structural changes taking place in the economy (Okoń-Horodyńska et al., 2012).

Thus, the common denominator of the patent system and digital reality includes such components as datafication, networking, and collection and processing of huge data repositories – which also characterize the structure of the system. In the network economy, the data flowing from IT systems is produced by individuals, businessess and institutional users, obtained from the archives kept by public institutions and companies and collected by an increasing number of sensors placed in devices, personal items and in private and public space. This forces the introduction of new solutions in the field of data integration from various sources or systems, providing the basis for making optimal decisions, often in real time. Everything takes place within networks of diversified reach (Radomska, 2019).

The process of activating innovation through patent systems is similar. Entities explore the network resources of the system searching for new knowledge and verifying the knowledge already possessed in such a way as to constantly create new solutions through knowledge diffusion. Thus, economic benefits are achieved (creating new solutions), along with social objectives (increasing the level of innovation) and marketing goals (image of an innovative entity) by using the data generated in enormous amounts by networks and obtained from geographically, subjectively and objectively dispersed nodes. Integration and archiving of this type of data stimulate the innovation process, allow to plan and manage it based on data on the one hand and often to adapt products to the needs and expectations of the consumer (i.e., introduce personalization) on the other hand. The popularization of the Internet and the increase in the importance of the new business model of platforms make the whole process more dynamic by creating virtual multilateral markets based on data and knowledge derived from patent systems.

What strongly links the patent system with digital management is also the transformation of the innovation process towards combinatorial innovation. The classic "supply-side" approach to inventive activity proposed at the beginning of the 20th century by Joseph Schumpeter assumed that its first stage was an invention which was the product of creativity, often of an individual. In subsequent stages, it goes to the market and at this point there is a possibility of its dissemination, and further diffusion transforms it into a socio-economic phenomenon (Śledziewska & Włoch, 2020). Schumpeter assumed the linearity of the course of the entire process, and his approach is referred to as 3I, with three components: invention, innovation and imitation.

However, in the digital economy, the linear approach has been negated. According to W. Brian Arthur, innovations are created on the basis of other, already existing innovations; they constitute their creative combination (Arthur, 2009). This tendency was visible earlier, but its current intensification is related to the significant acceleration of the knowledge circulation, made possible by the popularization of the Internet. This acceleration is also due to the dematerialization of the main "substrate" of innovative activities, namely data. In addition, the image of an individual, isolated inventor is a thing of the past – today, innovations result from cooperation of many entities with diversified competences and sources of financing.

The literature on the subject also indicates that the use of patent information has a fundamental impact by strengthening the work efficiency of engineers and scientists, increasing the level and quality of managerial economics (e.g., by developing the competences of employees) and eliminating the trap of duplicating research, design and construction works already at a very early stage. A correctly conducted process of analyzing the patent literature makes possible:

- technology monitoring and scanning;
- in-depth technological intelligence;
- forecasting the development of technology by analyzing the directions and trends of theoretical and implementation works;
- technology evaluation from an individual perspective and assessing the competitive position of researchers, institutions, regions or countries;
- identification of those areas of knowledge that are necessary for effective R&D;
- tracking technology fusion cases and emerging new research and technology areas;
- acquiring and sharing knowledge that shapes the absorption capacity of individual entities
- use of technology from patent applications that have never been granted, have lost their legal validity in some countries or from patents for which exclusive rights have expired.

(Szatkowski, 2016)

However, it should be remembered that the effective use of patent information depends on the fulfilment of certain system conditions and having specific predispositions also on the part of the inventor. These include technological maturity, openness to new technologies and the ability to absorb them, wide dissemination of information on technical innovations, having a search system for the latest technical achievements, high dynamics of implementation and modernization of new technologies, openness to scientific and technical cooperation, the functioning of motivation systems using elements of human capital management, risk propensity, the existence of an extensive system of market research, including the interception of information about market and consumer expectations (Niklewicz-Pijaczyńska, 2019). These are the conditions that connect the system with the competences of employees in the new digital reality.

8.5 The patent system as a barrier to diffusion of innovation

Despite the above-described potential to stimulate the process of innovation diffusion, there are also significant objections against patent systems. First of all, there are voices that exaggerated respect for the principles of industrial property is increasingly limiting the innovative activity of American or European technology companies, while Chinese start-ups do not encounter such barriers. Paradoxically, the ability to quickly copy competing solutions and modify them is even considered emblematic of entrepreneurship (Lee, 2018).

However, the problem of respecting patent protection has many shades. A. Bryant, the former chairman of Intel, now at General Electric, has repeatedly mentioned this, as over 14 (!) years he was forced to fight for his patent on a light bulb with its infringers, confessing bitterly that his opponents were able to prevent him from profiting from that particular patent until the rights to it were almost useless (Teece, 2018). It should also be remembered that the scope of a patent can significantly vary depending on the statutory regulations in force in a given country – for example, in some countries, protection is given to general IT concepts and in some to specific source codes or algorithms. Thus, there is a dangerous incentive to monopolize ideas with a high degree of generality, while IT specialists who actually create a computer programme have no chance of entering the market. This is related to the increasingly frequent problem: some companies transform their business models so that they are entirely based on creating new technologies, patenting inventions and then licensing rights without manufacturing any product (Denton, 2011). These types of strategies do not pose a threat in themselves, but using licenses as a tool to influence competition does.

The American Supreme Court pointed out that the monopoly obtained through a patent is often disproportionate to the value of the technical information disclosed in the application. This is related to a significant threat, namely the practice of patent trolling: the companies with the "non-manufacturing" status buy or otherwise acquire patents, and then derive financial benefits from them, by pursuing their claims for patent infringement. In this situation, inventors frequently submit partial patent applications to preventively protect their rights and reduce the risk of a patent being obtained by third parties for solutions that improve their own inventions. Major barriers to entry arise for enterprises which, having no experience or legal and economic background, are exposed to brutal attacks by patent trolls. In the long run, this leads to disadvantageous consequences. Many inventions with great economic potential never end up in the system, while exclusive rights are granted for solutions with negligible market value, or solutions are submitted to the patent office only for strategic purposes. Levin points out that today patents rarely represent great value, except in special cases, such as new drugs, chemical products and simple mechanical inventions (Levin et al., 1987), and Mansfield asserts that many of them can be created at low cost (Mansfield, 1985; Mansfield et al., 1981).

However, the thesis presented by the American court about the harmful impact of the patent monopoly on the market is strongly rejected, among others, by D.J. Teece, arguing that patents are not self-enforcing, because they allow to capture only a fraction of the benefits that society derives from introducing innovations into the market (Teece, 2018). Also, Arrow found the monopolization argument debatable, writing:

> Patent royalties are generally so low that the profits from exploiting one's own invention are not appreciably greater than those derived from the use of others' knowledge. It really calls for some explanation, why the firm that has developed the knowledge cannot demand a greater share of the resulting profits.
>
> (Arrow, 1962; Teece, 2018)

Arrow thus indicates that in many cases imitation is often just as profitable as innovation. In the source literature, there are more and more opinions that economists often mistakenly assume automatic monopolization of the market after obtaining a patent, while due to the characteristics of the digital economy, this happens extremely rarely. Obtaining a patent depends on a complex combination of factors such as time, technical and technological standards as well as institutional conditions (Teece, 2018). Even meeting all requirements is sometimes not enough, because, as the example of Thomas Edison shows, there is no doubt that "technological DNA needs to be married to business and entrepreneurial DNA for inventors to succeed". Thus, just being a pioneer is not the path to wealth, and the legislator needs to be aware of the challenges that innovators face in gaining sufficient benefits to continue their work in the future. To sustain, a society's innovation engine should reasonably support not only the creation of value resulting from innovation but also block their capture by third parties. Otherwise, not only the motivation to undertake innovative activity will become blurred, but also the future society will suffer (Teece & Sherry, 2016).

On the other hand, a practice that is clearly dangerous for the shaping of competition in the digital age is the pursuit of patenting companies to misuse their monopolistic position by adopting prohibited practices, such as, inter alia, creating patent thickets and granting cross-licenses. The use of the patent system in this type of anti-competitive strategies, e.g., by pharmaceutical companies, disrupts the process of diffusion of innovation, leading to a reduction in the quality of life and loss of social trust in the entire system. These practices are most often used by market-dominant entities, which make them particularly dangerous. Meanwhile, in the era of digital economy, small and medium-sized enterprises (SMEs) should be supported, especially those that invest in information and communication technology (ICT) solutions. Currently, many of them are unable to oppose such practices, access data or invest in modern technologies. They also often do not have the knowledge that would allow to introduce modern solutions into their business activities. One of the ways to solve the problem is the cooperation of the state with the private sector to support business in building ICT competences, creating public-private partnerships and cooperation aimed at data exchange, for which inexpensive and reliable connectivity is essential (UN, 2019).

The doubts surrounding patenting are also related to the fact that the number of patents granted by international systems is often significantly higher than the number granted by national systems. For example, the number of patents granted by the European Patent Office (EPO) and recognized in Poland is twice as many as those granted by the Polish Patent Office. The reasons for this may be varied – a different substantive qualification of the conditions for obtaining protection rights, procedural delays or, as mentioned above, different scopes of protection. It may also indicate that entities are not interested in local patenting but in a patent with a possibly wide, supra-regional scope. This is particularly important in the case of solutions related to IT that are created globally – therefore, the process of standardizing plays a major role in the approach to patenting. In the absence of standards, companies pool their patent resources on an open basis, e.g., in the form of an open innovation network, where ideas are made available to all who use them to create free software. This is where another gap appears in terms of gaining real influence of public policy on patent issues. It should focus on awarding public contracts for solutions based on open standards, without patent risk. However, one cannot ignore the fact that researches conducted so far on the correlation between open innovation systems and the emergence of inventions indicate that such a relationship is negligible, and innovation we are dealing with in this case is primarily characterized by continuity. This may mean that while openness of innovation processes favours the diffusion of knowledge understood broadly, the development of breakthrough inventions is connected with a particularly strong relationship with research and development activities and with the traditional system of industrial property protection. This is very important because patents and other intangible assets constitute a large part of the resources owned by technology companies and the source of their competitive strength.

The argument that the level of a country's innovativeness is assessed on the basis of the number of patents is also repeatedly articulated – meanwhile, it is urgent to change the way of defining the concept of innovation, not referring it to the number of patents granted in a given field, in view of the fact that due to the frequent depreciation of patents they ceased to be a measure of the innovation value. If the idea protected by them has not been actually implemented – its benefit is negligible.

The problem that strongly links the patent system with the digital economy also lies in geographic concentration of patents in two countries: the

United States and China, which hold 75% of global patents related to blockchain technology, account for 50% of global spending on works related with the Internet of Things, 75% of the cloud technology market and 90% of market value of the largest digital platforms. The 2019 UN report highlights the growing gap between developed and developing countries. This is manifested, among others, by half the world being offline. In developing countries, only 1/5 of people use the Internet, while in developed countries it is 4/5, and in developing countries there are disparities in access to technology between women and men (UN, 2019).

On the other hand, the main accusation raised with regard to the problems with sharing patent knowledge is delays in their verification, development and publication. The remedy in this case could be the autonomization of routine activities increasing the productivity of patent officers – for example, in 2015, delays in the US patent system were recorded in 500,000 cases. The Deloitte report on the use of artificial intelligence in the American public administration emphasizes that real benefits may come from a radical reduction in the amount of paperwork focused on documenting and recording information – currently, these activities take American officials half a billion hours a year (Śledziewska & Włoch, 2020).

Moreover, the period of the granted patent exclusivity requires a thorough review. Currently, it is 20 years from the date of obtaining the patent, which, considering the dynamics of technology ageing, is an absurdly long period. In addition, despite the efforts, there is still no uniform patent database that researchers and engineers could use to search for technical knowledge and verify their solutions. However, if such a database existed, another problem related to its use would still be present – lack of universal access to inexpensive and high-speed Internet, resulting in digital exclusion of individuals and teams with enormous innovative potential that will never be realized.

Finally, it is worth while to mention another most current context in which the problem of patent policy is addressed. It is about the public discourse on the issue of introducing the "basic income". It is discussed in connection with the threat of technological unemployment being a consequence of the progressive digitalization of the economy. As rightly indicated by G. Standing, the wealth inherited nowadays by society consists primarily of intangible assets, such as intellectual property. They are a source of rent related to their natural or deliberately induced scarcity, and income generated solely by virtue of their possession goes to individuals or enterprises. Meanwhile, many patented solutions originate from publicly funded research. Many of them are based on prior knowledge and solutions. Thus, it is society that has conceived today's rent collected entirely by individuals, and it is actually society that bears the risk that intellectual property protection systems, paradoxically created by the state and international regulations, are supposed to counteract. Standing sees this situation as unfair, proposing that the intellectual exclusivity rent obtained in this way be encumbered with a kind of social dividend. It would be paid to the public as a basic income, thus becoming one of the tools to counteract the negative effects of technological unemployment (Standing, 2021).

8.6 Conclusion

Inventive activity, being the core of digital economies, is conditioned by access to data sets from various sources. However, this is often not possible, because technological knowledge treated as valuable intellectual property is strongly, and not always in accordance with the rules of competition, protected against use by third parties. The way to solve the above problem may be to change the rules and improve the functionality of patent systems that constitute a unique set of advanced engineering knowledge necessary for the creation of new solutions. The goal is to improve its functionality in such a way that it responds to the needs of the innovation market more effectively than before. This is necessary because patent systems in their current structure allow access to the knowledge necessary to create new solutions, but at the same time they significantly block the process of their further diffusion. Therefore, the proposed changes aim at the implementation of several recommendations. First, strengthening the network effect – the more users of the patent resources, the greater the effectiveness of those resources and their ability to attract further innovators. Second, strengthening the role of patent databases by raising the possibilities for global data collection, verification, control and analysis. Third, building user loyalty through a wide range of services and opportunities that over time will make withdrawal from the system unprofitable, and often too risky. Fourth, reviewing its rules so that when patents are granted, they encourage their holders to share intellectual property, convinced that their interests are sufficiently protected.

When designing these changes, it should be remembered that the described problem is complex. Any modifications undertaken in this respect should be implemented with caution and after careful analysis of empirical data from many interrelated research areas. However, the introduction of such modifications is both reasonable and necessary in view of the huge potential of patent databases that are distinguished from other shared knowledge resources by several characteristics. These include the obligation to provide technical data in the scope of the requested protection, free-of-charge provision of unique information, ongoing updating of the global state of the art, substantive verification of documentation and providing data from a very long period, which enables data aggregation at any level and the use of IT tools facilitating knowledge flow regardless of geographical constraints. This makes patent databases an exceptionally useful resource for the diffusion of innovation, which are a substrate and a condition for further expansion of the digital economy.

References

7 European Public Service Union (2015). A new Digital Agenda for Europe: 2015. eu. https://eur-lex.europa.eu/legal-content/EN/TXT/PDF/?uri=CELEX:52010IP0133&from=EN

Acs, Z.J. & Audretsch, D.B. (1989). Patents as a Measure of Innovative Activity. *Kyklos*, *42*(2), 171–180. https://doi.org/10.1111/j.1467-6435.1989.tb00186.x.

Arrow, K.J. (1962). Comment. In R.R. Nelson (Ed.), *The Rate and the Direction of Inventive Activity: Economic and Social Factors* (pp. 353–358). Princeton University Press. https://www.jstor.org/stable/j.ctt183pshc.

Arthur, B.W. (2009). *The Nature of Technology: What It Is and How It Evolves*. Free Press. ISBN: 1416544062.

Audretsch, D.B. (1995). Intellectual Property Rights: New Research Directions. In H. Albach & S. Rosenkranz (Eds.), *Intellectual Property Rights and Global Competition. Towards a New Synthesis* (pp. 36–74). WZB Berlin. Available at: https://www.piie.com/publications/chapters_preview/5072/05iie5072.pdf.

Biga, B. (2017). Niedoceniane-przeceniane zasoby niematerialne przedsiębiorstwa. In B. Biga, H. Izdebski & J. Hausner (Eds.), *Open Eyes Book 2*. Fundacja GAP. Available at: https://oees.pl/en/materialy-do-pobrania/?doing_wp_cron=1688139339.6876430511474609375000.

Brynjolfsson, E., Rock, D. & Syverson, C. (2018). *AI and the Modern Productivity Paradox: a Clash of Expectations and Statistics*. MIT IDE Research Brief. http://ide.mit.edu/sites/default/files/publications/IDE%20Research%20Brief_v0118.pdf.

Dahlman, C., Mealy, S. & Wermelinger, M. (2016). *Harnessing the Digital Economy for Developing Countries*. OECD. http://www.oecd-ilibrary.org/docserver/download/4adffb24-en.pdf.

Denton, A. (2011). Intellectual Property Rights in Today's Digital Economy. *GSR11 Discussion Paper*. International Telecommunications Union. https://www.itu.int/ITU-D/treg/Events/Seminars/GSR/GSR11/documents/05-Intellectual-property-E.pdf.

Ernst, H. (2003). Patent Information for Strategic Technology Management. *World Patent Information*, *3*, 233–242. https://doi.org/10.1016/S0172-2190(03)00077-2.

Firlej, K. & Żmija, D. (2014). Transfer wiedzy i dyfuzja innowacji jako źródło konkurencyjności przedsiębiorstw przemysłu spożywczego w Polsce. Uniwersytet Ekonomiczny w Krakowie. Available at: https://depot.ceon.pl/bitstream/handle/123456789/6732/Ksi%20%20ka-K.-Firlej-D.-%20mija-Transfer-wiedzy-i-dyfuzja-innowacji-jako-%20rod%20o-konkurencyjno%20ci-przedsi%20biorstw-przemys%20u-spo%20ywczego-w-Polsce.pdf?sequence=4.

Haeussler, C., Harhoff, D. & Mueller, E. (2014). How Patenting Informs VC Investors – The Case of Biotechnology. *Research Policy*, *8*, 1286–1298. https://doi.org/10.1016/j.respol.2014.03.012.

Jaffe, A., Fogarty, M.S. & Banks, B.A. (1998). Evidence from Patents and Patent Citations on the Impact of NASA and Other Federal Labs on Commercial Innovation. *Journal of Industrial Economics*, *46*(2), 183–205. https://www.jstor.org/stable/117548.

Jaffe, A., Trajtenberg, M. & Henderson, R. (1993). Geographic Localization of Knowledge Spillovers as Evidenced by Patent Citations. *Quarterly Journal of Economics*, *108*(3), 577–598. https://doi.org/10.2307/2118401.

Jeon, J., Lee, C. & Park, Y. (2011). How to Use Patent Information to Search Potential Technology Partners in Open Innovation. *Journal of Intellectual Property Rights*, *5*, 385–393. Available at: https://nopr.niscpr.res.in/bitstream/123456789/12688/1/JIPR%2016(5)%20385-393.pdf.

Johnson, D.K.N. (2002). The OECD Technology Concordance (OTC): Patents by Industry of Manufacture and Sector of Use. *OECD Science, Technology and Industry Working Papers 5*. OECD Publishing. https://doi.org/10.1787/521138670407.

Keller, W. (2001). Knowledge spillovers at the world's technology frontier. *Center for Economic Policy Research*. https://repec.cepr.org/repec/cpr/ceprdp/Dp2815.pdf

Kinsella, S. (2001). Against Intellectual Property. *Journal of Libertarian Studies*, *15*(2), 1–53. https://www.movingtofreedom.org/journals/jls/15_2/15_2_1.pdf.

Krasser, R. & Bernhard, W. (2008). *Patentrecht. Ein Lehr und Handbuch zum deutschen Patent und Gebrauchmusterecht. Europäischen und Internationalen Patentrecht*. C.H.Beck. ISBN: 3406555055.

Lanjouw, J., Pakes, A. & Putnam, J. (1998). How to Count Patents and Value Intellectual Property: The Uses of Patent Renewal and Application Data. *Journal of Industrial Economics*, *46*(4), 405–432. https://doi.org/10.1111/1467-6451.00081.

Lee, K.F. (2018). *AI Superpowers: China, Silicon Valley, and the New World Order*. Houghton Mifflin Harcourt. ISBN: 132854639X.

Levin, R.C., Klevorick, A.K., Nelson, R.R., Winter, S.G., Gilbert, R. & Griliches, Z. (1987). Appropriating the Returns from Industrial Research and Development. *Brookings Papers on Economic Activity*, *1987*(3), 783–831. Available at: https://www.brookings.edu/wp-content/uploads/1987/12/1987c_bpea_levin_klevorick_nelson_winter_gilbert_griliches.pdf.

Mansfield, E. (1985). How Rapidly Does New Industrial Technology Leak Out? *Journal of Industrial Economics*, *34*(2), 217–223. https://doi.org/10.2307/2098683.

Mansfield, E., Schwartz, M. & Wagner, S. (1981). Imitation Costs and Patents: An Empirical Study. *Economic Journal*, *91*(364), 907–918. https://doi.org/10.2307/2232499.

Newton, W. & Partington, C.F. (1830). Full Descriptions of Principles and Details of Every New Patent, also Original Communications on Objects Connected with Science and Philosophy, Particularly Such as Embrace the Most Recent Inventions and Discoveries. *The London Journal of Arts and Sciences*, *IV*(XIX). https://books.google.pl/books?id=1UgEAAAAQAAJ&pg.

Niklewicz-Pijaczyńska, M. (2019). *System patentowy w gospodarowaniu wiedzą. Ekonomia wiedzy technicznej skodyfikowanej*. E-Wydawnictwo. Prawnicza i Ekonomiczna Biblioteka Cyfrowa. https://doi.org/10.34616/23.19.019.

Okoń-Horodyńska, E., Sierotowicz, T. & Wisła, R. (2012). *Pomiar aktywności patentowej gałęzi gospodarki z wykorzystaniem tablic konkordancyjnych*. PTE. ISBN: 978-83-88700-60-6.

OECD (2018). *The Seoul Declaration for the Future of the Internet Economy*. 18.06.2018 Ministerial Session. https://www.oecd.org/digital/consumer/40839436.pdf.

Oslo Manual (2018). *Guidelines for Collecting, Reporting and Using Data on Innovation* (4th edition). OECD Publishing. https://doi.org/10.1787/9789264304604-en.

Parker, G.G., Van Alstyne, M.W. & Choudary, S.P. (2016). *How Networked Markets Are Transforming the Economy-and How to Make Them Work for You*. W. W. Norton & Company. ISBN: 0393249131.

Popp, D. (2005). Lessons from Patents: Using Patents to Measure Technological Change in Environmental Models. *Ecological Economics*, *54*(2–3), 209–226. https://doi.org/10.1016/j.ecolecon.2005.01.001.

Radomska, E. (2019). Rozwój gospodarki cyfrowej i społeczeństwa cyfrowego w aspekcie dynamicznych zmian w otoczeniu zewnętrznym na przykładzie Wielkiej Brytanii. https://doi.org/10.26399/meip.1(64).2019.05/e.radomska, https://mysl.lazarski.pl/fileadmin/user_upload/oficyna/Mysl_Ekonomiczna_i_Polityczna/meip-64/Mysl_EiP_1-19_9Radomska.pdf.

Ray, G.F. (1969). The Diffusion of New Technology. *National Institute Economic Review*, *48*(1), 40–83. https://doi.org/10.1177/002795016904800105.

Rogers, E.M. (2003). *Diffusion of Innovations*. Free Press. ISBN: 0743222091.

Standing, G. (2021). *Dochód podstawowy. Jak możemy sprawić by się udało*. Wydawnictwo Krytyki Politycznej. ISBN: 978-83-665-8641-3.

Szatkowski, K. (2016). *Zarządzanie innowacjami i transferem technologii*. PWN. ISBN: 9788301185404.

Śledziewska, K. & Włoch, R. (2020). *Gospodarka cyfrowa. Jak nowe technologie zmieniają świat*. Wydawnictwo Uniwersytetu Warszawskiego. Available at: https://delab.uw.edu.pl/wp-content/uploads/2020/04/Katarzyna-%C5%9Aledziewska-Renata-W%C5%82och-Gospodarka-cyfrowa.pdf.

Tapscott, D. (1995). *The Digital Economy. Rethinking Promise and Peril in the Age of Networked Intelligence*. McGraw-Hill. ISBN: 0070622000.

Teece, D.J. & Sherry, E.F. (2016). *The IEEE's New IPR Policy: Did the IEEE Shoot Itself in the Foot and Harm Innovation?* http://businessinnovation.berkeley.edu/wp-content/uploads/2014/07/14-The-IEEEs-New-Policy_Teece_Sherry_8-3-16_2_Clean.pdf.

Teece, D.J. (2018). *Profiting from Innovation in the Digital Economy: Standards, Complementary Assets, and Business Models in the Wireless World*. https://escholarship.org/content/qt58h69717/qt58h69717.pdf

Toffler, A. (1998). *Szok przyszłości*. Wydawnictwo Zysk i S-ka.

UN (2019). *Digital Economy Report*. https://cyberpolicy.nask.pl/wp-content/uploads/2019/12/Digital-Economy-Report-2019_analiza-CyberPolicy.pdf.

Wendt, J. (2010). Model dyfuzji innowacji i inne problemy badań w geopolityce i geostrategii. In J.A. Wendt & Z. Lach (Eds.), *Geopolityka. Elementy teorii, wybrane metody i badania*. Instytut Geopolityki. Available at: http://geopolityka.net/wp-content/uploads/2012/05/Geopolityka_Elementy_teorii.pdf.

World International Property Organisation [WIPO] (2013). STANDARD ST.9. Recommendation Concerning Bibliographic Data on and Relating to Patents and SPCS. *Handbook on Industrial Property Information and Documentation*, 3.9.0–3.9.12. http://www.wipo.int/export/sites/www/standards/en/pdf/03-09-01.pdf.

Varian, H. (2009). *Hal Varian on How the Web Challenges Managers*. McKinsey & Company High Tech. https://www.mckinsey.com/industries/technology-media-and-telecommunications/our-insights/hal-varian-on-how-the-web-challenges-managers.

Part III

Nature of resources

9 Behind the transparency of 'data reuse'

Beata Mäihäniemi[1]

9.1 Introduction

Anna is joining a Facebook group on postpartum depression and then, shortly afterwards, sees a link to an article on how walks in nature fight depression. She clicks on it and it takes her to third-party's website that is connected to Facebook by a 'like' button. Facebook may deduct from this combo a piece of very sensitive information about her personal health that she would not like to be revealed later on and to be eventually sold to advertisers. Moreover, in some cases, the act of data repackaging will not affect only Anna, but several other users. When the data she reveals results from her interaction with other users, she will then reveal data not only about herself but also about her Facebook friends.

The situation described above could be classified as 'repacking data'. It happens when data from at least two separate sources once gathered for different purposes, and in different settings, is combined into a bundle to create a new piece of information that may, as a result, become sensitive information, which can be sold later on.

This chapter focuses on political economy of data use, and its economic and distributional outcomes. I argue here that the choice of a data governance model may also have political implications. As most of the gatekeepers are US-based companies and the applicable regulations are imposed in the EU, home to only few (if any) gatekeepers (large online platforms). Moreover, allowing the continuation of the rights-based approach, with the consent mechanism as its main core, means approving further commodification of data and data harvesting. Users may not be aware of the consequences of consenting to such a repackaging. Instead, giving preference to data commons would allow more companies, also small and medium-sized, to benefit from data pools and increased data sharing and not rely on self-preferences of users that can largely be biased or manipulated.

The regulatory options for tackling data repackaging will vary, depending very much on whether this data repackaging happens in the spirit of seeing data as a commodity or commons which is a starting point for the discussion in this chapter. Moreover, it seems that there is a need to introduce some

DOI: 10.4324/9781003450160-13

rules of thumb for data repackaging. As it will be shown, repackaging data differs significantly from repackaging physical goods, therefore minimal requirements for providing information on the origin of datasets when repackaging sensitive data are needed. These are also elaborated on in this chapter. Finally, I reflect on the current state of regulation and give some recommendations as to direction in which it should develop to capture the benefits of collective data governance.

9.2 Gatekeepers, consent mechanisms and data repackaging

Major problems may arise where extensive data repackaging is done through intermediaries and by gatekeepers. A gatekeeper is a dominant online platform within the meaning of Article 3 of the Digital Markets Act (hereinafter the DMA), which sets out the conditions for the designation of gatekeepers. A gatekeeper must cumulatively fulfil the following three conditions. First, it must have a significant impact on the internal market. Second, it must operate a core platform service which serves as an important gateway for business users to reach end users; and third, it should enjoy an entrenched and durable position in its operations, or foreseeably enjoy such a position in the near future (DMA, 2022, Article 3[1]).

Data repackaging by gatekeepers is done mostly to monetize further on the already gathered data. As mentioned earlier, 'repacking data' happens when data from at least two separate sources once gathered for different purposes and, in different settings, is combined into a bundle to create a new piece of information that may, as a result, become sensitive information, which can be sold later on.

While the goals of many gatekeepers are highly altruistic, this may not be the reality in practice. For example, Google claims to be aiming at 'maximizing access to information' (Google, n.d.). Google also states that

> Google's mission is to organize the world's information and make it universally accessible and useful. That's why Search makes it easy to discover a broad range of information from a wide variety of sources.
>
> (ibid.)

Similarly, Facebook states that it is 'building a community and bringing the world closer together' (Facebook, n.d.). Nevertheless, despite their altruistic goals, these dominant online platforms have become major data refineries, where producing knowledge is only a secondary goal, while their primary goal is producing wealth. This is accomplished by facilitating new ways of extracting data, data collection and monetizing users' choices and behaviours (Cohen, 2019, p. 71). Such data collection is enabled by the so-called digital unconscious, which denotes a situation where users' vulnerabilities, such as moods, health, stress levels and professional or personal success, are taken advantage of to manipulate and discriminate against them. This in turn diminishes their privacy, identity and autonomy (Hildebrandt, 2015, p. 65).

Therefore, on the one hand, it may be unclear where and for what purposes our data is being collected and reused in the future.

As long as 'private interest of data controllers is prioritized over public interest; and this is true for both personal and non personal data' (Zygmuntowski et al., 2021, p. 13), data flow will remain impeded. Personal sovereignty, self-determination over data and digital emancipation promise conscious citizens, however, due to inequalities, users' data is sold on uneven and non-transparent terms (ibid., p. 20). Users are given a choice to consent to the large platform gathering their data, but this choice is weak. In a data economy, users seem to be treated as resources 'to be themselves cultivated, processed, and consumed' (Cohen, 2019, p. 71).

An approach where data owners are (seemingly) given control over their data as a personal object and individually decide on selling their information is questionable, especially when dealing with large dominant online platforms, although most platforms rely on consent, which also has its roots in the idea of autonomy. However, even where consumers receive a consent notice or privacy policy which informs them about data collection, storage and processing, they only have a choice to agree directly or indirectly (Nouwens et al., 2020, p. 1). Moreover, our choices do not always reflect our real personal preferences. At worst, online platforms manipulate us into keeping the data flowing, fuelling an information-hungry business model. That manipulation often results from so-called dark patterns in platform design (Waldman 2020, p. 107).

Relying on consent as a basis for data collection allows gatekeepers to gather enormous amounts of data that will stay under private ownership and therefore will not feed to data flow to sufficient extent. As pointed out by Waldman (2020), 'consent cannot operate in a world of passive, secret data collection' (p. 106). Some attempts to circumvent this problem have already been made at the EU level. For example, Article 5(8) of the DMA addresses tying the performance of a contract or a service to a request for consent to process personal data that is not necessary for the performance of that contract and service, i.e., the fact that the consent is given due to information asymmetry between the user and the gatekeeper.

Moreover, some forms of data governance would work better in addressing abundance of data and the problem with consent being an insufficient solution to excessive unfair data collection. Therefore, Kerber (2021) proposes to apply a solution of 'open data', where data is seen as something similar to commons, an infrastructure that is based on the non-rival character of data (ibid., p. 12). Similarly, Cohen (2019) evaluates a solution of 'governance of commons' that offers specific rules for keeping a resource open to community affiliates. Such a solution may also offer rules on how to use the resource responsibly and sanctions for abusing the affiliation to the commons (ibid., p. 63).

9.3 Is personal data a commodity or commons?

A discussion is ongoing whether data is private property (a commodity) or a commons, which is a traditional economic distinction. Actually, in terms of both, we can identify property rights, however, they are much more complex when it comes to commons as it has been pointed out by Ostrom (1990). In this part, I will first refer to economic arguments related to classifying data as private property or as commons. As it will be shown, to address and possibly limit the reuse of data by gatekeepers, the nature of data has to be understood, and there is a need to refrain from treating data as anything approximating commodity.

When it comes to the idea of data as private property, a commodity – this is dubious, since data is not autonomous (Zygmuntowski et al., 2021, p. 9). Data can be defined as a 'mere technology-based recording of reality, [that] may misrepresent, oversimplify, or distort it. Nevertheless, digital systems rely on input to function' (ibid.). Commodified data would then be distanced from the individuals who provided it or from the social relations and value creating process it comes from (Jessop, 2007, p. 115).

There is a wide discussion about whether personal data can be seen as a kind of property (see e.g., Chrobak, 2018) and can carry property rights, leaning towards the conclusion that data will probably not be treated as property. Property rights can be defined as 'exclusive authority to determine how a resource is used, whether that resource is owned by government or by individuals' (Alchian 2018) (see also Demsetz, 2002, 1967).

According to Käll (2020), data cannot be captured as an object of property alone or by a traditional understanding of property, since data is constantly dematerialized and produced in such a way that it can be captured as an object of economy and law (ibid., pp. 1–2). Unlike traditional property, data is an object that is disconnected from something material; it is a resource that is extracted but can belong to a data subject (ibid., p. 6). Second, data, unlike traditional property objects, holds 'affective control', meaning that it can simultaneously create and oversee effects (ibid., pp. 8–9). For example, data that is gathered on a consumer can then be repackaged and used for further nudging of this consumer's behaviour in a direction desired by a data collector (ibid.). Where data, like any other information, can be both an input and output of its production process, this makes property rights and market-based production a less appealing option and encourages creating further information from these data (Benkler, 2003, p. 1253).

Hildebrandt offers an approach to data that is based on property in the non-legal sense, where users' autonomy is increased by giving them more control over their data with the help of technical, legal and economic tools. These tools allow sharing, trading or monetizing data, which can be done by licensing specific data flows. Such an approach is only one of the available options next to no individual control and harm redress carried out ex post. Finally, Hildebrandt also points out the third possibility of EU-style data protection, which limits data gathering and narrows the set of purposes for which data can be gathered in a transparent way (Hildebrandt, 2015, p. 201).

According to Kerber (2021), data should not be seen as 'property' since the data 'owner' does not hold the rights to a set of data. Instead, they hold so-called bundles of rights to data, rooted in the economic theory of property rights. This concept can be applied to multiple users and hence is more suitable for a non-rivalrous resource. Therefore, preferred solutions for data governance are open data and traditional exclusive rights. Both specify and assign bundles of rights to a set (or stream) of data. They also offer detailed solutions to accommodate situations that fit between open data and traditional exclusive rights. Moreover, they tackle trade-off problems that arise in different markets and contexts where data is used. Consequently, it would be more appropriate to use the term 'governance' instead of 'property' (ibid., p. 2).

Consequently, many arguments speak against treating data as property or as a commodity. Instead, some kind of commons may offer a better way to govern data. Data as commons occurs then, if the resource is governed jointly and shared by a group of users. Governance corresponds with seeing data as a 'commons' where 'no single person has exclusive control over the use and disposition of any particular resource in the commons' (Benkler, 2003, pp. 1273–1274). Information governed as commons is unowned and free for all to use for market or non-market-based enterprises (ibid.). Sustainable commons is a result of both legal and policy endeavours (on the idea of commons, see e.g. Butler, 1982; Hardin, 1968; Rose, 1986). Additionally, it also requires developing a physical layer for the sharing of data. This would complement the option where infrastructure is owned. The idea of core, unbiased common infrastructure, open to all and used by all, could then be applied to govern information (ibid.).

If we govern data as commons, this will mean that there is a dedicated and trusted data-sharing space that has been established in the public interest. Public actors are then stewarding data (Zygmuntowski et al., 2021, p. 10). Here, public data commons could ensure that digital utilities are operated on equal terms and protected in data flows but also can be used to advance innovation and for monitoring purposes (ibid., p. 21, on data commons see also Madison et al., 2022).

According to Dulong de Rosnay and Stalder (2020), data commons are an alternative to market-based approaches and represent a situation where resources are made of data, information, culture and knowledge, while all of the resources are either created and/or maintained online. Data commons are also shared in such a way that their enclosure is limited, and everyone can access and build upon them (ibid., p. 2). The difference between these and tangible commons, such as a forest, and digital commons, such as Wikipedia or free software, is that the latter cannot be overused or materially exhausted. However, they can still be undersupplied, be protected by insufficient legal frameworks, be polluted or have poor quality or be difficult to find (ibid., p. 2).

Digital commons are about resources that are non-rival and that can be used at the same time by a number of people. They still need to be continually maintained, they can be destroyed and they need governance and participation rules (Dulong de Rosnay & Stalder, 2020, p. 7). The monitoring task includes in particular ensuring that governance rules are shared and can be translated into quality control, accountability etc. Digital commons need to be protected by legal rules from enclosure or appropriation (ibid., p. 14).

The distinction between seeing data as a commodity or commons will then affect a choice of a data governance model to address data repackaging. We can indicate several ways of governing data; it can be treated more like a commodity or commons, depending on who oversees it: individuals or public agencies, or private companies. As pointed out by Zygmuntowski et al. (2021), there is a need for change as regards data mining practices, because they are now 'failing individuals and society'.

Seeing data as a commodity strengthens asymmetries of power when data is repacked by gatekeepers based on consent from users. Instead, establishing data commons would contribute to the very much-needed institutional and trust-based mechanism for data governance, at the same time enhancing common welfare and protecting fundamental rights of individuals (ibid., p. 14).

9.4 Legal regulations and cases on data repackaging for gatekeepers

What are the current EU-wide regulations and case law on what could be referred to as repackaging?

Older tools such as the General Data Protection Regulation (2016/679; hereinafter the GDPR) or competition law offer limited means for restricting the specific use of data or the ways in which it is exploited, in particular, they are based on a right-oriented approach, so that they tend to fictionally commodify data, meaning they rely on people's own perceptions as to their privacy preferences or products/services preferences, or, as regards competition law, only work in addressing specific cases of data repackaging, in that particular context.

9.4.1 The role of GDPR

Personal data is defined in legal terms as 'any information relating to an identified or identifiable natural person' (General Data Protection Regulation, Article 4[1]). This is used as a working definition here, as an analytical tool and a legal definition, although it is not free from flaws.

The primary role in regulating the repackaging of data is still played by the GDPR. It proposes a set of rules and principles for processing data, which are applicable to both private and public companies. It has a large impact both on digital markets and on governmental practices (Lindroos-Hovinheimo, 2021). However, as pointed out by Lindroos-Hovinheimo (2021), combining data protection principles from the GDPR with data sharing or open data flows may be challenging. In particular, combining the

GDPR with the Data Governance Act which regulates data-sharing intermediaries to encourage them to facilitate data flows is one of the challenges of new regulations meeting old ones (ibid.). This is because the GDPR limits the purpose of data gathering in a certain way, for example by laying down a close set of processing options and other principles of lawfulness, fairness and transparency, data minimization, accuracy, storage limitation, integrity and confidentiality and accountability (Regulation 2016/679 [GDPR], Article 5).

However, privacy rights, including data protection regulations, can only limit specific uses of data, but not the overall exploitation and selling of data itself (Käll, 2020, p. 3). The role of the GDPR in tackling the excessive reuse of data for commercial purposes may be quite limited as a consequence. The GDPR allows the rematerialization of data by giving consumers the power to get their data back, in the form of a legal concept that makes this possible. However, it is doubtful whether these legal constructions can stop the processes of dematerialization, commodification and affective control that currently turn data into a specific form of property (or property-to-be) (ibid., pp. 9–10).

Similarly, Kerber sees control rights over personal data in the GDPR as strong only in theory, such as the possibility to exclude others from using your data by denying consent. However, the GDPR does not confer any rights to data in the way that property rights do with regard to physical property; as rights to data are not exclusive since they need to be balanced against several fundamental values and interests associated with the use of personal data, so that the processing of personal data is based on legitimate interests on the basis of Article 6(1) of the GDPR (Kerber, 2021, p. 16). Moreover, data protection seems insufficient as an aim for data governance, as different data governance models may have negative consequences; moreover, the positive network or spillover effects may be wider than privacy alone (Zygmuntowski et al., 2021, p. 11). Other aims can be put before data protection in European law, such as public interests (if promoting public interests is done in the form of parliamentary law, in a democratic way) (ibid., p. 12). Finally, the application of GDPR may prevent companies from starting to share initiatives, as they would need to apply a number of data governance techniques used to separate personal and non-personal data, and even identify and trace rights and privileges that have been granted or obtained for every piece of data (ibid., p. 13).

9.4.2 Data repackaging in light of case law on competition

There are not many case laws on repackaging in the strict sense. First, a good point of reference for the issue of repackaging from the perspective of competition law is the recent acceptance of commitments offered by Amazon to the European Commission which are barring it from using marketplace seller data and ensuring equal access to Buy Box and Prime. Amazon, 'a titan of 21st century commerce' (Kahn, 2022, p. 712), has multiple business objectives in addition to being a retailer, as it is also

> a marketing platform, a delivery and logistics network, a payment service, a credit lender, an auction house, a major book publisher, a producer of television and films, a fashion designer, a hardware manufacturer, and a leading provider of cloud server space and computing power.
>
> (ibid., p. 713)

The European Commission opened two investigations into Amazon in 2019 and 2020. The Commission's competition concerns were over Amazon's use of non-public marketplace seller data and over a possible bias in granting sellers access to its Buy Box and its Prime programme. Amazon had been collecting non-public marketplace seller data as it had been entering into standard agreements with sellers that included Amazon's right to analyze and use third-party seller data. According to the European Commission, such use of accumulated marketplace seller data could affect competition (European Commission, 2019). Amazon also gave a preferential treatment to its own retail offers and those of marketplace sellers that used Amazon's logistics and delivery services (*Amazon Marketplace* & *Amazon – Buy Box*; European Commission, 2020; European Commission, 2022a).

Instead of the Commission filing a decision finding that Amazon was using the retail data in an abusive way, Amazon voluntarily offered two rounds of commitments (Case *Amazon Marketplace*; European Commission, 2020; European Commission, 2022c) and hence was not fined. The second round commitments were made legally binding at the end of December 2022. These include the need for Amazon to ensure that independent carriers can directly contact their Amazon customers, thus being enabled to provide equivalent delivery services to those offered by Amazon (European Commission, 2022c).

The second case that can be indicated considering data repackaging is investigations into Facebook in Germany. It refers to concern about what can be done with data that has been collected on and off social media. The German Competition Authority found the practice of gathering users' data while they visit third-party websites to constitute anticompetitive exploitation of users and hence to constitute a violation of data protection rules at the same time. However, in August 2019, the Higher Regional Court of Düsseldorf reversed the ruling against Facebook. Unlike the German Competition Authority, the Court found no exploitation of users because, as it concluded, gathering users' data on third-party websites does not weaken the consumer economically nor imply a loss of control on the part of the user. Thereafter, the case went to the Federal Court which ruled that there is an abuse of dominance but that it stems from the loss of control by users (see *Judgement of the Bundeskartellamt of 6 February 2019: Facebook*, *Judgement of Oberlandesgericht Düsseldorf of 26 August 2019*; *Federal Court of Justice of Germany*, 2020; *Facebook Inc. and Others v Bundeskartellamt*, see also Wiedemann, 2020). The Higher Regional Court of Düsseldorf sent a request for a preliminary ruling to the European Court of Justice (hereinafter ECJ) on the matter of excessive data collection on third-party websites. The ECJ has, in its ruling, stressed several important issues. These include the observation that where data processing by Facebook involves special categories of data such as ones revealing racial or ethnic origin, political opinions, religious beliefs or sexual orientation, and the processing of which is in principle prohibited by the GDPR (...) (i)t will be for the national court to determine whether some of the data collected may actually allow such information to be revealed, irrespective of whether that information concerns a user of that social network or any other natural person (Court of Justice of the European Union, 2023).

The Court also clarifies that merely visiting websites and apps that may reveal sensitive information does not denote that the user wishes to reveal such an information. Similarly, where a user is entering information into third party websites or apps or clicking or tapping on buttons, that are integrated into them, these should not be used by Facebook unless the user expresses her consent for making that publicly available (ibid.). As to non-personal data, these can only be gathered by Facebook where 'data processing is objectively indispensable such that the main subject matter of the contract cannot be achieved if the processing in question does not occur' (ibid.). In the opinion of the ECJ, personalized advertising would not classify as the legitimate interest that would justify data gathering without the user's consent (ibid.).

An important question is whether competition law can limit data repackaging. This is because, as pointed out earlier, competition law is primarily designed for scarce resources, whereas data is abundant. Competition is increasingly measured by consumer prices which became its 'major metric' (Kahn, 2022, p. 720). One challenge about applying competition law to data is that the law is more suitable for physical resources. There has been much discussion on whether data can be priced and at what price. But how can data be priced if it is not scarce but abundant instead? Competition law is largely designed for resources that are countable and easy to define, ones that can be measured and monetized in economic terms. However, applying competition law to data may prove problematic. The lack of a price on data may pose challenges when it comes to defining in which relevant geographical product markets the abusive behaviour of excessive data collection has occurred, which is a crucial step in defining dominance, a prerequisite for assessing the abuse of dominance. Likewise, the essential facilities doctrine could be used as a theory of harm meaning a form of refusal to supply. However, considering the abundance of data, it may be difficult to qualify data as a facility essential for entry into the market and making contracts. Even though access to data could be granted based on the refusal to deal concept, such as the so-called exceptional circumstances test or the essential facilities doctrine (Mäihäniemi, 2020), this has not been done as yet (Mäihäniemi, 2017, pp. 36–37).

9.4.3 Digital Markets Act and data repackaging

In order to tackle the challenges arising from gatekeepers' unwanted behaviour in digital markets, the EU has also introduced an *ex-ante* regulation concerning gatekeepers' data-gathering practices. Some of the solutions include data portability, data interoperability, bans on dominant platforms combining data from third-party websites with that gathered via the main service and so forth. Many of these measures have been introduced in the sectoral regulation of online markets, such as the DMA, which only regulates gatekeepers, namely dominant online platforms (Digital Markets Act, 2022; see also Bongartz et al., 2021; de Streel & Larouche, 2021; Dunne, 2021).

The main point of the DMA is to ensure a competitive and fair market in the digital sector and to protect companies and consumers from unfair practices of the 'gatekeepers' of the EU internal market (Ministry of Finance Finland, n.d.). The DMA also promotes the high quality of digital products and services, reasonable and competitive prices and users' freedom of choice (ibid.). The DMA is only applied to carefully defined gatekeepers, to be designated by the European Commission, and which comprise dominant online platforms that were defined in part 2. In practice, this boils down to only a small number of firm, none of which is even based in Europe and many of which, although based in the US, still have their data processing infrastructure elsewhere. The European Commission has now on September 6, 2023 designated six gatekeepers under the Digital Markets Act; namely, Alphabet, Amazon, Apple, ByteDance, Meta, and Microsoft. Designation touches upon 22 different core platform services, such as Facebook, Google Maps, Amazon, etc. The gatekeepers have now half a year to comply with DMA (European Commission 2023a). Therefore, in the case of Amazon, its behaviour can be tackled using not competition law, but specific provisions of the DMA that enter into force as of early May 2023. From that time, within two months, companies providing core platform services, the list of which is provided in the DMA, have to notify the Commission and provide all relevant information. The Commission will then, within additional two months, adopt a decision designating a specific gatekeeper. Designated gatekeepers, within six months from the Commission's decision that designates them, will have to comply with the obligation laid down in the DMA (European Commission, n.d.). In particular, in the above-mentioned Amazon case, the data governance provisions contained in Article 6(2) and 6(10) of the DMA could have application.

Article 6(2) prevents data silos, namely, by stating that a gatekeeper may not use business users' non-public data to compete with them (Article 6[2] Digital Markets Act). This article is directly inspired by the Amazon investigations. Data that is not publicly available would consist of data regarding third-party sellers' listings and transactions that have been either inferred from or collected through Amazon, for the purposes of its retail operations (ibid.).

The second obligation, laid down in Article 6(10) of the DMA, requires gatekeepers to provide business users with real-time access to their data generated on the platform. This has to be done at their request, free of charge, with effective, high-quality, continuous and real-time access to (also personal) data.

These two provisions point out that data, although gathered by gatekeepers, still belongs to users and not to the online platform (Kerber, 2021, p. 21). Therefore, having rights over data does not necessarily mean owning data. Business users could still 'get real-time access to all aggregated and non-aggregated data without any limitations on how they are using it, i.e., they get a full bundle of rights on the data and are free how to use them' (ibid.). Although these obligations can be seen as necessary for protecting competition, they can also be interpreted as a decision that the de facto holder of data (here the provider of platform services) is not the 'rightful owner' of this data because it is the business users that have generated the data within their activities. This change in the assignment of the bundle of rights pertaining to this data from the platform to the business users could therefore also be justified as a matter of fairness (as the second main objective of the DMA), especially also due to the 'unequal bargaining power' situation between the gatekeeper and the business users (ibid.). The above-mentioned Amazon investigations by means of competition law measures show that the DMA could work well in addressing issues that were originally investigated based on competition law revolving around the commodity of data.

Regarding the Facebook v. Germany case, the provisions of Article 5(2) (a–d) of the DMA are directly inspired by these investigations in that they require the user's consent for combining personal data. They ban processing and use of end-users' personal data by gatekeepers. In particular, they ban processing end-users' personal data collected from third-party services for the purpose of providing online advertising services without prior consent (Article 5[2][a] DMA). This law is directly linked to the German Facebook case. Moreover, it prevents combining personal data obtained by core platform services with data obtained by any other first-party or third-party services without express user consent (Article 5[2][b] DMA). It also bans cross-use of personal data from the relevant core platform service in other services provided separately by the gatekeeper, including other core platform services and vice versa (Article 5[2][c]) as well as signing in end users to other services of the gatekeeper in order to combine personal data (Article

5[2][d]). Article 5(2) of the DMA can then be seen as a provision that regulates the reuse of data and one that gives some kind of ownership rights to the users.

9.4.4 Other regulations applicable to data repackaging

The Data Act proposal of 2022 defines the rules for sharing data, the requirements to be fulfilled for access by public bodies, international data transfers, cloud switching and interoperability. The aim of the Data Act is to give individuals and businesses more control over their IoT (Internet of Things) device data through a reinforced data portability right, copying or transferring data easily from across different services, where the data is generated through smart objects, machines and devices (European Commission, 2022b). The importance of the Data Act is comparable to that of the GDPR. While the GDPR defines the processing of personal data, the Data Act applies to all data, taking into account data protection. At best, the regulation thus creates regulatory symmetry because in practice data materials often contain both personal data and other data (Lehtonen et al., 2022).

The Data Act grants every user the right to access and port to third parties, the data generated through their use of connected products and related services (including both personal and non-personal data) (Cooper & Oberschelp de Meneses, 2022). The user is also able to share this data with third parties. However, users and third parties should not share such data with gatekeepers (within the meaning of the DMA) (Article 5[2] Proposal of Data Act). Moreover, gatekeepers may not 'solicit or commercially incentivise a user in any manner, including by providing monetary or any other compensation, to make data available to one of its services that the user has obtained pursuant to a request under Article 4(1)' (ibid., point [a]). In this manner, the Data Act effectively limits the reuse of data by gatekeepers to a significant extent, offering yet another tool that gives the user not so much a property right with regard to their data as a form of governance and limitation.

The important input of the Data Act is that it aims to tackle the power imbalance between SMEs and larger enterprises as they are

> unable to negotiate fair and balanced data-sharing agreements due to their weaker position in relation to stronger market players, but also as there are barrier to switching between competitive and trustworthy cloud and edge services in the EU, and that they do not have such a wide possibility to combine data from different sectors.'(European Commission 2023b).

For example, in Finland, a bus company recently had to re-purchase its data from the software company that built its online payment services to obtain access to the data. The Data Act could tackle such problems, without the need for the EU to delve into prioritizing data. It specifically provides that data which users have contributed, and which is accessed at the request of a third party, should not then be shared with gatekeepers.

The Digital Services Act (Regulation 2022/2065) also indirectly tackles the issue of repackaging data. It puts a ban on advertising on online platforms by profiling children (Article 28(2) DSA) or based on special categories of personal data such as ethnicity, political views or sexual orientation (Article 4[13], 4[14] and 4[15], and Article 9 and Recitals [51] to [56] of the GDPR). It aims at increased transparency of all forms of advertising on online platforms and influencers' commercial communications.

Non-commercial use of data is regulated in the recent Data Governance Act (hereinafter DGA, Regulation 2022/868). The DGA regulates the reuse of data held by public sector bodies, such as state, regional or local authorities. It lays down rules facilitating data sharing, especially between gatekeepers and the public sphere to advance public well-being. The aim of the Data Governance Act is then to regulate the reuse of specific kinds of protected public-sector data and to encourage data altruism to boost the data economy (Council of the EU, 2022a). This can be described as a data cooperative where individuals are encouraged to share their data for mutual, public benefit and qualified as non-commercial use of data. Specific mechanisms enabling the reuse of data, which are created by the Data Governance Act, include a common European data space and an interoperable internal data market. Small and medium-sized enterprises will also benefit from better data interoperability, standardization and simplified access to public sector data (ibid.).

9.4.5 Overview of regulations

In this part, it is shown that the GDPR or competition law, which is very much based on the idea of commodifying data, is not the optimal solution for data governance in the case of repackaging. When data is owned and controlled (either by individuals who create it or by private dominant companies who gather it) a number of issues arise. Newly introduced regulations, such as the DMA, give data users more power over their data and promote collaborative projects using data, and prevent gatekeepers from obstructing such activities, but they do not encourage data pools or data sharing. New regulations, such as the Data Act, give users the right to access their data and share it, but without indicating a property right to data.

However, the DMA places limitations on what gatekeepers can do with data obtained through the main services they provide, as they operate as two-sided platforms, connecting businesses and regular online users. For example, data governance arrangements should include a ban on using customers' business data to expand gatekeeper's core services and on combining data from the core service with data obtained from third-party services that are connected to a gatekeeper by an advertising campaign.

However, the DGA goes a step further and in fact advocates some kind of data commons and collective data governance.

9.5 Rules of thumb for transparent repackaging of data

9.5.1 Challenges to assessing the origins of datasets. Repackaging physical goods v. data

When personal data is repackaged by gatekeepers, it becomes increasingly non-transparent as no mention of its origin is provided. This situation contrasts with repackaging traditional (physical) goods, where information is usually provided on the package. Information on the package of a physical article would at least include basic information on the product in the language of the country of destination, what the product is made of, its expiration date and so on. When data is repackaged and many datasets are often combined, there is no information on what the new datasets are composed of, where they originate from and so forth. In particular, gatekeepers should increase transparency when it comes to operations that consist in processing sensitive data. This includes information on the origins of datasets being repackaged. Thus far, only the ways in which the data is gathered, the rules on which data should not be gathered, or the limiting principles on data have been presented (General Data Protection Regulation, Articles 5 and 6, the essential facilities doctrine in competition law, refusal to deal, etc.).

Assessing the origin of datasets may be difficult for several reasons. First, data is not pure, raw information about the user, but more the result of interactions with people (Evans, 2022). There can be several interactions involving several sets of data, which results in even more interactions. Raw data is a rare occurrence (see e.g., Gitelman, 2013). Moreover, where data is pre-cooked in advance, and framed for further use for different purposes, physical structures and the law may further blur its nature, dematerialize it and leave it unprotected and vulnerable. Picturing data as a resource that can easily be 'extracted' renders the infrastructures used in its objectification invisible (Käll, 2020, p. 6). This demonstrates a need to make the infrastructure and the law more transparent.

Second, data is also non-rivalrous and can therefore be used simultaneously by multiple users, and for different purposes at the same time. Consequently, there is a need to acknowledge the different purposes of data and its benefits outside the market (Käll, 2020, p. 4). If we wish to use data outside the market as well, then we may need to reconsider and possibly rematerialize it (ibid.). Hence, where data can be used in many different ways in the future, this means that it may be difficult to assess its quality or it can be assessed only in a specific context.

Unlike the repackaging of data, repackaging physical goods does not involve dealing with the issues of pre-cooking, abundance or non-rivalrous goods. Physical goods are scarce and some of them may require special protection by laws on intellectual property rights or competition. However, would such transparency of origin work in cases where non-physical goods and abundant goods are repackaged? It seems that due to the abundance of data, it would not be practical to require that every time datasets made of personal data are repackaged, information on their context should be provided. Such transparency would be recommended and should preferably be mandated by law when the dataset contains sensitive personal information or data from areas where digital literacy is at a relatively low level.

Sensitive data would be understood as personal data revealing racial or ethnic origin, political opinions and religious or philosophical beliefs; trade-union membership; genetic data, biometric data processed solely to identify a human being; health-related data or data concerning a person's sex life or sexual orientation (European Commission, b.; Article 4[13], [14] and [15], and Article 9 and Recitals [51] to [56] of the GDPR; see also e.g. Google judgement on how they defined data [*Lloyd v Google LLC.*]). If there are doubts about whether data is sensitive, then it should be classified as such (*OT v Vyriausioji tarnybinės etikos komisija*, see also Brautigam, 2022). The preliminary ruling in the case OT v. Vyriausioji tarnybinės etikos komisija analyzed, among other things, the question of whether publishing the name of a spouse constitutes revealing sensitive data, as in this case it appeared that the couple were not heterosexual. Where such data is published online, it can then be used for other, secondary uses and affect the fundamental rights of a person (ibid).

Where (also sensitive) data is reused without the permission of a user and the user is not sufficiently informed about where data has been gathered and reused, such behaviour could then be categorized as an exploitative abuse of dominance, e.g. exploitative business terms as demonstrated in the German investigations of Facebook practices that we have mentioned previously in this chapter. Here, the issue of gathering a user's sensitive data on a third-party website that is connected to Facebook, for example through a 'like' button, and combining it with other personal data gathered on Facebook's main social media website can be problematic. The Oberlandesgericht Düsseldorf (a higher court) raised this issue in one of its questions addressed to the European Court of Justice in its request for a preliminary ruling (*Facebook Inc. and Others v. Bundeskartellamt*, 2021). The Oberlandesgericht Düsseldorf asked

> If an internet user merely visits websites or apps (…) such as flirting apps, gay dating sites, political party websites or health-related websites, or also enters information into them, for example when registering or when placing orders, and another undertaking, such as Facebook Ireland, uses interfaces integrated into those websites and apps, such as 'Facebook Business Tools', or cookies or similar storage technologies placed on the internet user's computer or mobile device, to collect data about those visits to the websites and apps and the information

> entered by the user, and links those data with the data from the user's Facebook.com account and uses them, does this collection and/or linking and/or use involve the processing of sensitive data for the purpose of that provision?
>
> (ibid., q 2a).

What is more, the Oberlandesgericht Düsseldorf was also concerned about consent given to a dominant undertaking such as Facebook (ibid., q 6). The GDPR provides the basis for consent for data reuse. Consent as to data collection is defined in Articles 6 and 7 of the GDPR. However, where consent for data collection is given to a gatekeeper, it may be questionable whether such consent is strong enough to be valid. This can be concluded from the German investigations of Facebook as well as the Guidelines on consent (European Data Protection Board, 2020). The latter state that where there is an asymmetry of power, for example when we are dealing with public companies, then this consent could be seen as weak due to such asymmetry (ibid., para. 16). Similar conclusions could be drawn in a situation where a user is facing a gatekeeper. In its ruling on Google Search, the General Court compared Google to a public company (*Google and Alphabet v Commission*). Therefore, based on a clearly visible asymmetry of power, we could conclude that the consent given to Google (or any other gatekeeper) may be weak and its validity duly questionable.

Excessive data collection, as in the case of Facebook, is conducted without the consent of users and carried out in such a way that the data on the activities of users on third-party websites may be combined with the data collected on the main social media, which must be deemed problematic (see e.g. Mäihäniemi, 2022a; Mäihäniemi, 2022b). There is a concern that excessive data collection is an abuse of dominance and is inconsistent with the GDPR, or is detrimental to users because they cannot determine how their data is used. However, the case does not explore repackaging in detail and the need for increased transparency regarding this operation. It focuses instead on the way in which data is excessively collected. It does, however, investigate the issue of consent for the dominant undertaking to gather data and stresses that this consent might be 'weak'. It also questions whether gathering sensitive data is the right way to proceed (*Facebook Inc. and Others v Bundeskartellamt*). This investigation concerns an abuse of dominance that would not only consist of exploitative business terms but also refers to data protection regulations.

9.5.2 *Minimum requirements for repackaging data*

What then would be the bare minimum in terms of information to be provided while repackaging data? Requirements on providing the 'origin' of repackaged data could significantly increase the transparency of the process of repackaging itself. However, it may be challenging to identify all the ingredients in datasets without conducting a detailed analysis with the assistance of computer scientists. Furthermore, data may be provided in different formats and these technical difficulties may blur the transparency of data repackaging. The origin of data, similarly to a country of origin in the case of traditional physical goods, is the context in which the data were originally collected. The context always changes and is specific to the use of a given dataset.

Minimum requirements on transparency regarding the context of data collection and the further reuse of datasets could bring much-needed clarity to the context in which a dataset is repackaged and indicate whether increased protection of such a dataset is needed. This solution would work as a pre-scan to assess the possible issues that may arise with regard to sensitive personal data, or data originating from developing countries. It would also address the abundance of data, as not all of the datasets would have to be 'pre-scanned', excluding, e.g., the cases where datasets are repackaged between different countries, companies and so on in an effort to boost the European economy. As competition law rules were created for the free movement of goods and services when the European Union was conceived, creating one's own rules for data repackaging could similarly boost the EU economy.

To accompany the context requirements for the reuse of sensitive data and data gathered in areas where digital literacy is still developing, some form of protection against repackaging such sensitive datasets without the knowledge and consent of the holder of an original dataset should be offered.

In the case L'Oréal SA et al. v. eBay et al. (C-324/09), the original package of a physical article, namely luxurious perfume produced by L'Oréal SA, had been removed and the product was sold online in third countries where the trademark was not registered, through the online marketplace eBay. The question arose as to whether eBay should be responsible for infringing L'Oréal SA et al.'s trademark right. In connection with the case, the High Court of England put several preliminary questions to the Court of Justice of the European Communities (today's European Union), asking, for example, whether the removal of boxes or other outer packaging from perfumes and cosmetics without the consent of a holder of a trademark gives the trademark holder the right to oppose the commercialization of unboxed products (*L'Oréal SA and Others v eBay International AG and Others*, opinion of Advocate General Jääskinen, delivered on 9 December 2010). According to Jääskinen, these second-hand transactions and offers of cosmetic products may be allowed, and legal users of a trademark cannot be opposed, as in the context of durable goods such as cars and boats. These transactions would be of a non-commercial nature.

This case could be interpreted in such a way that sensitive datasets could only be reused without the consent of the original holder for non-commercial use. It should then be obligatory to provide information on the context when dealing with datasets that include sensitive data or ones gathered in geographical areas that are not yet advanced in terms of digital literacy. Provided that such data could be used for non-commercial purposes such as research. However, as with data spaces and data altruism, companies could decide to enforce such a positive code of conduct and follow good practice. This approach could then spread voluntarily throughout data-based industries but would require a legal framework for its adoption.

9.6 How applicable legislation evolves and how it changes business dynamics in Europe and elsewhere?

As stressed in this chapter, many of the older regulations, such as competition law, try to address data as a commodity and it does not seem to work optimally since detaching data from its context is a dubious endeavour. However, it may be extremely difficult to make a shift in the EU towards a collective data governance model. This is because a consent mechanism has been allegedly lobbied for by gatekeepers, and it seems to ensure they are able to gather large amounts of data for further repackaging. Once the consent mechanism and commodifying data have become a new form of a preferred, 'default' option for dealing with gatekeepers, and there are actually no other options to replace them, then it seems that the concept of data as commons may offer a good alternative for solving the problem, however, it would require designing a brand-new network of data intermediaries.

The role of the public sector cannot be underestimated. It can offer a trust-based mechanism, rules as well as additional laws to accommodate data sharing in a collective manner. It can operate both as a facilitator and custodian, offering governance rules and at the same time enforcing these (Zygmuntowski et al., 2021. p. 19). The use of intermediary indicates that there exists a new trustworthy sharing mechanism (Janssen et al., 2020). However, creating a new form of data intermediaries on a large scale would require substantial resources as well as regulation to support the operation of such intermediaries. Governance by a public sector is not unproblematic either, as it would need to adhere to extremely high standards of responsibility, legal criteria etc.

The extension of digital rights to include collective ones, where trust is placed in collective governance of data is already designed for public institutions in the EU to some extent. Here, the EU could pave the way for other jurisdictions. While gatekeepers are now being targeted with new regulations that offer a new way to deal with data – data governance, some of the solutions are advancing collective rights more than others, e.g., the idea of 'data altruism' and creating common data spaces. The idea of 'data altruism' originates from the Data Governance Act and means that an individual can voluntarily donate their personal data for common interest. This will be accomplished through 'personal data spaces', where data is only used for purposes agreed to by the individuals donating the data, such as medical research (Dr2 Consultants, 2020). However, the idea of data altruism and data governance requires specific tools and specific questions to be tackled. This involves increasing the transparency of the origins of datasets that are being repackaged, and perhaps the possibility of covering at least sensitive datasets with some form of protection, such as a bundle of rights or an identifier akin to a trademark.

The choice of data governance model largely depends on a political setting, as we can observe the so-called systems competition between commercial data governance in the form of American companies, that are mostly very large online platforms or very large search engines, and the European model that claims to give a user more self-determination over the use of their data but in fact gives scarce possibilities that are restricted to data protection. In China, we can observe politically controlled system that is governed by a party. In the US, it is driven mostly by market forces (see e.g., Bradford 2023).

Changing the default of the data governance model, consent, can be seen as an attack on American companies and generally as a political move as have been seen by many recent endeavours of the European Union. This is very much due to the fact that Europe itself does not have its own large online platforms, except for example SAP. Further changes to data governance model, which has been popular as gatekeepers were able to take advantage of a weak consent due to asymmetry of power, may be political in nature and perhaps could lead to the exit of most of the gatekeepers from Europe. However, economic and distributional outcomes, such as a choice to regulate data as a commodity or commons or repackaging data using higher standards than in the case of physical goods, have important implications for our ability to safely increase the data flow, increase the competitiveness of small- and medium-sized enterprises and allow competition with gatekeepers and should be therefore advanced by the European Union on a larger scale to show the lead for other jurisdictions. The US has already followed European footsteps with the increasing regulation of online platforms by Biden's antitrust team: Lina Khan, Tim Wu and Jonathan Kanter, however, it is doubtful it will also reach a status of a regulatory empire such as the EU.

The EU's lead in global platform/data regulation affects certain economic and distributional outcomes of policy on data. This could be seen as a process of 'unilateral regulatory globalization' where a single state's law and regulations are transplanted to other jurisdictions, affecting their legal standards. The law and regulations can then migrate into other jurisdictions if the state where they originate from actively imposes them, or they can be transplanted to a state that willingly adopts them (Bradford, 2012; Bradford, 2020). Especially the law originating from the European Union is very influential. For example, the GDPR is also widely implemented beyond the European Union.

The European choices may therefore have large implications beyond its borders. However, clear mechanisms, such as the rules of thumbs introduced in this chapter, need to be still advanced for these purposes and the idea of data altruism developed beyond its application to data in the public sphere.

One should be especially careful with repackaging sensitive datasets – these could only be reused without the consent of the original holder for non-commercial use.

9.7 Conclusion

The chapter argues that there is a need to advance data commons further in the European Union on a larger scale; however, this endeavour stumbles upon a number of obstacles, such as a design of older regulations around the idea of consent of the user as a basis for (also excessive or unfair) data gathering. This leads to the countless possibilities of data repackaging, often not known to users. Transparency is therefore needed, especially for a repackaging of sensitive data or where sensitive data can be derived from non-sensitive datasets.

As I have shown, data governance by data commons may work much better than the rights-based approach which does not take into account a number of behavioural heuristics and biases that users face while making a decision to consent to data gathering in return for seemingly free service. Involving public institutions in data commons could increase trust in data sharing and repackaging. The choice of a data governance model is also political, the EU could in fact pave the way for other jurisdictions to replace the 'American' model of consent, which then became a standard transplanted to the GDPR, with data commons and clearer rules for data repackaging.

Note

1 The author would like to thank the following co-workers from the Legal Tech Lab, University of Helsinki, for their valuable comments: I would also like to thank Alexander Mörelius-Wulff for his help with the references, and Lynn Nikkanen for doing the language checking. I am also grateful to Professor Claes Granmar, University of Stockholm, for his comments.

This research has been conducted under a project funding granted by the Academy of Finland, decision number 324116 (2019).

References

Armen A. Alchian, Property Rights, *EcoLib, Collection: Basic Concepts*, 5 Feb 2018 https://www.econlib.org/library/Enc/PropertyRights.html

Benkler, Y. (2003). Freedom in the Commons: Towards a Political Economy of Information. *Duke Law Journal*, *52*(6), pp. 1245–1276.

Bongartz, P., Langenstein, S., & Podszun, R. (2021). The Digital Markets Act: Moving from Competition Law to Regulation for Large Gatekeepers. *Journal of European Consumer and Market Law*, *10*(2), pp. 60–67.

Bradford, A. (2012). The Brussels Effect. *Northwestern University Law Review*, *107*(1), pp. 1–68.

Bradford, A. (2020). *The Brussels Effect: How the European Union Rules the World.* Faculty Books.

Bradford, A. (2023). *Digital Empires. The Global Battle to Regulate Technology*. OUP.

Bräutigam, T. (2022, August 15). What Is in a Name? CJEU Gives a Wide Definition of What Constitutes Processing of Sensitive Personal Data. *Bird & Bird*. https://www.twobirds.com/en/insights/2022/global/what-is-in-a-name-cjeu.

Butler, L.L. (1982). The Commons Concept: An Historical Concept with Modern Relevance. *William and Mary Law Review*, *23*, pp. 835–935.

Chrobak, L. (2018). Proprietary Rights in Digital Data? Normative Perspectives and Principles of Civil Law. In M. Bakhoum, B. Conde Gallego, M.O. Mackenrodt, & G. Surblytė-Namavičienė (Eds.), *Personal Data in Competition, Consumer Protection and Intellectual Property Law – Towards a Holistic Approach?* (pp. 253–272). Springer.

Cohen, J.E. (2019). *Between Truth and Power. The Legal Constructions of Informational Capitalism*. Oxford University Press.

Cooper, D. & Oberschelp de Meneses, A. (2022, February 28). European Commission Publishes Draft Data Act. *Covington*. https://www.insideprivacy.com/european-union-2/13667/.

Council of the EU. (2022a, May 16). *Council Approves Data Governance Act*. Press release. https://www.consilium.europa.eu/fi/press/press-releases/2022/05/16/le-conseil-approuve-l-acte-sur-la-gouvernance-des-donnees/.

Court of Justice of the European Union (4 July 2023), PRESS RELEASE No 113/23, Luxembourg, Judgment of the Court in Case C-252/21 | Meta Platforms and Others (General terms of use of a social network). A national competition authority can find, in the context of the examination of an abuse of a dominant position, that the GDPR has been infringed. https://curia.europa.eu/jcms/upload/docs/application/pdf/2023-07/cp230113en.pdf

Demsetz, H. (2002). Toward a Theory of Property Rights II: The Competition between Private and Collective Ownership. *The Journal of Legal Studies, 31*(S2): The Evolution of Property Rights, pp. S653–S672.

Demsetz, H. (1967). Towards a Theory of Property Rights. *The American Economic Review*, *57*(2), pp. 347–359.

de Streel, A. & Larouche, P. (2021). The European Digital Markets Act: A Revolution Grounded on Traditions. *Journal of European Competition Law & Practice*, *12*(7), pp. 542–560.

Dr2 Consultants. (2020, April 12). Data Governance Act: Main Elements and Business Implications. https://dr2consultants.eu/data-governance-act-main-elements-and-business-implications/

Dulong de Rosnay, M. & Stalder, F. (2020). Digital Commons. *Internet Policy Review*, *9*(4). https://doi.org/10.14763/2020.4.1530.

Dunne, N. (2021). The Role of Regulation in EU Competition Law Assessment. *LSE Law, Society and Economy Working Papers 09/2021*. London School of Economics and Political Science. https://papers.ssrn.com/sol3/papers.cfm?abstract_id=3871315.

European Commission (2023a, September 6) Commission designates six gatekeepers under the Digital Markets Act, https://digital-markets-act.ec.europa.eu/commission-designates-six-gatekeepers-under-digital-markets-act-2023-09-06_en

European Commission (2023b, June 28) Data Act – Questions and Answers. Questions and answers, https://ec.europa.eu/commission/presscorner/detail/en/qanda_22_1114

European Commission. (2019, July 17). *Antitrust: Commission Opens Investigation into Possible Anti-competitive Conduct of Amazon.* Press release. https://ec.europa.eu/commission/presscorner/detail/en/IP_19_4291.

European Commission. (2020, November 10). *Antitrust. Commission Sends Statement of Objections to Amazon for the Use of Non-public Independent Seller Data and Opens Second Investigation into Its E-commerce Business Practices.* Press release. https://ec.europa.eu/commission/presscorner/detail/en/ip_20_2077.

European Commission. (2022a, July 14). *Antitrust: Commission Seeks Feedback on Commitments Offered by Amazon Concerning Marketplace Seller Data and Access to Buy Box and Prime.* https://ec.europa.eu/commission/presscorner/detail/en/ip_22_4522.

European Commission. (2022b, February 23). *Data Act – Questions and Answers.* https://ec.europa.eu/commission/presscorner/detail/en/qanda_22_1114.

European Commission. (2022c). *Antitrust: Commission Accepts Commitments by Amazon Barring It from Using Marketplace Seller Data, and Ensuring Equal Access to Buy Box and Prime.* https://ec.europa.eu/commission/presscorner/detail/en/ip_22_7777.

European Commission. (n.d.). *How Much Data Can Be Collected?* https://ec.europa.eu/info/law/law-topic/data-protection/reform/rules-business-and-organisations/principles-gdpr/how-much-data-can-be-collected_en.

European Data Protection Board. (2020). *Guidelines 05/2020 on Consent under Regulation 2016/679.* https://edpb.europa.eu/sites/default/files/files/file1/edpb_guidelines_202005_consent_en.pdf.

Evans, B. (2022, May 27). There Is No Such Thing as 'Data'. What We Have Are Innumerable Different Collections of Information, Each of Them Specific to a Particular Application. *Financial Times.* https://www.ft.com/content/c93725c4-5e34-4b3b-aae8-dd4c241abebd?shareType=nongift.

Facebook. (n.d.). *About.* https://about.facebook.com/company-info/.

Gitelman, L. (2013). *"Raw Data" Is an Oxymoron.* MIT Press.

Google. (n.d.). *Our Approach to Search.* https://www.google.com/search/howsearchworks/our-approach/#:~:text=Google's%20mission%20is%20to%20organize,a%20wide%20variety%20of%20sources.

Hardin, G. (1968). The Tragedy of the Commons. *Science, 168*, pp. 1243–1248.

Hildebrandt, M. (2015). *Smart Technologies and the End(s) of Law. Novel Entanglements of Law and Technology.* Edward Elgar Publishing.

Janssen, H., Cobbe, J., & Singh, J. (2020). Personal Information Management Systems: A User-Centric Privacy Utopia? *Internet Policy Review*, 9(4). https://doi.org/10.14763/2020.4.1536.

Jessop, B. (2007). Knowledge as a Fictitious Commodity: Insights and Limits of a Polanyian Perspective. In A. Buğra & K. Ağartan (Eds.), *Reading Karl Polanyi for the Twenty-first Century* (pp. 115–133). Palgrave Macmillan US. https://doi.org/10.1057/9780230607187_7.

Kahn, L.M. (2022). Amazon Antitrust Paradox. *Yale Law Journal, 126*, pp. 710–805. https://www.yalelawjournal.org/pdf/e.710.Khan.805_zuvfyyeh.pdf.

Käll, J. (2020). The Materiality of Data as Property. *Harvard International Law Journal Frontiers, 61.* https://harvardilj.org/wp-content/uploads/sites/15/Kall-PDF-format.pdf.

Kerber, W. (2021, April 26). Specifying and Assigning "Bundles of Rights" on Data: An Economic Perspective. *SSRN*. https://ssrn.com/abstract=3847620 or http://doi.org/10.2139/ssrn.3847620.

Lehtonen, K., Halenius, L., & Rastas, T. (2022, February 16). The Data Act Promises the Same Keys to Success to Everyone Participating in the Data Economy. *Sitra*. https://www.sitra.fi/blogit/datasaados-lupaa-yhtalaiset-menestyksen-avaimet-kaikille-jotka-osallistuvat-datatalouteen/.

Lindroos-Hovinheimo, S. (2021, March 1). Data protection Clashes with Data Sharing: How will the EU Reconcile Its Two Aims? *European Law Blog*. https://europeanlawblog.eu/2021/03/01/data-protection-clashes-with-data-sharing-how-will-the-eu-reconcile-its-two-aims/.

Madison, M.J., Frischmann, B., Sanfilippo, M.R., & Strandburg, K.J. (2022). Too Much of a Good Thing? A Governing Knowledge Commons Review of Abundance in Context. *Frontiers in Research Metrics and Analytics*, 7. https://doi.org/10.3389/frma.2022.959505.

Mäihäniemi, B. (2022a). Attention Being Bought and Sold by Online Platforms. User's Self-determination in Governing Their Own Data as a Dimension of Consumer Welfare in Antitrust? In V. Šmejkal (Ed.), *EU Antitrust: Hot Topics & Next Steps: Proceedings of the International Conference Held in Prague on January 24–25, 2022* (pp. 83–92). Faculty of Law of the Charles University.

Mäihäniemi, B. (2022b). The Role of Behavioural Economics in Shaping Remedies for Facebook's Excessive Data Gathering. *Computer Law & Security Review*, *46*, pp. 1–15.

Mäihäniemi, B. (2020). *Competition Law and Big Data. Imposing Access to Information in Digital Markets. New Horizons in Competition Law and Economics.* Edward Elgar.

Mäihäniemi, B. (2017). *Imposing Access to Information in Digital Markets Based on Competition Law: In Search of a Possible Theory of Harm in the EU Google Search Investigations* (pp. 36–37). University of Helsinki.

Ministry of Finance, Finland. (n.d.). EU Digital Statutes Lay the Ground Rules for Operating in the Digital Age. https://vm.fi/en/digital-statutes-in-the-eu.

Nouwens, M., Liccardi, I., Veale, M., Karger, D., & Kagal, L. (2020). Dark Patterns after the GDPR: Scraping Consent Pop-Ups and Demonstrating Their Influence. In *Proceedings of the 2020 CHI Conference on Human Factors in Computing Systems* (pp. 1–13). ACM. https://doi.org/10.1145/3313831.3376321.

Ostrom, E. (1990). *Governing the Commons*. Cambridge University Press. https://ec.europa.eu/commission/presscorner/detail/en/ip_22_7777.

Rose, C.M. (1986). The Comedy of the Commons: Custom, Commerce, and Inherently Public Property. *The University of Chicago Law Review*, *53*(3), pp. 711–781.

Waldman, A.E. (2020). Cognitive Biases, Dark Patterns, and the 'Privacy Paradox'. *Current Opinion in Psychology*, *31*, pp. 105–109.

Wiedemann, K. (2020). A Matter of Choice: The German Federal Supreme Court's Interim Decision in the Abuse-of-Dominance Proceedings Bundeskartellamt v. Facebook (Case KVR 69/19), Published Online: 16 November 2020.

Zygmuntowski, J.J., Laura, Z., & Nemitz, P.F. (2021). Embedding European Values in Data Governance: A Case for Public Data Commons. *Internet Policy Review*, *10*(3). https://policyreview.info/pdf/policyreview-2021-3-1572.pdf.

Legal documents

Amazon - Buy Box (Case AT.40703) Commission Decision [not yet published] (Autumn 2022).

Amazon Marketplace (Case AT.40462) Commission Decision [not yet published] (Autumn 2022).

Council of the EU. (2022b). Proposal for Regulation of the European Parliament and of the Council on Harmonised Rules on Fair Access to and Use of Data (Data Act). COM(2022) 68 final 2022/0047 (COD).

Case C-184/20. *Judgement of the Court (Grand Chamber) of 1 August 2022: OT v Vyriausioji tarnybinės etikos komisija*. The Court of Justice of the European Union.

Case T-612/17. *Judgment of the General Court (Ninth Chamber, Extended Composition) of 10 November 2021: Google and Alphabet v Commission (Google Shopping)*, not yet published.

Case C-252/21. *Request for a Preliminary Ruling from the Oberlandesgericht Düsseldorf (Germany) Lodged on 22 April 2021 — Facebook Inc. and Others v Bundeskartellamt*, OJC 320, 9.8.2021, pp. 16–18.

Case VI-Kart 2/19 (V). *Judgement of Oberlandesgericht Düsseldorf of 24 March 2021:*.... www.justiz.nrw.de/nrwe/olgs/duesseldorf/j2021/Kart_2_19_V_Beschluss_20210324.html.

Federal Court of Justice of Germany. (2020, June 23). *Federal Court of Justice Provisionally Confirms Allegation of Facebook Abusing Dominant Position*. Press release no. 080/2020. www.bundeskartellamt.de/SharedDocs/Publikation/EN/Pressemitteilungen/2020/23_06_2020_BGH_Facebook.pdf?__blob=publicationFile&v=3.

European Parliament. (2020). *Legislative Resolution of 5 July 2022 on the Proposal for a Regulation of the European Parliament and of the Council on Contestable and Fair Markets in the Digital Sector (Digital Markets Act)* (COM(2020)0842 – C9-0419/2020 – 2020/0374(COD).

Directive 2019/1024. *On Open Data and the Re-use of Public Sector Information*. European Parliament and Council. https://eur-lex.europa.eu/legal-content/EN/TXT/PDF/?uri=CELEX:32019L1024&from=EN.

Case B6-22/16. *Judgement of the Bundeskartellamt of 6 February 2019: Facebook, Exploitative Business Terms Pursuant to Section 19(1) GWB for Inadequate Data Processing*. Bundeskartellamt. https://www.bundeskartellamt.de/SharedDocs/Entscheidung/EN/Fallberichte/Missbrauchsaufsicht/2019/B6-22-16.pdf?__blob=publicationFile&v=.

Case VI-Kart 1/19 (V). *Judgement of Oberlandesgericht Düsseldorf of 26 August 2019:* .... https://perma.cc/WFJ2-JWEM.

Case C-657/11. *Judgement of the Court (Third Chamber) of 11 July 2013: Belgian Electronic Sorting Technology NV v Bert Peelaers and Visys NV*. The Court of Justice of the European Union.

Case C-324/09. *Judgement of the Court (Grand Chamber) of July 2011: L'Oréal SA and Others v eBay International AG and Others*. The Court of Justice of the European Union.

European Commission. (n.d.a). https://commission.europa.eu/strategy-and-policy/priorities-2019-2024/europe-fit-digital-age/digital-markets-act-ensuring-fair-and-open-digital-markets_en.

Proposal for a Regulation of the European Parliament and of the Council on Harmonised Rules on Fair Access to and Use of Data (Data Act). COM/2022/68 final.

Regulation 2016/679. *On the Protection of Natural Persons with Regard to the Processing of Personal Data and on the Free Movement of Such Data, and Repealing Directive 95/46/EC (General Data Protection Regulation).* European Parliament and Council.

Regulation (EU) 2022/868 of the European Parliament and of the Council of 30 May 2022 on European Data Governance and Amending Regulation (EU) 2018/1724 (Data Governance Act) (Text with EEA Relevance) PE/85/2021/REV/1. *OJ L 152, 3.6.2022*, pp. 1–44.

Regulation (EU) 2022/1925 of the European Parliament and of the Council of 14 September 2022 on Contestable and Fair Markets in the Digital Sector and Amending Directives (EU) 2019/1937 and (EU) 2020/1828 (Digital Markets Act) (Text with EEA Relevance). PE/17/2022/REV/1. *OJ L 265, 12.10.2022*, pp. 1–66.

Regulation (EU) 2022/2065 of the European Parliament and of the Council of 19 October 2022 on a Single Market For Digital Services and amending Directive 2000/31/EC (Digital Services Act) (Text with EEA Relevance). PE/30/2022/REV/1. *OJ L 277, 27.10.2022*, pp. 1–102.

UKSC 50. *Judgement of the Supreme Court of 19 November 2021: Lloyd v Google LLC.* The Supreme Court of the United Kingdom. https://www.supremecourt.uk/cases/docs/uksc-2019-0213-judgment.pdf.

10 Data extractivism

Social pollution and real-world costs

Christopher W. Chagnon and Sophia E. Hagolani-Albov

10.1 Introduction

There have been striking changes in the world since the early- to mid-2000s. Geopolitically, there has been the War on Terror, the Pink Tide, and other events. Perhaps a starker change has been the way that 'smart' computerized technology has become increasingly embedded in and central to peoples' lives. As processes of embedding have intensified, the amount of personal data (referred to as 'data'[1] for the remainder of the chapter) generated from the use of these devices has increased exponentially; more specifically data about the people using these devices. This data is valuable. It has become a trite tautology to state 'data is the new oil'; however, it does have a similarly significant impact on the world market. Currently, seven of the ten most valuable companies in the world (measured by market capitalization) are technology companies (Statista, 2021a). Two were founded in the 1970s (Microsoft, Apple), four in the 1990s (Amazon, Alphabet, Tencent, and Alibaba), and one in the 2000s (Meta) (Cantale & Buche, 2018; Leskin, 2020). These companies all have data harvesting, processing, usage, and sales at the core of their business models. The other companies are Saudi Aramco, the world's largest oil company (#3); Tesla (#8); and Berkshire Hathaway (#10).

As with other strategic resources, companies have pushed to expand the sites and volume of extraction as the value and potential uses of data have become more widely appreciated. However, unlike traditional resource extractive companies where tools of extraction often do not have a direct use for the end user and sites are linked to physical geographic features (often far from the end users), data extraction is often hidden and embedded in consumer goods and services. As such, the push to expand sites of data extraction can be seen in the proliferation of smart devices, the 'Internet of Things',[2] and apps for smart devices (Couldry & Mejias, 2019). Beyond expanding the potential sites of extraction and updating the technology of extraction to increase volume, many companies design their software and services to maximize data extraction. This is often done by trying to increase the amount of time users engage with the software and through

DOI: 10.4324/9781003450160-14

background tracking of what the user does on their devices (Alter, 2017; Binns et al., 2018).

The concept of 'extractivism' was developed to analyze the damages done by extremely destructive modes of resource extraction to maximize profits (Durante et al., 2021). Analysis was initially focused on hydrocarbon and mineral extraction but has been expanded to areas such as forestry and agriculture, and more recently (and somewhat controversially) into areas beyond 'natural' resources (Chagnon et al., 2022). This includes (but is not limited to) the harvesting of data, called 'data extractivism'. Although previous work has tied data extractivism to the expansion of other forms of extractivism, environmental damage, and real-world violence, work outlining the social damage caused by data extractivist models has been limited (Chagnon et al., 2021; Dunlap & Jakobsen, 2020). This chapter highlights ways that data extractivist approaches cause, what could be termed, 'social pollution', with an emphasis on the European context.

This chapter proceeds as follows. First, there is a brief overview of the concept of extractivism and earlier work that laid the groundwork for development of data extractivism. Next there is a discussion of data as a resource and how the business structures surround the harvesting, processing, and deployment of data function similarly to the business structures in other extractivisms. The chapter then pivots to an extended discussion of the social impacts and the more general social pollution that is a result of the data extractive environment. The chapter then traces responses to data extractivism in the European Union (EU) and ends with concluding remarks and recommendations for further research.

10.2 Background

10.2.1 A brief overview of extractivism

A detailed explanation of the nuances of extractivism as a concept is beyond the scope of this article (see Chagnon et al., 2022; Ye et al., 2020); however, this section will provide a brief look at some aspects of its background and defining features. Extractivism, from the Spanish *extractivismo*, developed out of the Latin American context and draws upon a variety of work, including social ecology, dependency theory, and Indigenous resistance (Gudynas, 2021). The term dates to at least the 1970s as a description of the hydrocarbon and mineral export sectors; however, the current conceptualization came together in the late 2000s (Gudynas, 2021). As Chagnon et al. (2022, p. 1) write, 'Extractivism as a concept forms a complex ensemble of self-reinforcing practices, mentalities, and power differentials underwriting and rationalizing socio-ecologically destructive modes of organizing life through subjugation, violence, depletion, and non-reciprocity'.

There have been numerous definitions of extractivism from various authors. These definitions can vary significantly in length, characteristics, and level of analysis. However, Chagnon et al. (2022, p. 4) identify four common threads:

1 Extractivism involves appropriation of natural and human resource wealth, producing a drain that damages or depletes its source in a potentially irreversible way.
2 Extractivism is premised on capital accumulation and centralization of power. It can occur because of relational power disparities (inequalities/imbalances) and alienation.
3 Drain, associated with extractivisms, can be analyzed as resource and wealth flows in time and space (at and through different nested levels, including local, state, regional, and global).
4 Extractivism is a modality of capital accumulation in current global capitalist development that conditions, constrains, and pressures lives of virtually all humans and other-than-humans. However, it is not dependent on or synonymous with global capitalism and has been embedded in other systems.

Durante et al. (2021, p. 20) provide a succinct, comprehensible, and useful definition: extractivism is 'a particular way of thinking and the properties and practices organized toward the goal of maximizing benefit through extraction, which brings in its wake violence and destruction'.

10.2.2 Previous work on data extractivism

There are numerous works that use the term 'data extractivism' somewhere in their text; however, few engage robustly with extractivism literature, and none systematically link the types of damages from extractivism to the social damages of data extractivism. The term 'data extractivism' was likely coined by Evgeny Morozov in approximately 2016 (Morozov, 2016). Morozov's engagement with the concept of data extractivism has been largely through opinion articles and essays that focus on current trends and events in technology news (Morozov, 2017). As such, although the systems, actions, changes, and motivations discussed in the articles fit in very well with extractivism, there is no direct engagement with extractivism academic literature or theory.

The first article to discuss applying the lens of extractivism to data was written in 2015 by Gago and Mezzadra, although the article does not directly use the term 'data extractivism'. The article engages with extractivism literature, but the discussion is very limited—only three sentences—and it does not delve into social damages. This article exhibits the frustrating linguistic trend that has been repeated in numerous works of using the term 'data mining' to describe the harvesting of data (seemingly to create stronger semantic connections with extractive industries). This can be confusing, as 'data mining' is a well-established term defined by the Oxford English Dictionary (2010) as 'the practice of analysing large databases in order to generate new information', rather than the process of collecting or harvesting data to put into datasets (Gago & Mezzadra, 2015).

Another article touching on the application of extractivism to data was written in 2017 by Mezzadra and Neilson. Like the 2015 article, while it does engage with extractivism literature, it does not use the term 'data extractivism'. The article discusses the potential to apply the concept of extractivism to several areas, including data among many others. It not only provides a more in-depth discussion than Gago and Mezzadra (2015), but it also demonstrates a problem that repeatedly arises in discussions of data extractivism: conflating the discussion of *harvesting* data with discussion of *using* data (Mezzadra & Neilson, 2017). Of course, the dangerous usages of data are incredibly important to study (and are a popular topic of research). However, conflating these two areas can make it difficult to effectively address the damages from extractivist approaches to data harvesting and is not in-line with extractivism research. This is like an extractivism analysis of an iron ore mine mixing in significant discussion of bicycle safety because iron ore is used in the production of steel, which is used to make bicycles. While bicycle safety is important, it is a very separate issue from damages caused by the extraction of iron ore.

Couldry and Mejias (2019) touch on the concept of data extractivism as part of their broader systemic conceptualization of data colonialism. They directly use the term data extractivism and engage with extractivism literature; however, the damages of modes of data extraction are not their focus. However, Chagnon et al. (2021) discuss data extractivism directly, and differentiate data extractivism from other potential digital extractivisms, illustrating the connection between data extractivism and other forms of extractivism and highlighting the data extractive system. However, it only briefly touches upon social damages of data extractivism, focusing on the violent uses of data in algorithms.

10.3 Data and extractivism

Data is not a new resource, but only recently has technology progressed enough to make it profitable to extract data on an industrial scale (Couldry & Mejias, 2019). Arguably, the collection of data goes back to at least the censuses of Babylon 5,800 years ago (Population Reference Bureau, 2021). As methodologies and technologies improved, the breadth, depth, and volume of data also increased; however, it was mostly in the hands of the public sector in the form of censuses because collecting such data is incredibly expensive and labor-intensive. As Couldry and Mejias (2019) explain, in the 1980s, private sector data collection capabilities matched and began to surpass the public sector. As technology continued to evolve, the true value of data was increasingly realized (Couldry & Mejias, 2019, pp. 118–129). It was not until the 1990s, arguably even the late 2000s, when smart devices began to proliferate, and data made the leap from being collected to being harvested on a mass industrial scale.

It is difficult to know precisely how much data is being harvested by tech giants, whether their primary focus is software (Facebook), hardware (Samsung), or both (Apple, Alphabet/Google, Amazon, etc.). However, the volume is undoubtedly high for tech companies that operate in extractivist ways. For example, in 2014, Facebook harvested over four petabytes of data *every day* (Bronson & Wiener, 2014). One petabyte is equivalent to over 1,000 terabytes, or over 1,000,000 gigabytes. These numbers are so large that it is hard to put into perspective or really be able to translate what these really mean in terms of storage and the related infrastructure. To explain it another way, one petabyte is the equivalent of 500,000,000,000 pages of standard printed text or 2.5 years of high-definition film footage (Puiu, 2021; Spurlock, 2019). Two petabytes are estimated to be the equivalent of all the information in all the academic research libraries in the United States (Puiu, 2021). The number of Facebook users has more than doubled since 2014 (Statista, 2021b). Considering that, and the fact that technology has continued to speed up, the current figure for Facebook alone is likely much higher than four petabytes.

10.3.1 Business structure

Ye et al. (2020) make two observations about the structure of extractivist businesses. First, the businesses create a 'monopoly' over resources, which mean concentrating the benefits to 'a limited number of beneficiaries, whilst the costs are externalized'. Second, these companies depend on 'close intertwinements between state and private capital groups (be they national or international)' (Ye et al., 2020, p. 2).

The use of the term 'monopoly' would seem to be unnecessarily limiting, even to the extent that it would exclude most instances of extractivism and arguably, 'oligopoly' would work just as well. Regardless, this reflects very accurately the state of big tech companies. Data extraction is dominated by five companies—Amazon, Apple, Google/Alphabet, Facebook, and Microsoft. One could argue that they all represent different monopolies, as they all deal in data, but from different angles. Couldry and Mejias (2019, p. 50) refer to these companies as monopoly-monopsony hybrids, meaning they control the markets for both the production and purchase of data. They point out that there are other major players and different sectors in what they term the 'cloud empire'—infrastructure, devices, transmission, data brokers, etc.—but these five companies hold sway over most of the global market (Couldry & Mejias, 2019).

There is also clear evidence of close intertwining between big tech companies and states. A significant example is the efforts by big tech companies to scrap or soften the EU's forthcoming Digital Markets Act (DMA) (Regulation [EU] 2022/1925) and Digital Services Act (DSA) (Regulation [EU] 2022/2065) (Espinoza, 2022). Currently, tech companies are the biggest lobbying sector in the EU, spending over €97 million annually on lobbying EU institutions, outspending pharmaceutical, fossil fuel, finance, and chemical lobbies (Bank et al., 2021). Between December 2019 and March 2022, lobbyists from big tech companies have held at least 48 meetings with officials from the European Parliament and European Commission (Meaker, 2022). Beyond this, big tech companies also have partnerships with and pour millions of euros annually into prominent think tanks and leading European universities to influence public and policy discussions around industry regulation (Bank et al., 2021; Clarke et al., 2021). A leaked document from Google in 2020 unveiled tactics the company employed to influence the DMA and DSA debate, including the previously listed methods, which also enlisted help from US officials from embassies in Europe and the Office of the United States Trade Representative (Satariano & Stevis-Gridneff, 2020). There are numerous other examples of this intertwining globally, including Google successfully lobbying the United States government to ignore the findings of a Federal Trade Commission antitrust investigation that recommended suing the company for breach of antitrust laws; or when Chinese tech companies openly tried to hire Communist Party members to build stronger ties with the government (Pham, 2018; Winkler et al., 2015).

10.4 Social impacts of data extractivism

Although it is important to show how the structures and features of data extraction match those found in the more established extractivist sectors, showing how the impacts are similar is perhaps more important. This is because previously accepted extractivisms have an easier 'eye test'; that is, the negative impacts they cause are very visually striking—for example, an open-pit mine, a mountainside ground into rubble, or a forest being turned into a plantation (Kröger, 2020). Data extractivism, although constant and increasingly ubiquitous, is harder to see—while one may have information constantly being harvested, they do not see the packets of information flying off to other parts of the world in the same way one can see coal trucks rumbling down a highway. As such, it can be harder to connect negative impacts to data extractivism. While there are negative impacts of data extractivism related to the environment, particularly in the form of pollution and environmental degradation caused by the devices and infrastructure needed to continue data extractivism and the inequalities that are exacerbated by data extractive activities, they are beyond the scope of this chapter. Thus, this section will focus on the negative impacts of data extractivism on the human social environment.

10.4.1 Social pollution

As data is harvested from human social interactions, the damage resulting from the extractivist approach to data also happens in the human social environment. This damage to the social environment is very visible if one knows what to look for; however, given how widespread the impacts are and how rapidly these systems have developed. For this article, 'social pollution' means the harmful and destructive impacts extractivist approaches to data have on societies.

This conceptualization of social pollution is related to several similar terms that have been used in connection to the socio-cultural harms of technology, data, and the online space. 'Data pollution', one of the earliest, entered the academic literature in 1986 with Zimmerli's philosophical examination of data and its potential side streams. Early in the piece, he makes an important distinction of 'pollution of data and pollution by data' (Zimmerli, 1986, p. 291). There is a deeper exploration into the former type of data pollution; however, it is his treatment of the latter that is the genesis of data pollution as we conceptualize it through the lens of extractivism. Zimmerli indicates,

> by means of...regionalized ethical principles such as those of "informed consent", it is possible in the field of data dissemination and application to judge the morality of the actions of those individuals or institutions who undertake the actions in question.
>
> (1986, p. 303)

Ben-Shahar (2019) discusses 'data pollution', though places it as the negative impacts of data breaches or data leaks, rather than to the collection of data. Meel and Vishwakarma (2020) discuss 'information pollution' in relation to the malicious introduction and spread of fake news and misinformation, yet their focus is not on the social impacts but on the patterns of spread. A similar usage of the term 'social pollution' can be found in news articles related to the work of the Observatory on Social Media (formerly called 'Truthy'), seeming to refer to the negative social impacts of social media, yet the explicit term is not used by the organization (Pai, 2014). The following sections will go through some of the facets of social pollution associated with data extractivism.

10.4.2 Homogeneity

A fundamental aspect of data extractivism is that its platforms and devices are projects of homogeneity. Although it is common, especially in the Global North, to think of approaches to technology as universal and monolithic, Milan and Treré (2019) point out this is not inherently the case. Just as there are many different epistemologies in the world, the way that people use the internet, devices, and modes of datafication are also numerous within a culture and unique to different cultures. However, big tech companies do push to homogenize as they expand their reach and data harvesting globally, offering the same look, functions, and features that were designed for the Global North with minimal concern for localization. Mobile phones are an excellent example of this. Cameras on mobile phones made by most companies in the Global North are built with cameras and photo processing software that is optimized for light skin and take poorer quality photos of people with dark skin. A Chinese phone company, Transsion, was able to grab a large chunk of mobile markets across Africa due to having cameras that were designed to photograph people with darker skin, as well as other features that were in demand in African markets (Christensen, 2018).

Data extractivism also pushes out, dominates, or changes pre-existing methods of social interaction and communication. This can be through marginalizing cultures through limited localization. For example, Facebook Free Basics only works in the dominant languages of multilingual countries (Salazar, 2017). It can also be through pushing out or acquiring competitors, such as when Facebook purchased WhatsApp and Instagram. Likewise, it can change modes of social life like the growth of ecommerce, which currently comprises 20% of all global retail sales (Keenan, 2022).

10.4.3 Toxifying the social environment

Data extractivism also creates a toxic social environment more broadly. One of the fundamental ways that this happens is that data extractive systems are designed to be highly addictive to keep people engaged and harvest more data (Andersson, 2018; Andreassen & Pallesen, 2014). Both platforms and devices can cause this addiction and dependency, and while long-term concrete impacts are still unknown due to how relatively new these systems are, there are studies that suggest they have a negative impact on the following: memory of information (Barr et al., 2015), memory of one's own life (Tamir et al., 2018), attention span (Nikken & Schols, 2015), sleep quality (Li et al., 2021), and ability to delay gratification (Wilmer & Chein, 2016). In addition, this is more insidious because companies know that these negative externalities exist and are still pushing these products. For example, internal research from Meta found that Instagram has a severe negative impact on the mental health of teenage girls (Wells et al., 2021).

Couldry and Mejias (2019) focus on a loss of autonomy as a social environmental impact of data extractive systems. This is not autonomy in the sense of being incapable of doing something without the assistance of a device. Rather, it is the shrinking ability to have space away from data extractive systems, space that is purely for ourselves. Couldry and Mejias (2019) specifically link this to Hegel's concept of freedom being the ability to be simply with oneself. That is, to have a space where one's thoughts, feelings, and actions are not known, shared, or mitigated by the outside world. Such spaces are important for mental and spiritual growth. Data extractive systems impact this autonomy in several ways. One is that it is substantially harder to be truly alone—to be somewhere where one's movements, words, and other interactions would not be harvested by some sort of device.

10.4.4 Polarization/echo chambers

One of the most prominent and easy-to-recognize forms of social pollution from data extractivism are polarization and echo chambers. This is a rich area of study, and this section will briefly look at some major aspects which demonstrate how this social pollution happens. Ossewaarde (2019) points out that a 'digital community' differs significantly from a physical community. Physical communities rely on face-to-face interactions, duties, traditions, social constraints, and responsibilities. Digital communities are based on streams of information and entertainment, they are constantly shifting and changing, and in these online spaces it is easier to walk away from conversations and avoid challenges (Ossewaarde, 2019). However, it is significantly easier to form a large digital community compared to a large physical community. Putnam (2000) points out that communities shifting toward homogeneity is not a new phenomenon, but it is significantly easier for people with extremist or conspiratorial views to find a large community online. The issue is not simply people with more extremist or conspiratorial views, but that the psychological characteristics of community engagement people exhibit in physical communities are mirrored in online communities (Sunstein, 2017).

The creation of echo chambers can lead to toxic online environments and can be linked to several aspects of social psychology (Jiang et al., 2021). One aspect is homophily, the tendency of people to trust and prefer to be around people who share similar ideas (Zafarani et al., 2014). Another aspect is confirmation bias, the tendency of people to seek out, favor, and recall information that supports their pre-existing ideas, while also discounting or ignoring information that goes against their pre-existing ideas (Lord et al., 1979). There are also issues of how people confront cognitive dissonance, which is when a person's beliefs and their actions do not align. One of the easiest ways people deal with cognitive dissonance is to confirm with others that they are correct in their actions and beliefs (Jiang et al., 2021). As such, it is very easy for people to end up in echo chambers online. Within these echo chambers, it is easy for false information to spread. As Ossewaarde (2019, p. 27) states, 'such information packed in deceptive clichés, stereotypes, slogans, prejudices and ready-made images, obscures realities of domination and prevents their criticism.' Even in these echo chambers, it is not that people are totally cut off from other views. Rather, different views are shared in these groups to be ridiculed, critiqued, and dismissed, potentially leading to greater polarization (Bright et al., 2020).

Social psychological phenomena within these groups can lead to radicalization and the spread of false information (Sunstein, 2017). These communities do not exist in a vacuum; rather, they overlap and bleed into each other as individuals join multiple communities and share information among them. This can lead to the phenomenon of 'group polarization': when people discuss a topic as a group, people in the group are likely to have more extreme positions than they had prior to being part of the group discussion (Iandoli et al., 2021). This can be people in a group with diverse ideas on a topic all shifting toward a particular idea from their original point, or it can be people who generally agree eliminating dissenting thought and becoming more extreme (Wang et al., 2018). This happens for two reasons. One is persuasive arguments and information; that is, the people presenting the argument have more arguments that support one side of an issue and lack arguments for the other side. The second is reputational concerns pushing people to accept the dominant opinion to be viewed more favorably by the rest of the group. It is worth noting that this is not limited to long discussions but also occurs with brief exposure to viewpoints (Sunstein, 2017, pp. 71–73).

Being in a group that largely agrees with itself will push members toward more extreme views (Strandberg et al., 2017). This happens even more easily online because it is so easy to entirely block out opposing views. People build trust in these groups, and what people spread, or share, is more likely to be believed. This, in turn, can exacerbate the phenomenon of biased assimilation, where people are more likely to believe information that supports their prior beliefs and conversely makes it easy to reject or ignore information that goes against those beliefs (DiFonzo et al., 2014). These features coming together can create informational and reputational cascades of group behavior. Informational cascades are when people do not necessarily have a set opinion on a subject but decide to look at what others in their trusted community think and mimic that opinion. This can lead to the rapid spread of false information and conspiracy theories (Wang et al., 2018). This can link with reputational cascades, where people in a community will go along with (or at least not oppose) the dominant community opinion, even if they disagree with it, because they do not want to lose social standing (Sunstein, 1999).

With all this in mind, one can start to understand how easy and natural it is for very strong and large echo chambers to come into being online. However, this is a phenomenon that is being actively driven and exacerbated by companies to increase engagement (and the data that comes from this engagement). With the release of the 'Facebook Papers', a leak of over 1,300 internal Facebook documents to media outlets by an internal whistleblower, this toxic environment, and the social pollution it causes, can be seen as a feature of the data extractive system rather than a bug (Cameron et al., 2022). The documents show that Facebook was fully aware that the way their algorithms are designed, and their policies of moderation, are causing social damage and violence, but chose not to substantively change them because such changes would impact profitability. A clear example is Facebook's well-advertised shift to emphasize 'meaningful communities', a change in the

Facebook algorithm to promote content from groups (including new groups that the user was not a part of) on newsfeeds and de-prioritize content from Facebook friends. This change included giving greater algorithmic weight to angry reactions on posts than simple likes. Facebook employees approached founder and CEO Mark Zuckerberg both before the launch with concerns and after the launch with data that the changes were exacerbating problems of polarization and toxification. However, the changes significantly increased user engagement and amount of time spent online (increasing the amount of data that could be harvested), so no substantive actions were taken to address the issue (Hagey & Horwitz, 2021). This issue is exacerbated by Facebook knowingly underspending on content moderation and its XCheck program, which exempts 'pretty much anyone regularly in the media or who has a substantial online following, including film stars, cable talk show hosts, academics, and online personalities with large followings' from content moderation (Horowitz, 2021). Facebook has also pressured partner fact-checking services to retroactively tone down fact checks. This is all done out of the fear that accidentally moderating acceptable content could lead to negative news stories, which could impact profitability. This has allowed high-profile people to share misinformation, which can then spread quickly through groups with impunity (Horowitz, 2021).

In the European context, the connection between social media and polarization has been the topic of significant research (Dixon & Juan-Torres, 2018). One of the most famous is the impact of online polarization on the Brexit vote (Del Vicario et al., 2017). Karlsen et al. (2017) note that online echo chambers in Norway have 'trench warfare dynamics'. Schaub and Morisi (2020) find that the spread of broadband internet and subsequent rise of social media echo chambers have played a significant role in the rise of the populist Five Star Movement party in Italy and the Alternative for Germany populist right-wing party in Germany. There have also been discussions of online environments enabling anti-immigrant attacks in Sweden (Törnberg & Wahlström, 2018).

10.5 Responses in Europe

The EU is widely considered to be at the forefront of regulation of big tech companies. The first major piece of legislation was the General Data Protection Regulation (GDPR), which passed the European Parliament in 2016 and came into effect for all organizations in 2018. The GDPR requires websites to receive informed consent from users for processing their information and gives them an option to opt out, as well as outlines the privacy rights of users. Violators can be fined up to 4% of their global annual revenue (Wolford, 2022). At least 17 countries in the world have adopted GDPR-like legislation (Simmons, 2022). However, while the GDPR is pioneering, it has also been the subject of significant criticism. Some have pointed out that the 'informed consent' pop-ups on websites do not really inform users;

rather, they are simply another button to click, with many designed to make opting-out more difficult than opting-in to data tracking (Utz et al., 2019). Another point of criticism has been related to the enforcement of the GDPR being left to individual states, with many not having enough specialists in their Data Protection Agencies to effectively regulate the industry (Ryan, 2020). Beyond this, there have been criticisms that investigations and subsequent fines take too long to progress and are too small to actually impact the behavior of businesses (Satariano, 2020). To date, the largest GDPR fine was handed down in Luxembourg in 2021 on a case opened in 2018, fining Amazon €746 million (Data Privacy Manager, 2022). Although this amount seems significant, it only accounts for about 0.17% of annual global revenue (Boice, 2022).

The DMA and DSA legislations have also been heralded as a groundbreaking step in the regulation of tech companies. The DMA (Regulation [EU] 2022/1925) focuses on large 'gatekeeper' companies (companies with €75 billion market capitalization, or €7.5 billion in annual turnover for the past three years, or have at least 45 million monthly users in the EU and 10,000 annual business users). Regulations in the law include a prohibition on sharing data across owned platforms (for example, data that Meta collects on Instagram cannot be combined with data collected by Facebook) without specific user consent, allowing interoperability of instant messaging services, rules about transparency of pricing and allowing sellers on platforms to sell on multiple platforms, and ensuring the right of users to unsubscribe from core platform services. The DMA will be enforced by the European Commission, and first-time violations can carry fines of up to 10% of global annual turnover (Regulation [EU] 2022/1925).

The DSA (Regulation [EU] 2022/2065) focuses on accountability of tech companies and user rights. Regulations include greater obligations for platforms to take down disinformation, harmful speech, and illegal content, potentially requiring sharing how their algorithms work with regulators, limits on targeted advertising, transparency rules for sellers in online marketplaces, and provisions for researchers to access data from platforms. Enforcement for large companies will be under the jurisdiction of the European Commission, and member states will have oversight of other platforms established in their countries (Regulation [EU] 2022/2065). As these laws have not yet come into effect (they will be applicable to all parties in 2024), it is impossible to currently gauge their efficacy. However, with the previously mentioned massive lobbying and influence campaign, there are reasons to fear that the legislation could be watered down, or enforcement could be relatively light and slow as it has been for the GDPR. While under this one can request information about algorithms and a greater emphasis on content moderation, it is conceivable that issues of social pollution stemming from modes of data harvesting could be addressed. However, given that companies will still be exempt from liability from damages caused by modes of harvesting data, and the focus seems to be more on *what* is done with the data after it is harvested rather than *how* the data is harvested, the likelihood of it being used to tackle issues of social pollution is unclear (Regulation [EU] 2022/2065).

10.6 Conclusion

The breakneck pace of technological advancement and encroachment of technology into social spaces has changed societies around the globe in ways that were unimaginable a few decades ago. The rapid rise of big tech companies to join the ranks of resource extractive companies as some of the most valuable companies and active government lobbyists in the world has also presented significant changes and challenges for governance. While there has been an explosion of critical research questioning pro-tech orthodoxy which dominated early days of the industry, most of the research around data harvesting has been focused on the terrifying implications of what is and can be done with data rather than the damages caused by how data is harvested. This is not to claim that the study of the current and potential uses of data is not valuable; quite the contrary: use of data is distinct but intimately related to extractive modes of harvesting. However, utilizing the concept of extractivism to analyze the destructive data-harvesting modalities of big tech companies can help provide a more nuanced picture of the current and potential damage done and aid in the search for alternatives and ways to prevent or mitigate that damage. This chapter has touched on a variety of damages caused by data extractivism by presenting a concept and examples of damage data extractivist modalities cause to the social environment in the form of social pollution. Although this is a start, there remains potential for future work to further identify and delineate forms of social pollution produced by different types of tech companies, as well as utilize the concept of data extractivism for empirical case studies.

Notes

1 This article uses the definition of data from Couldry and Mejias (2019, p. xiii), 'information flows that pass from human life in all its forms to infrastructures for collection and processing', mentioned here to avoid confusion in relation to academic, geologic, or other types of data.

2 '"The Internet of Things" describes the network of physical objects—"things"—that are embedded with sensors, software, and other technologies for the purpose of connecting and exchanging data with other devices and systems over the internet. These devices range from ordinary household objects to sophisticated industrial tools' (Oracle 2022).

References

Alter, A. (2017). *Irresistible - The Rise of Addictive Technology and the Business of Keeping Us Hooked*. Penguin Press. ISBN: 1594206643.

Andersson, H. (2018, July 4). Social Media Apps Are 'Deliberately' Addictive to Users. *BBC News*. https://www.bbc.com/news/technology-44640959.

Andreassen, C., & Pallesen, S. (2014). Social Network Site Addiction - An Overview. *Current Pharmaceutical Design*, *20*(25), 4053–4061. https://doi.org/10.2174/1381 6128113199990616.

Bank, M., Duffy, F., Leyendecker, V., & Silva, M. (2021). *The Lobby Network: Big Tech's Web of Influence in the EU*. Corporate Europe Observatory. Available at: https://corporateeurope.org/sites/default/files/2021-08/The%20lobby%20 network%20-%20Big%20Tech%27s%20web%20of%20influence%20in%20 the%20EU.pdf.

Barr, N., Pennycook, G., Stolz, J. A., & Fugelsang, J. A. (2015). The Brain in Your Pocket: Evidence That Smartphones Are Used to Supplant Thinking. *Computers in Human Behavior*, *48*, 473–480. https://doi.org/10.1016/j.chb.2015.02.029.

Ben-Shahar, O. (2019). Data Pollution. *Journal of Legal Analysis*, *11*, 104–159. https://doi.org/10.1093/jla/laz005.

Binns, R., Lyngs, U., Van Kleek, M., Zhao, J., Libert, T., & Shadbolt, N. (2018). Third Party Tracking in the Mobile Ecosystem. *Proceedings of the 10th ACM Conference on Web Science*. https://doi.org/10.1145/3201064.3201089.

Boice, M. (2022, March 29). 15 Amazon Statistics You Should Know in 2022. *JungleScout*. https://www.junglescout.com/blog/amazon-statistics/#:~:text=2.,up%20 %2421.3%20billion%20from%202020.

Bright, J., Marchal, N., Ganesh, B., & Rudinac, S. (2020). Echo Chambers Exist! (But They're Full of Opposing Views). ArXiv:2001.11461. https://doi.org/https:// doi.org/10.48550/arXiv.2001.11461.

Bronson, N., & Wiener, J. (2014, October 22). Facebook's Top Open Data Problems - Facebook Research. *Facebook Research*. https://research.fb.com/blog/2014/10/ facebook-s-top-open-data-problems/.

Cameron, D., Wodinsky, S., & DeGeurin, M. (2022, April 18). Read the Facebook Papers for Yourself. *Gizmodo*. https://gizmodo.com/facebook-papers-how-to-read-1848702919.

Cantale, S., & Buche, I. (2018, January 18). How Tencent Became the World's Most Valuable Social Network Firm – With Barely Any Advertising. *The Conversation*. https://theconversation.com/how-tencent-became-the-worlds-most-valuable-social-network-firm-with-barely-any-advertising-90334.

Chagnon, C. W., Durante, F., Gills, B. K., Hagolani-Albov, S. E., Hokkanen, S., Kangasluoma, S. M. J., Konttinen, H., Kröger, M., LaFleur, W., Ollinaho, O., & Vuola, M. P. S. (2022). From Extractivism to Global Extractivism: The Evolution of an Organizing Concept. *The Journal of Peasant Studies*, *49*(4), 1–33. https://doi.org/1 0.1080/03066150.2022.2069015.

Chagnon, C. W., Hagolani-Albov, S. E., & Hokkanen, S. (2021). Extractivism at Your Fingertips. In J. Shapiro & J.-A. McNeish (Eds.), *Our Extractive Age: Expressions of Violence and Resistance* (1st ed.). Routledge. ISBN: 9780367650520.

Christensen, C. P. (2018). Africa Calling: How Transsion Rose to Dominate the African Phone Market - CKGSB. *CKGSB Knowledge*. https://english.ckgsb.edu.cn/ knowledges/africa-transsion-african-phone-market/.

Clarke, L., Williams, O., & Swindells, K. (2021). How Google Quietly Funds Europe's Leading Tech Policy Institutes. *New Statesman*. https://www. newstatesman.com/science-tech/2021/07/how-google-quietly-funds-europe-s-leading-tech-policy-institutes.

Couldry, N., & Mejias, U. A. (2019). *The Costs of Connection: How Data Is Colonizing Human Life and Appropriating It for Capitalism*. Stanford University Press.

Data Privacy Manager (2022). 20 Biggest GDPR Fines So Far [2019, 2020, 2021 & 2022] – Data Privacy Manager. *Data Privacy Manager*. https://dataprivacymanager.net/5-biggest-gdpr-fines-so-far-2020/.

Del Vicario, M., Zollo, F., Caldarelli, G., Scala, A., & Quattrociocchi, W. (2017). Mapping Social Dynamics on Facebook: The Brexit Debate. *Social Networks*, *50*, 6–16. https://doi.org/10.1016/j.socnet.2017.02.002.

DiFonzo, N., Suls, J., Beckstead, J. W., Bourgeois, M. J., Homan, C. M., Brougher, S., Younge, A. J., & Terpstra-Schwab, N. (2014). Network Structure Moderates Intergroup Differentiation of Stereotyped Rumors. *Social Cognition*, *32*(5), 409–448. https://doi.org/10.1521/soco.2014.32.5.409.

Dixon, T., & Juan-Torres, M. (2018). *Is the Internet Eroding Europe's Middle Ground?: Public Opinion, Polarisation and New Technologies* (Ser. ESPAS Foresight Reflection Paper Series). European Political Strategy Centre. Available at: https://espas.secure.europarl.europa.eu/orbis/sites/default/files/generated/document/en/Foresight%20Reflection%20Polarisation%20paper_V04.pdf.

Dunlap, A., & Jakobsen, J. (2020). *The Violent Technologies of Extraction: Political Ecology, Critical Agrarian Studies and the Capitalist Worldeater*. Palgrave Pivot. https://doi.org/10.1007/978-3-030-26852-7.

Durante, F., Kröger, M., & LaFleur, W. (2021). Extraction and Extractivisms: Definitions and Concepts. In J. Shapiro & J.-A. McNeish (Eds.), *Our Extractive Age: Expressions of Violence and Resistance* (1st ed.). Routledge. ISBN: 9780367650520.

Espinoza, J. (2022, January 11). Google in Last-Ditch Lobbying Attempt to Influence Incoming EU Tech Rules. *Financial Times*. https://www.ft.com/content/8c7527bc-7ab4-41cd-ba94-3145208da9c3.

Gago, V., & Mezzadra, S. (2015). Para una crítica de las operaciones extractivas del capital: patrón de acumulación y luchas sociales en el tiempo de la financiarización. *Nueva Sociedad*, *255*. Available at: http://economiainternacional.sociales.uba.ar/wp-content/uploads/sites/84/2018/08/Gago-y-Mezzadra-2015.pdf.

Gudynas, E. (2021). *Extractivisms: Politics, Economy and Ecology*. Fernwood Publishing. ISBN: 1773631764.

Hagey, K., & Horwitz, J. (2021, September 15). Facebook Tried to Make Its Platform a Healthier Place. It Got Angrier Instead. *The Wall Street Journal*. https://www.wsj.com/articles/facebook-algorithm-change-zuckerberg-11631654215?mod=article_inline.

Horowitz, J. (2021, September 13). Facebook Says Its Rules Apply to All. Company Documents Reveal a Secret Elite That's Exempt. *The Wall Street Journal*. https://www.wsj.com/articles/facebook-files-xcheck-zuckerberg-elite-rules-11631541353?mod=article_inline.

Iandoli, L., Primario, S., & Zollo, G. (2021). The Impact of Group Polarization on the Quality of Online Debate in Social Media: A Systematic Literature Review. *Technological Forecasting and Social Change*, *170*. https://doi.org/10.1016/j.techfore.2021.120924.

Jiang, B., Karami, M., Cheng, L., Black, T., & Liu, H. (2021). *Mechanisms and Attributes of Echo Chambers in Social Media*. International Conference on Social Computing, Behavioral-Cultural Modeling, & Prediction and Behavior Representation in Modeling and Simulation. Virtual, Springer.

Karlsen, R., Steen-Johnsen, K., Wollebæk, D., & Enjolras, B. (2017). Echo Chamber and Trench Warfare Dynamics in Online Debates. *European Journal of Communication*, *32*(3), 257–273. https://doi.org/10.1177/0267323117695734.

Keenan, M. (2022, November 24). Global Ecommerce Explained: Stats and Trends to Watch. *Shopify Plus*. https://www.shopify.com/enterprise/global-ecommerce-statistics.

Kröger, M. (2020). *Iron Will: Global Extractivism and Mining Resistance in Brazil and India*. University of Michigan Press. https://doi.org/10.3998/mpub.11533186.

Leskin, P. (2020, February 27). Bill Gates, Mark Zuckerberg, and Jeff Bezos: Here's How Old the Founders of 23 Tech Giants Were When They Started Their First Companies. *Business Insider*. https://www.businessinsider.com/ages-of-tech-founders-when-they-started-their-first-companies-2019-4?r=US&IR=T.

Li, X., Fu, S., Fu, Q., & Zhong, B. (2021). Youths' Habitual Use of Smartphones Alters Sleep Quality and Memory: Insights from a National Sample of Chinese Students. *International Journal of Environmental Research and Public Health*, *18*(5), 2254. https://doi.org/10.3390/ijerph18052254.

Lord, C. G., Ross, L., & Lepper, M. R. (1979). Biased Assimilation and Attitude Polarization: The Effects of Prior Theories on Subsequently Considered Evidence. *Journal of Personality and Social Psychology*, *37*(11), 2098–2109. https://doi.org/10.1037/0022-3514.37.11.2098.

Meaker, M. (2022, March 25). Europe's Digital Markets Act Takes a Hammer to Big Tech. *Wired*. https://www.wired.com/story/digital-markets-act-messaging/.

Meel, P., & Vishwakarma, D. K. (2020). Fake News, Rumor, Information Pollution in Social Media and Web: A Contemporary Survey of State-of-the-Arts, Challenges and Opportunities. *Expert Systems with Applications*, *153*. https://doi.org/10.1016/j.eswa.2019.112986.

Mezzadra, S., & Neilson, B. (2017). On the Multiple Frontiers of Extraction: Excavating Contemporary Capitalism. *Cultural Studies*, *31*(2–3), 185–204. https://doi.org/10.1080/09502386.2017.1303425.

Milan, S., & Treré, E. (2019). Big Data from the South(s): Beyond Data Universalism. *Television & New Media*, *20*(4), 319–335. https://doi.org/10.1177/1527476419837739.

Morozov, E. (2016). *Digital Democracy and Technological Sovereignty: Left Answers to the Smart Attack of Neoliberalism (Lecture by Evgeny Morozov)*. YouTube. Rosa Luxemburg-Stiftung. https://www.youtube.com/watch?v=pLO2I9QHfz0.

Morozov, E. (2017). *Digital Intermediation of Everything: At the Intersection of Politics, Technology and Finance*. Council of Europe.

Nikken, P., & Schols, M. (2015). How and Why Parents Guide the Media Use of Young Children. *Journal of Child and Family Studies*, *24*(11), 3423–3435. https://doi.org/10.1007/s10826-015-0144-4.

Oracle (2022). What Is the Internet of Things (IoT)? *Internet of Things*. https://www.oracle.com/internet-of-things/what-is-iot/.

Ossewaarde, M. (2019). Digital Transformation and the Renewal of Social Theory: Unpacking the New Fraudulent Myths and Misplaced Metaphors. *Technological Forecasting and Social Change*, *146*, 24–30. https://doi.org/10.1016/j.techfore.2019.05.007.

Oxford Dictionary of English (2010). Data Mining. In *Oxford Dictionary of English*. Ebook Edition.

Pai, A. (2014, October 17). The Government Wants to Study 'Social Pollution' on Twitter. *The Washington Post*. https://www.washingtonpost.com/opinions/truthy-project-is-unworthy-of-tax-dollars/2014/10/17/a3274faa-531b-11e4-809b-8cc0a295c773_story.html.

Pham, S. (2018, November 4). Why China's Tech Giants Are Cozying Up to the Communist Party. *CNN*. https://edition.cnn.com/2018/11/02/tech/china-tech-communist-party/index.html.

Population Reference Bureau (2021). *Milestones and Moments in Global Census History – Population Reference Bureau* [Press Release]. Population Reference Bureau. https://www.prb.org/resources/milestones-and-moments-in-global-census-history/.

Puiu, T. (2021, December 28). How Big Is a Petabyte, Exabyte Or Yottabyte? What's the Biggest Byte for That Matter? *ZME Science*. https://www.zmescience.com/science/how-big-data-can-get/.

Putnam, R. D. (2000). Bowling Alone: America's Declining Social Capital. *Culture and Politics*, 223–234. https://doi.org/10.1007/978-1-349-62397-6_12.

Regulation (EU) 2022/1925. *On Contestable and Fair Markets in the Digital Sector and Amending Directives (EU) 2019/1937 and (EU) 2020/1828 (Digital Markets Act)*. European Parliament and Council. https://eur-lex.europa.eu/legal-content/en/TXT/?uri=COM%3A2020%3A842%3AFIN.

Regulation (EU) 2022/2065. *On a Single Market for Digital Services and Amending Directive 200/31/EC (Digital Services Act)*. European Parliament and Council. https://eur-lex.europa.eu/legal-content/EN/TXT/?uri=celex%3A32022R2065.

Ryan, J. (2020). *Europe's Governments Are Failing the GDPR* (Report). Brave. https://brave.com/static-assets/files/Brave-2020-DPA-Report.pdf.

Salazar, G. (2017). Free Basics in Real Life: Six Case Studies on Facebook's Internet "On Ramp" Initiative from Africa, Asia and Latin America. *Global Voices Advox Working Paper*. https://advox.globalvoices.org/wp-content/uploads/2017/07/MEXICO.pdf.

Satariano, A. (2020, April 27). Europe's Privacy Law Hasn't Shown Its Teeth, Frustrating Advocates. *New York Times*. https://www.nytimes.com/2020/04/27/technology/GDPR-privacy-law-europe.html.

Satariano, A., & Stevis-Gridneff, M. (2020, December 14). Big Tech Turns Its Lobbyists Loose on Europe, Alarming Regulators. *New York Times*. https://www.nytimes.com/2020/12/14/technology/big-tech-lobbying-europe.html.

Schaub, M., & Morisi, D. (2020). Voter Mobilisation in the Echo Chamber: Broadband Internet and the Rise of Populism in Europe. *European Journal of Political Research*, *59*(4), 752–773. https://doi.org/10.1111/1475-6765.12373.

Simmons, D. (2022). 17 Countries with GDPR-like Data Privacy Laws. *Comforte Blog*. https://insights.comforte.com/countries-with-gdpr-like-data-privacy-laws.

Spurlock, R. (2019). Petabyte - How Much Information Could It Actually Hold? *Cobalt Iron Blog*. https://info.cobaltiron.com/blog/petabyte-how-much-information-could-it-actually-hold.

Statista (2021a). *Biggest Companies in the World by Market Cap 2021*. Statista. https://www.statista.com/statistics/263264/top-companies-in-the-world-by-market-capitalization/.

Statista (2021b). *Facebook: Daily Active Users Worldwide*. Statista. https://www.statista.com/statistics/346167/facebook-global-dau/.

Strandberg, K., Himmelroos, S., & Grönlund, K. (2017). Do Discussions in Like-Minded Groups Necessarily Lead to More Extreme Opinions? Deliberative Democracy and Group Polarization. *International Political Science Review*, *40*(1), 41–57. https://doi.org/10.1177/0192512117692136.

Sunstein, C. R. (1999). The Law of Group Polarization. *SSRN Electronic Journal*. https://doi.org/10.2139/ssrn.199668.

Sunstein, C. R. (2017). *#Republic: Divided Democracy in the Age of Social Media*. Princeton University Press. https://doi.org/10.2307/j.ctv8xnhtd.

Tamir, D. I., Templeton, E. M., Ward, A. F., & Zaki, J. (2018). Media Usage Diminishes Memory for Experiences. *Journal of Experimental Social Psychology*, *76*, 161–168. https://doi.org/10.1016/j.jesp.2018.01.006.

Törnberg, A., & Wahlström, M. (2018). Unveiling the Radical Right Online; Exploring Framing and Identity in an Online Anti-immigrant Discussion Group. *Sociologisk Forskning*, *55*(2–3), 267–292. https://doi.org/10.37062/sf.55.18193.

Utz, C., Degeling, M., Fahl, S., Schaub, F., & Holz, T. (2019). (Un)informed Consent. *Proceedings of the 2019 ACM SIGSAC Conference on Computer and Communications Security*. https://doi.org/10.1145/3319535.3354212.

Wang, Q., Yang, X., & Xi, W. (2018). Effects of Group Arguments on Rumor Belief and Transmission in Online Communities: An Information Cascade and Group Polarization Perspective. *Information & Management*, *55*(4), 441–449. https://doi.org/10.1016/j.im.2017.10.004.

Wells, G., Horwitz, J., & Seetharaman, D. (2021, September 14). Facebook Knows Instagram Is Toxic for Many Teen Girls, Company Documents Show. *The Wall Street Journal*. https://www.wsj.com/articles/facebook-knows-instagram-is-toxic-for-teen-girls-company-documents-show-11631620739.

Wilmer, H. H., & Chein, J. M. (2016). Mobile Technology Habits: Patterns of Association among Device Usage, Intertemporal Preference, Impulse Control, and Reward Sensitivity. *Psychonomic Bulletin & Review*, *23*(5), 1607–1614. https://doi.org/10.3758/s13423-016-1011-z.

Winkler, R., Kendall, B., & Mullins, B. (2015, March 19). Inside the U.S. Antitrust Probe of Google. *Wall Street Journal*. https://www.wsj.com/articles/inside-the-u-s-antitrust-probe-of-google-1426793274.

Wolford, B. (2022). *What Is GDPR, the EU's New Data Protection Law?* GDPR.EU. https://gdpr.eu/what-is-gdpr/.

Ye, J., van der Ploeg, J. D., Schneider, S., & Shanin, T. (2020). The Incursions of Extractivism: Moving from Dispersed Places to Global Capitalism. *The Journal of Peasant Studies*, *47*(1), 155–183. https://doi.org/10.1080/03066150.2018.1559834.

Zafarani, R., Abbasi, M. A., & Liu, H. (2014). *Social Media Mining: An Introduction*. Cambridge University Press. Available at: http://www.socialmediamining.info/SMM.pdf.

Zimmerli, W. C. (1986). Who Is to Blame for Data Pollution? On Individual Moral Responsibility with Information Technology. *Philosophy and Technology II*, 291–305. https://doi.org/10.1007/978-94-009-4512-8_21.

11 FinTech future trends

Secondary data review

Yevheniia Polishchuk

11.1 Introduction

Digitalization has affected to a greater or lesser degree all spheres of life: that of ordinary citizens, small- and medium-sized businesses, large companies, governments, non-governmental organizations, etc. For some, digitalization offers new opportunities, while for others, on the contrary, it is a challenge that needs to be overcome. Digitalization also affects the financial sector where a separate FinTech industry emerged. In its beginning, FinTech was distinguished by breakthrough innovations in the field of finance (mostly in the field of payments); then financial intermediaries began to notice the fact that competitors were growing next to them and could occupy a separate niche, thus taking away their market share. This forced banks to invest significant funds in the development of FinTech services based on their organizations. Regulators of the financial services market also began to pay attention to a fast-growing industry that went beyond their regulatory competences and thereby created a number of risks for consumers. Moreover, large corporations began to enter the FinTech industry, which posed financial stability risks, as such important market players always have a great potential to influence the development of the market and the economy in general.

There is a large number of published studies that describe the role of FinTech in various spheres: reveal the impact of FinTech on transforming the economy in general, changes that take place in financial markets and growing robo-advising; leveling the asymmetry of information; reducing poverty in certain vulnerable groups (including refugees) in the context of Sustainable Development Goals (SDGs); overcoming the crisis caused by the COVID-19; application of FinTech for the purposes of public authorities, etc. For instance, Hill (2018) in his book describes the future trends in financial services driven by FinTech.

Social aspects of FinTech application are also analyzed in the literature to show new areas and provide a larger context. The greater the FinTech penetration, the better indicators of the financial market in developing countries – such findings are revealed by Aduba, Asgari, and Izawa (2022), based on an analysis of more than 60 economies. Babina, Buchak, and Gornall (2022)

DOI: 10.4324/9781003450160-15

argue that FinTech opens access to customer data and mitigates the asymmetry of information.

Importantly, FinTech played a crucial role in overcoming poverty in Sub-Saharan African countries at the beginning of its implementation. However, continued development of FinTech slows down the pace of poverty reduction (Emara, 2022). Another sphere where FinTech has a crucial impact is robo-advising. Big data analysis is useful in making more reasonable investment decisions as D'Acunto and Rossi (2022) argue in their paper.

Recently, attention focused on the COVID-19 impact on developments in the FinTech industry. During the pandemic, banks were consulted by FinTech companies on how to provide consumers with financial services in such conditions. Therefore, the financial market has changed: neo-bank (nonbank) FinTechs appeared, banks began to pay more attention to innovations in finance (Hill, 2021).

FinTech is a disruptive innovation in the financial market; therefore, financial regulators strengthened their supervision of FinTech (Anagnostopoulos, 2018). FinTech has certain success in providing administrative services to public authorities (Sambros et al., 2020). Velasco (2021) studied the role of FinTech for immigrants, based on the Mexican case. FinTech (paytech) supports immigrants' households via transferring remittances. Increasing welfare, access to better jobs, and, finally, forming immigrants' financial behavior are the strengths of FinTech implementation in the country. For refugees, FinTech can be the only way to receive micro-financial aid or get a loan – this is emphasized by Bhagat and Roderick (2020). They demonstrate that, in Kenya, FinTech extended financial inclusion among refugees. On the other hand, Makina and Salami (2019) prove that there are negative consequences of FinTech intensive use by vulnerable groups (e.g., over-indebtedness and increased propensity to spend). They also argue that there is a link between financial inclusion and FinTech development.

In recent years, the FinTech industry, like most industries, has experienced the coronavirus crisis, which stimulated some participants to develop, while others, on the contrary, were forced to curtail their activities. Currently, the FinTech industry is developing under conditions of post-pandemic consequences, transformation of the banking sector, changes in the portrait of consumers, innovations in the regulation of the financial services market, as well as challenges in the labor market where there are few interdisciplinary specialists.

Despite the uncertainty surrounding work of the participants in the FinTech industry (consulting companies, scientists, government organizations, industry associations), an attempt is made to determine future trends, taking into account certain signals that are already visible in the market. By anticipating these trends, the resources and efforts of market participants can be reasonably allocated, and regulators can pay attention to weak areas of FinTech potentially posing the risk of subsequent shocks and crises. The data were collected using open-access sources and explored using an analytical framework which was previously developed and included such categories as: the FinTech industry response to COVID-19 shock; FinTech and regulation; FinTech and its impact on the banking system; and employment and skills desired in the FinTech industry. This study aims to identify signals, propose forecasts, and predictions for the FinTech industry, to provide a basis for making further recommendations, enabling the stakeholders of the FinTech ecosystem to develop their industry, and avoid and mitigate risks.

11.2 Methodology

A variety of methods are used to assess FinTech. Each has its advantages and drawbacks. A secondary data review (SDR) has been used as the main exploratory method. This method was chosen because it allows to identify trends by providing valuable insights into patterns and changes over time. Moreover, an SDR is suitable for examining data that has already been collected and includes a large sample size, providing a more representative picture of the phenomenon under study. The collected FinTech data were processed using DEEP (Data Extraction and Evaluation Platform) software.[1] The software is specifically developed to facilitate the process of SDR and analysis. Its extensive array of features encompasses tools for data extraction, cleansing, and analysis, as well as collaborative and project management functionalities.

DEEP was used to continue analysis of data from a wide range of sources, such as academic journals, social media platforms, and government reports. An SDR allows to browse various types of reports and identifies future trends. Therefore, the most recent analytical reports (2016–2022) prepared by the global financial tigers, consulting companies, FinTech associations, market players, central banks, and certain financial institutions are selected for analysis. The methods of research which were used by the companies that prepared the reports included survey, online survey, a systematic literature review, and descriptive statistics with cross-country analysis. Publications were included in the analysis only if they originated from reliable organizations and described studies based on appropriate methodology. The SDR method can be more useful for identifying and characterizing the future trends in FinTech development if based on specific signals which are observable now.

11.3 Presentation of analysis results

11.3.1 FinTech development: general aspects

FinTech is a rapidly growing industry that has transformed the way financial services are delivered to consumers and businesses. FinTech involves the use of technology to provide innovative solutions that enhance financial transactions, payments, and investments.

The recent paper "Pulse of FinTech H2'2021" (KPMG, 2021) describes the growth of FinTech deals in Americas, EMEA, and Asia-Pacific regions to reveal important insights. For these purposes, cross-country (regional) analysis provided by PitchBook Data, Inc. was chosen as a method for collecting data that gave the opportunity to reach conclusions as to prospects of FinTech in developing countries. The authors observed that investors showed a keen interest in cryptocurrency, wealthtech, blockchain, and cybersecurity. Global FinTech investment reached $210 billion by the end of 2021. Venture capital was the most popular form of investment in 2021. FinTech focused on banking replacements. Moreover, the application of data analytics in FinTech was the central topic for the players. Following trends for the near future are predicted: banks planning to develop embedded solutions as a component of larger offering; FinTech companies assuming an additional role of data organizations; increasing regulatory scrutiny of embedded finance offerings; environmental, social, and governance (ESG) FinTechs would grow, especially those related to circular economy, climate change, and decarbonization; underdeveloped regions would be perceived as more favorable for FinTech deals; and unicorns would lose their favorable position in developed countries, remaining strong in developing ones (KPMG, 2021, pp. 7–8).

The key findings of "CeFPro's Global FinTech Research Reportket (2021–2022)" (CeFPro, 2022) are presented below. The text discusses the top three FinTech opportunities for financial services firms in 2027. The data for that analysis was collected using various methods, including capital investment measurement, technology rankings, expert opinions of analysts within the research company, surveys, and one-to-one and group discussions. According to the study, cybersecurity is considered the most important opportunity with 87% of respondents rating it highly, followed by advanced data and analytics at 82%, and artificial intelligence (AI) at 81%. On the other hand, such areas as edge computing and 5G, regulatory compliance, and private digital/cryptocurrency are considered to become less important in 2027. The COVID-19 pandemic has had a mixed impact on FinTech companies. On the positive side, some companies have benefited from the shift to digital channels and online banking, but on the negative side other areas such as client relationships, consulting, retail banking, and wealth management have faced challenges. There are also discussions about cybersecurity as both an investment opportunity and an obstacle. While it is considered a top priority for investment over the next 12 months, it may also limit the development of companies if not addressed properly (CeFPro, 2022, pp. 9–12).

The "Digital Wealth Management Report" (FinTech Futures, 2020b, pp. 4–8) presents the results of interviews with FinTech leaders. It emphasizes the role of wealth managers in FinTech. Changes in client behavior must be followed by changes to the business models adopted by consulting companies. The behavior of investors changes, affecting their approach to investment: they pay attention to the nature of the companies they wish to invest in (in particular, millennials expect specific environmental and social outcomes). A shift in demographics also impacts on future strategies of wealth management; for instance, the group of high-net-worth individuals (HNWIs) includes a growing proportion of women and of young people who prefer using digital FinTech solutions in asset management. As a result, one third of HNWIs prefer to control their investment via FinTech solutions, the others prefer an individual approach. Advisors are planning to implement new FinTech products for managing several clients at the same time, using APIs. This will enable wealth managers to shorten the time of interactions and make them agile, mobile, etc. HNWIs require more personalized service – it means better fitting the client's needs. In addition, wealth managers demand more efficient methods of portfolio management. Now, clients expect not only to receive information but to obtain data reports useful in future decision-making. It means that the set of skills possessed by wealth managers must include data analytics and data visualization in the nearest future. At the same time, the wealth management industry must learn how to use the FinTech solutions to create space for personalized advisory services.

The PWC's report "Blurred lines: How FinTech is shaping Financial Services" (PWC, 2016) shows that five years ago (2016) FinTechs were perceived as small entities that followed banks and collected "financial scrap"; now, they are independent participants in the financial services market and valuable partners for banks. The banking sectors particularly disrupted by FinTech include consumer banking, fund transfer and payments, investment and wealth management, small and medium enterprises (SME) banking, brokerage services, insurance intermediary, market operators and exchanges, fund operators, investment banking and reinsurance. In 2016, the Global FinTech Survey was conducted based on a sample of 544 respondents from 46 countries. The respondents included Chief Executive Officers, Heads of Innovation, Chief Information Officers, and top-tier managers engaged in digital and technological transformation. The analysts aimed to predict trends in the banking industry, considering e.g. whether increasing ease of payments would be accompanied by renewed digital experience and whether future asset and wealth management would change from technology-enabled human advice to human-supported technology-driven advice. They also asked whether blockchain provided foundations for future FinTech or FinTech was tending to focus in the near future on digital infrastructure forming, using APIs, integration with open banking; some segments of the financial services market were going to be bankless and the biggest FinTech companies were planning to rely on super apps which would cover the gap in banking.

The report "Beyond FinTech: A Pragmatic Assessment of Disruptive Potential in Financial Services" (World Economic Forum, 2017) aims to answer questions as to the future of such FinTech sectors as PayTech, insurance, digital banking, lending, investment management, equity crowdfunding, and market infrastructure. One hundred and fifty interviews and ten international workshop sessions were conducted, encouraging collaborative dialog and discussion on insights and opportunities. The authors aim at identifying the key trends shaping the future of specific FinTech sectors. FinTech industry clients will contact financial companies less frequently as large players gain market share. Financial services providers will engage clients with different financial organizations from single channels – special platforms will appear. There are also value chain changes: (1) value chain movements in the FinTech industry will reflect the competitive pressure from all stakeholders of financial organizations, (2) profit redistribution is expected because of the changing value chain, and (3) de-verticalization of the value chain will be caused by sharing expenditures and industry-standard automation. Clients' preferences will make the role of financial intermediaries change. The role of real-time analytics will increase in activity assessment in the FinTech industry. At the same time, the issue of collecting, owing, and controlling data will become vital for all participants in the FinTech ecosystem. New technologies will entail a strong need for developing new talents and creating talent pools as the role of human capital in FinTech increases. FinTechs are becoming similar to LargeTechs and depend on them in purchasing critical infrastructure and technologies. Changes in regulatory provisions applicable to FinTech, in technologies and clients' preferences put in question increasing financial globalization. PayTechs wish to digitalize their services under such conditions as varied adoption of mobile payment and decreasing profitability (WEF, 2017, pp. 11–35).

11.3.2 FinTech industry response to the COVID-19 shock

The COVID-19 pandemic has had a significant impact on the global economy, including the FinTech industry. As governments around the world implemented social distancing measures and lockdowns, there was an unprecedented shift towards digital financial services. This shift has led to both opportunities and challenges for the FinTech industry which are described in the reports cited below. Importantly, most of the reports are based on surveys.

The paper "Creating financial inclusivity in a digital-first future" (FinTech Futures, 2021b) shows that COVID-19 forced people to use more actively digital financial services and 75% of users trust PayTech services; however, only 69% of adults are classified as accountholders. The experts recognize that users become more financially educated and more demanding. The consumers require easy, less expensive, and more comfortable access, and at the same time the requirement of security determines the first-priority characteristic of financial services. Financial inclusion depends on common efforts of private companies and regulators. The authors gave another forecast based on their interviews with FinTech key market players. The future of the FinTech industry looks promising, with an expected valuation of $3.7 trillion by 2025. Also, the industry is expected to benefit from advancements in cloud technologies and increased transparency, which will help reduce costs in financial services. Moreover, to provide hyper-personalized offerings, the industry will need to incorporate new sources of data and analysis, moving away from traditional lending methods. This will enable FinTech companies to provide tailored solutions that meet the specific needs of their customers. While the industry is evolving rapidly, it is important to remember about the older generation of clients who are considered to be "heavy users". This will prevent transforming financial inclusion into financial exclusion, as the industry moves towards more digital and tech-driven solutions (FinTech Futures, 2021b, pp. 6–9).

The next publication, "The Global Covid-19 FinTech Market Rapid Assessment Report" (World Economic Forum, 2020), based on an online survey of 1,385 FinTech firms operating in 169 countries, reflects the results of a rapid assessment of the COVID-19 impact on selected companies, industries, and regions. The highest growth rate of the FinTech industry is noticed in the Middle East and North Africa (40%), North America (21%), and Sub-Saharan Africa (21%). Despite the COVID-19 pandemic, FinTech continues to follow upward trends. In addition, the authors expect an increase in (1) cybersecurity risks and (2) the costs of FinTech services in those countries where the COVID-19 restrictions were more severe. The analysts reveal that there are mixed opinions on restoration of fundraising capability and interest from investors. On the one hand, negative expectations are caused by a fall in the value of the companies during the pandemic; on the other hand, those who predict growth assume that an upward trend must emerge after a decline (CCAF, World Bank and World Economic Forum, 2020, pp. 101–121).

The authors of the paper "The Global Covid-19 FinTech Regulatory Rapid Assessment Study" (Cambridge Judge Business School, 2020) considered how COVID-19 made regulators change their approach to practice within the FinTech industry. The regulators understand that COVID-19 accelerated the development of FinTechs; however, such a fast growth can pose risks related to their performance and generally weaken the financial system. They also recognize closer communication between regulators and market players, facilitating knowledge transfer among regulators at the local and international level and promoting regulatory initiatives. The results of an online survey with the participation of FinTechs, and semi-structural interviews with representatives of regulators, were used to identify the following signals: future investment in FinTech will be related to the building of digital infrastructure, for instance, creating data repositories; moreover, both regulators and FinTech will contribute to the development of financial literacy and financial inclusion (Cambridge Judge Business School, 2020, pp. 65–71).

The Financial Stability Board issued the paper "FinTech and Market Structure in the COVID-19 Pandemic" (Financial Stability Board, 2022) which emphasizes principally benefits for the market resulting from COVID-19. The greatest include wider financial inclusion and the diversity of financial services. COVID-19 has changed the market structure in retail financial services, which can affect future financial stability. In light of the results of the cross-country analysis of drivers of digitalization and regulatory changes (Financial Stability Board, 2022, pp. 16–19), the BigTechs in partnership with FinTechs aim at greater concentration in certain markets, which will limit activities of smaller players. Moreover, BigTechs are less transparent, and their partnerships are ready to take a greater risk, aiming to preserve profitability based on their joint performance (Financial Stability Board, 2022, pp. 16–19).

Based on the information presented in the report (Financial Stability Board, 2022), the following additional trends in the development of the FinTech industry can be indicated. The growth of BigTech companies in the financial technology industry can potentially increase financial stability risks. As these companies become more influential in the market, they may gain significant power and control over financial services, which can lead to market distortions and an increased systemic risk. It will be important for regulators to closely monitor and manage these risks thus ensuring that the industry remains stable and resilient. There is an expectation that regulators in the financial and non-financial sectors will deepen their cooperation in the coming years. This is likely to be driven by the growing intersection between traditional financial services and the technology industry. As FinTech companies continue to disrupt the financial landscape, regulators will need to work closely together to ensure that the industry is safe, transparent, and fair for all. One trend that is likely to continue in the coming years is the rise of contactless payments. As more people become comfortable with using mobile payments and digital wallets, the need for physical visits to bank branches is likely to decrease. This trend is likely to accelerate due to the COVID-19 pandemic, which has led to a surge in digital payments as people seek to avoid contact with cash and other physical payment methods. This shift towards digital payments will have significant implications for the financial industry, as banks and other financial institutions will need to adapt to meet the changing needs of their customers.

To sum up, the reports analyzed highlight the significant impact that the COVID-19 pandemic has had on the FinTech industry. The pandemic has accelerated the shift towards digital financial services, creating both opportunities and challenges for the industry. Overall, the COVID-19 pandemic has brought about significant changes to the FinTech industry, accelerating the shift towards digital financial services and creating new opportunities for innovation and growth. However, it will be important for the industry to remain vigilant and adaptable in the face of ongoing challenges, such as ensuring financial stability and inclusivity in a rapidly changing landscape.

11.3.3 FinTech and regulation

The FinTech industry has emerged as a rapidly growing industry, disrupting the traditional financial sector by introducing innovative digital solutions. However, with this rapid growth, there is also a need for regulation to ensure that FinTech companies operate in a safe and transparent manner, protecting the interests of consumers and maintaining the stability of financial markets. In this context, FinTech regulation has become an important area of focus for policymakers and regulators around the world. This includes such issues as licensing requirements, data privacy and security, consumer protection, and anti-money laundering measures. In this section, we will explore the role of regulation in the FinTech industry and its implications for innovation and growth.

The Staff Discussion Paper "FinTech: Is This Time Different? A Framework for Assessing Risks and Opportunities for Central Banks" (Aaron et al., 2017) reflects on investigation of the risks and opportunities for regulation by central banks which are caused by FinTech development, based on a systematic literature review. FinTech has impacted monetary and financial stability as central banks' regulation areas. Even though modern banks can launch FinTech innovations, they experience difficulties related to their business models. Moreover, central banks can play the role of a networker. The authors outline such networks as centralized, decentralized, and distributed systems which can be supported by digital tokens that additionally can modify the motivation mechanisms of financial intermediaries. Now, the transition from mobile banking to distributed ledger technology and artificial intelligence can be observed. The researchers also predict that with the changing financial intermediary sector, a change in the regulation area is expected. They assume that central banks will pay more attention to business models of FinTechs in order to adapt regulatory measures to the market needs. The authors predict that AI and a token-based system will be the core technologies for reducing costs and accelerating processes in financial sectors (Bank of Canada, 2017, pp. 14–26).

The report "Creating enabling FinTech ecosystems: the role of regulators" (AFI, 2020) reveals the main characteristics of the existing FinTech ecosystem across the world as well as describes the main stakeholders in that ecosystem. The key sections are dedicated to regulators and regulatory frameworks in national policies. In addition to traditional stakeholders in the FinTech industry, accelerators, incubators, and innovation labs are studied there as participants who are capable of supporting and providing the companies with required well-skilled personnel. To identify possible future developments, a case study, cross-country analysis, and 14 interviews with FinTech industry representatives from different countries were conducted. In conclusion, the authors state that cybersecurity units will become an indispensable component in the structures of traditional financial intermediaries. The trend towards capacity and skill building will develop in the nearest future. Local talent pools will cooperate with industry and business. Digital financial literacy is important for financial intermediaries to enable consumers to absorb financial products. Central banks will be more willing to cooperate with key stakeholders: associations that represent industry interests, academia, FinTech labs, FinTechs, consumers, investors, mobile network operators, and advisors (AFI, 2020, pp. 3–6).

The KPMG report "Regulation and supervision of FinTech. Ever-expanding expectations" (KPMG, 2019) highlights increasing regulation of the FinTech industry due to the risks identified (risks to consumers and investors, financial services and firms, financial stability) which FinTech brings together with new technologies and its rapid expansion. The report points out that governance framework aims at preventing possible shocks, while consulting companies may reduce different types of risks. Consulting companies assist financial organizations in launching FinTech services in their offerings, by identifying the main risks related to FinTech, building operational resilience of FinTech, and providing a technology matchmaking platform. Advisors may also contribute to end-to-end framework and AI solutions, to RegTech solutions, and solutions in financial services linking them with FinTech clients. Therefore, it is expected that the importance of global advisory firms as a part of the FinTech ecosystem will increase for both regulators and financial institutions, and the regulators will continue improving and adjusting the market of financial services to reduce the risks identified and protect consumers (KPMG, 2019, pp. 11–14).

Yet another KPMG's report on regulation "Regulation 2030" (KPMG, 2018, pp. 9–16) answers the following questions: will regulation push on, or be pushed back?; what will be the regulatory response to FinTech?; will regulation be used increasingly to deliver social objectives?; and what questions does this raise for society to address? The answers to these questions will constitute a basis for identifying future trends, including changes in regulation, and varying between different jurisdictions. This will lead to fragmentation of legislation from country to country and new regulation rules. What is more, principles and guidelines will limit the FinTech's impact on the financial sector and regulation will promote the use of FinTech services for social purposes. Some of them will be more favorable for FinTech development (for instance, supporting carbon reduction, climate change initiatives, financial inclusion and equality), while the other may be less favorable (for example, concerning certain trading activities, products, and target quotas) (KPMG, 2018, pp. 9–16).

In conclusion, the reports analyzed in this section highlight the critical role of regulation in the growth and development of the FinTech industry. Effective regulation can create opportunities for innovation while ensuring financial stability and consumer protection. Collaboration and forward-thinking approaches are necessary for regulators to strike a balance between promoting innovation and safeguarding the interests of all stakeholders in the FinTech ecosystem.

11.3.4 FinTech impact on the banking system

The emergence of Financial Technology (FinTech) had a significant impact on the banking industry, transforming traditional banking practices and disrupting established business models. FinTech companies have introduced new products and services, such as mobile banking apps, digital wallets, and peer-to-peer lending platforms, which are increasingly popular among consumers. The rise of FinTech has also led to increased competition in the financial sector, putting pressure on traditional banks to adapt to changing market conditions. This has prompted banks to embrace digital transformation and invest in new technologies to enhance their customer experience and improve operational efficiency.

In 2017, Consumers International prepared the report "Banking on the future: an exploration of FinTech and the consumer interest" (Consumers International, 2017) which demonstrates how FinTech has changed the banking system and made bankers review their concepts of future developments. FinTech has improved clients' experience, then reduced expenses, and made the financial system more transparent. For banks, FinTech is a challenge and an opportunity at the same time. Namely, it poses a challenge because it requires huge investment and offers an opportunity because the world of FinTech opens new sources and gives access to a bigger group of clients. The researchers warn about a negative effect of FinTech, which is related to cybersecurity risks. The main trends revealed are related to the technology of trustless transfer that questions the need for financial intermediaries, in particular banks. Where transfer of funds without an intermediary is already a proven technology, if banks continue to refuse to invest in the development of their own FinTech ecosystems, their settlement function may be significantly reduced. In addition, banks realized that FinTech would undermine their profitability, so their investment in this industry began to grow (Consumers International, 2017, p. 37).

The EY report "Unleashing the potential of FinTech in banking" (EY, 2017) analyzes the partnership imperatives and opportunities for banks and FinTechs. Market players prefer to create partnerships while there are pros and cons of banks' engagement with FinTech companies. Analyzing FinTech activity of 45 global banks in North America, Europe, and Asia-Pacific, excluding Japan, EY researchers assess that their simplification of internal processes and use of external utilities aim at cutting the cost of implementing FinTech solutions. The authors assume that the industry will create its own standards which should be matched with those imposed by the regulatory body. Moreover, it is recommended to utilize internal talents who can be future entrepreneurs inside the company. Therefore, certain skills should be developed with the help of financial institutions. Automation will enable employees to do more value-added work. Migration is expected from banks to technology companies – founders of FinTech (EY, 2017, pp. 11–22).

"FinTech vs FinTech? The rise of digitalization in banking" (FinTech Futures, 2021a). Interviews with CEOs of FinTechs were used to prepare that workpaper on the equal position of FinTech with banking. While five years ago, FinTechs were perceived as small and uncompetitive firms, now they are established market players. At the same time, it is more difficult now for FinTechs to disrupt the market, since five years ago competition was less intensive than today. The COVID-19 shock caused disruptions. As a result, 60% of banks closed their branches or shortened office hours, 41% increased the limit of contactless transactions, and 34% implemented fully digital processes in product use.[2] Nowadays, the transition from a simple payment method to a set of services can be observed. The biggest challenge for FinTechs is posed by the question of how to translate customer's demands into technology language. In this context, predictions are made about the future of the financial service market. It is expected to be characterized by fierce competition and driven by market needs and customer preferences. The market is likely to see a reduction in the number of innovative projects, with a greater focus on identifying trends that meet the demands of consumers. Cloud-based systems will continue to gain popularity, with more companies outsourcing file sharing, communication, anti-fraud, and business management services. However, the focus in FinTech development is expected to shift from technology to culture and people, with a greater emphasis on creating customer-centric solutions and fostering a culture of innovation. Overall, the future of FinTech is likely to be shaped by a combination of market forces, technological advancements, and cultural shifts (FinTech Futures, 2021a, pp. 3–7).

The report "Banking and Payments in 2022: Digital transformation and trends in financial technology" discusses the FinTech impact on banking system development. The report presents the results of a study on digital transformation in the banking system. A survey was conducted with the participation of more than 50 senior managers from the FinTech sector. The respondents indicated that the biggest problems of today's banking are manual processes, legacy systems, poor interoperability with existing systems, meeting regulatory requirements, and slow operational/non-technological processes. About 44% of banking organizations do not use AI, machine learning (ML), and APIs; however, 19% of them are planning to implement those systems in the nearest future. At the same time, about 12% of the respondents have no plans to use such technologies as AI, ML, and APIs. Banks avoid manual processes because they reduce competitiveness, increase costs, and the number of errors. Most of the respondents consider scalability and regulatory pressure to be the main obstacles on the path of their growth during the next three years (FinTech Future, 2022, pp. 6–8).

All the reports discussed create a common narrative which suggests a new trend. The future of FinTech in banking is likely to be shaped by market needs, technological advancements, and cultural shifts, leading to a greater focus on creating customer-centric solutions and fostering a culture of innovation.

11.3.5 Employment and skills desired in the FinTech industry

The emergence of FinTech has created a range of new job opportunities and driven demand for new skills in the financial services industry. FinTech companies require a set of diverse skills, including technical expertise in such areas as software development, data analysis, and cybersecurity, as well as business and financial acumen. The rapid pace of technological innovation in FinTech has also created demand for workers who are adaptable, innovative, and capable of learning new skills quickly.

Based on the results of a market survey of the FinTech industry, the report "The Power of Data Analytics in FinTech Solutions" (FinTech Future, 2020a) identifies the most required skills of future candidates for positions in the FinTech industry. The author underlines the importance of technical and data analytics skills which should be displayed by potential employees. Not only the requirements of progress must be met but also those of clients and regulators. In addition, FinTechs expect a reduction in costs achieved by implementing data analytics solutions. The expert finds indications showing that the deployment of embedded analytics will be the most demanded skill in future recruitment by FinTechs. In addition, a system should be sought which will provide a flexible ability to adapt to clients' needs (FinTech Future, 2020a, pp. 3–8).

The paper "The Digital Skills Gaps in the FinTech Industry" (Coventry University, 2021) reveals a variety of gaps in FinTech skills caused on the one hand by fast-growing businesses and on the other hand by educational institutions' inability to prepare a sufficient number of specialists. Big data, Industry 4.0, and blockchain experts are the most demanded prospective workers in the industry. Importantly, small- and medium-sized enterprises are nowadays keen to hire those specialists. The Coventry University researchers argue that given an increasing number of programs targeted at FinTech, they are still insufficient to provide the market with the necessary pool of specialists. It is obvious that the main stakeholders will work to ensure that as many employees as possible appear on this path. Therefore, both short-term and long-term training programs will continue to set major trends. A revival of cooperation between the industry and educational sector is foreseen that will provide mutual benefits. The trend towards introducing dual education programs will continue (Coventry University, 2021, pp. 10–17).

The analyzed reports highlight the critical role of data analytics and digital skills in the FinTech industry. Effective use of data analytics is a key driver of innovation and competitive advantage in FinTech, helping firms to better understand their customers, improve operational efficiency, and manage risk. However, the digital skills gap presents a challenge for the industry, as companies struggle to find workers with the necessary technical expertise and business acumen to drive innovation and growth. Closing the digital skills gap and investing in data analytics capabilities will be essential for firms seeking to remain competitive in the dynamic and rapidly evolving FinTech landscape.

11.4 Conclusion

Generally, it is predicted that the FinTech industry will grow in the next three years. Investment in this area will be related to capacity building of digital infrastructure (data repositories), blockchain, cybersecurity environment, and cloud technologies. Nevertheless, technologies will play a crucial role in the FinTech industry development, people and culture will also remain in the focus of attention of financial intermediaries, FinTechs, and other stakeholders of the industry. Financial inclusion and financial literacy development will be promoted by the FinTech ecosystem.

Although regulators try to be closer to the industry, the financial and non-financial sectors, and more frequently participate and show their interest in the common area, the regulative pressure will increase. It is expected that the industry will create certain standards which must comply with the requirements set by regulators. Moreover, regulatory innovation is caused by the expansion of players in the FinTech ecosystem (BigTech companies such as Google, Amazon, Facebook and Apple), changes in business models of traditional financial institutions, and global changes (climate issues, poverty reduction, financial inclusiveness, circular economy, decarbonization). The last process has also led to new regulatory measures applicable to the financial services industry. Regulators are increasingly focused on ensuring that financial institutions are contributing to sustainable development goals and addressing ESG risks. Consequently, new regulations and reporting requirements have been introduced.

Financial intermediaries, FinTechs, and other market players must closely observe changes in the behavior of consumers, to identify possible trends that may emerge till 2030. The younger generation prefer to use FinTech solution for managing their wealth. Moreover, they require additional information and data visualization useful in future decision-making (data for analytics). Women have become wealthier and their investment style is less aggressive – they pay attention to projects delivering social objectives. FinTech solutions cater for the specific needs of the older generation, providing them with greater financial independence, security, and ease of use. These solutions also contribute to bridging the digital divide and promote financial inclusion of seniors who may have been left behind by traditional financial services.

COVID-19 has impacted FinTech industry ambiguously. The pandemic set long-term trends which will continue during the following years, and will mostly have positive effects, such as digital customer experience, payless technology, online banks and banking, ease of payments, and mobile-first strategies. At the same time, quarantine affected client relationships, consulting, retail banking, and wealthtech. Additionally, in the countries subject to more severe COVID-19 restrictions, the costs of FinTech services increased compared to less regulated territories during the pandemic. BigTech companies which expanded during the pandemic may achieve financial stability.

Banking investment in FinTech services will continue to increase. The main reason is to prevent losing the payment function used by those clients who may switch to FinTech offered by other financial intermediaries. In the future, talents may leave banks for technology companies – founders of FinTechs. Therefore, banks should pay more attention to forming talent pools inside their organizations. There are banks that do not consider investment in FinTech industry as this would eliminate manual processing.

As with all fast-growing branches, FinTech needs well-qualified personnel. Interdisciplinary programs combining finance/economics and IT will be strongly needed over the next years. On the one hand, a collaboration between the FinTech sector and academia aimed to prepare specialists and conduct research is needed to close the gaps in skills of prospective FinTech employees. On the other hand, consumers' digital financial literacy must be developed for them to absorb financial innovation.

Notes

1 See https://deephelp.zendesk.com/.
2 Digital Banking Maturity (Deloitte, 2020).).

References

Aaron, M., Rivadeneyra, F., & Soha, S. (2017). *FinTech: Is This Time Different? A Framework for Assessing Risks and Opportunities for Central Banks* [staff discussion paper]. Bank of Canada. Retrieved from https://www.bankofcanada.ca/wp-content/uploads/2017/07/sdp2017-10.pdf.

Aduba, J. J., Asgari, B., & Izawa, H. (2022). Causality between financial performance, FinTech, financial inclusion, and financial development in emerging and developing economies: A cross country analysis. *SSRN Electronic Journal*. https://doi.org/10.2139/ssrn.4113175.

AFI (2020). *Creating enabling FinTech ecosystems: the role of regulators*. https://www.afi-global.org/sites/default/files/publications/2020-01/AFI_FinTech_SR_AW_digital_0.pdf.

Anagnostopoulos, I. (2018). FinTech and Regtech: Impact on regulators and banks. *Journal of Economics and Business*, *100*, 7–25. https://doi.org/10.1016/j.jeconbus.2018.07.003.

Babina, T., Buchak, G., & Gornall, W. (2022). Customer data access and FinTech entry: Early evidence from open banking. *SSRN Electronic Journal*. https://doi.org/10.2139/ssrn.4071214.

Bhagat, A., & Roderick, L. (2020). Banking on refugees: Racialized expropriation in the FinTech era. *Environment and Planning A: Economy and Space*, *52*(8), 1498–1515. https://doi.org/10.1177/0308518x20904070.

Cambridge Judge Business School (2020). *The Global Covid-19 FinTech Regulatory Rapid Assessment Study*. Retrieved from https://www.jbs.cam.ac.uk/wp-content/uploads/2020/10/2020-ccaf-report-FinTech-regulatory-rapid-assessment.pdf.

CeFPro (2022). *Providing a Voice to the Market*. https://www.cefpro.com/fintech-leaders-2/.

Consumers International (2017). *Banking on the Future - Consumers International*. https://www.consumersinternational.org/media/154710/banking-on-the-future-full-report.pdf.

Coventry University (2021). *The Digital Skills Gaps in the FinTech Industry*. Retrieved from https://3yy7gm31u9o0it5f51gqn0j1-wpengine.netdna-ssl.com/wp-content/uploads/2021/03/J2218-20_IoC_Industry_Reports_FinTech-Industry_FINAL-Online.pdf.

D'Acunto, F. and Rossi, A. G., (2022). IT Meets Finance: Financial Decision Making in the Digital Era. Social Science Research Network. http://dx.doi.org/10.2139/ssrn.4100784

Deloitte (2020). *Digital Maturity. How Banks Are Responding to Digital (R)Evolution?* https://www2.deloitte.com/content/dam/Deloitte/ce/Documents/financial-services/ce-digital-banking-maturity-2020.pdf.

Emara, N. (2022). Asymmetric and threshold effects of FinTech on poverty in SSA countries. *SSRN Electronic Journal*. https://doi.org/10.2139/ssrn.4062335

EY (2017). *Unleashing the Potential of FinTech in Banking*. Retrieved from https://assets.ey.com/content/dam/ey-sites/ey-com/en_gl/topics/banking-and-capital-markets/ey-unleashing-the-potential-of-fin-tech-in-banking.pdf.

Financial Stability Board (2022). *FinTech and Market Structure in the COVID-19 Pandemic Implications for Financial Stability*. https://www.fsb.org/wp-content/uploads/P210322.pdf.

FinTech Future (2020a). *The Power of Data Analytics in FinTech Solutions*. https://www.FinTechfutures.com/files/2021/03/February-Data-Analytics-report-v4.pdf.

FinTech Future (2020b). *Digital Wealth Management Report*. https://www.fintechfutures.com/files/2020/07/Digital_Wealth_Management_Report_V4.pdf.

FinTech Futures (2021a). *"FinTech vs FinTech"? The Rise of Digitalisation in Banking*. https://www.FinTechfutures.com/2021/09/report-FinTech-vs-FinTech-the-rise-of-digitalisation-in-banking/.

FinTech Futures (2021b). *Creating Financial Inclusivity in a Digital-First Future*. https://www.FinTechfutures.com/2021/10/new-FinTech-futures-report-creating-financial-inclusivity-in-a-digital-first-future/.

FinTech Futures (2022). *Banking and Payments in 2022: Digital Transformation and Trends in FinTech*. https://www.FinTechfutures.com/2022/01/banking-and-payments-in-2022-digital-transformation-and-trends-in-financial-technology/.

Hill, J. (2018). *FinTech and the Remaking of Financial Institutions*. Academic Press.

Hill, J. A. (2021). Covid-19 and FinTech. *SSRN Electronic Journal*. https://doi.org/10.2139/ssrn.3777562.

KPMG (2018). *Regulation 2030*. https://assets.kpmg/content/dam/kpmg/xx/pdf/2018/03/regulation-2030.pdf.

KPMG (2019). *Regulation and Supervision of FinTech*. https://assets.kpmg/content/dam/kpmg/xx/pdf/2019/03/regulation-and-supervision-of-FinTech.pdf.

KPMG (2021). *Pulse of FinTech H2'21*. https://assets.kpmg/content/dam/kpmg/xx/pdf/2022/02/pulse-of-FinTech-h2-21.pdf.

Makina, D., & Salami, I. (2019). *Extending Financial Inclusion in Africa*. Elsevier Science & Technology.

PWC (2016). *Blurred Lines: How FinTech Is Shaping Financial Services*. https://www.pwc.com/il/en/home/assets/pwc_FinTech_global_report.pdf.

Sambros, S., Balan, O., & Lebedeva, V. (2020). Possibilities of application FinTech in improving the organization administrative services provision by local authorities. *Economics: Time Realities*, *1*(47), 48–52. https://doi.org/10.15276/etr.01.2020.6.

Velasco Arellano, S. (2021). FinTech, remittances and migrants' prosperity: A systematic review and exploration of the Mexican case. https://doi.org/10.14324/000.wp.10128014.

World Economic Forum (2017). *Beyond FinTech: A Pragmatic Assessment of Disruptive Potential in Financial Services*. https://www3.weforum.org/docs/Beyond_FinTech_-_A_Pragmatic_Assessment_of_Disruptive_Potential_in_Financial_Services.pdf.

World Economic Forum (2020). *The Global Covid-19 FinTech Market Rapid Assessment Study*. https://www3.weforum.org/docs/WEF_The_Global_Covid19_FinTech_Market_Rapid_Assessment_Study_2020.pdf.

Index

Note: **Bold** page numbers refer to tables; *italic* page numbers refer to figures and page numbers followed by "n" denote endnotes.

FSC
www.fsc.org
MIX
Papier | Fördert gute Waldnutzung
FSC® C083411

Kolibri 360 GmbH
Ferdinand-Jühlke-Straße 7
99095 Erfurt, Deutschland
produktsicherheit@kolibri360.de